INSURGENCY TR

INSURGENCY TRAP

Labor Politics in Postsocialist China

Eli Friedman

ILR PRESS

AN IMPRINT OF

CORNELL UNIVERSITY PRESS   **ITHACA AND LONDON**

Cornell University Press gratefully acknowledges receipt of a grant from the Hull Memorial Publication Fund of Cornell University as well as a Subsidy for Publication grant from the Chiang Ching-kuo Foundation for International Scholarly Exchange (USA), which generously assisted in the publication of this book.

First published 2014 by Cornell University Press
First printing, Cornell Paperbacks, 2014

Printed in the United States of America

Library of Congress Cataloging-in-Publication Data

Friedman, Eli, author.
    Insurgency trap : labor politics in postsocialist China / Eli Friedman.
        pages cm
    Includes bibliographical references and index.
    ISBN 978-0-8014-5269-7 (cloth : alk. paper) –
    ISBN 978-0-8014-7931-1 (pbk. : alk. paper)
    1. Labor unions—China—History. 2. Labor unions and socialism—China.
I. Title.
    HD6837.F77   2014
    322'.20951—dc23   2013046810

Cloth printing   10 9 8 7 6 5 4 3 2 1
Paperback printing   10 9 8 7 6 5 4 3 2 1

To my parents

Contents

Tables

Figures

Acknowledgments

Throughout this project I have benefited immensely from the guidance of Peter Evans. From the initial conception of the research all the way to the final submission, Peter has been an exemplary mentor, alternatively advising, instructing, cajoling, and simply leading by example. I have learned a tremendous amount from him, not just about sociology and doing good scholarship but also about how to act in the world. It goes without saying that this book would not have been possible without his support and guidance.

Ching Kwan Lee has selflessly offered her mentorship to me for many years. My intellectual debt to her is apparent enough in the following pages, and if I can count any scholarly or professional achievements, they are due in large part to her ongoing support. Kim Voss helped me think deeply about union organization and always provides timely reminders that Chinese labor politics may not be as unique as I think. And Kevin O'Brien has consistently provided me with some of the best feedback and suggestions on my work and how to make it comprehensible to others, as well as invaluable knowledge on conducting research in China. I also make special mention of Dylan Riley, who provided me with rigorous training in social theory. He helped me to see the world in a radically new light.

The intellectual environment at Berkeley is unparalleled, and while there I learned from an incredible group of fellow students: Abigail Andrews, Dan Buch, Ryan Calder, Jia-Ching Chen, Zongshi Chen, Julia Chuang, Barry Eidlin, Jonathan Hassid, Paul Hathazy, Daniel Immerwahr, Zach Levenson, Mike Levien, Kate Maich, Simon Morfit, Marcel Paret, Tianna Paschel, Alina Polyakova, Jeff Sallaz, Aaron Shaw, and Rachel Stern.

Numerous friends and colleagues in China helped facilitate my fieldwork and also provided camaraderie and intellectual stimulation, including Gao Haitao, He Gaochao, Huang Qiaoyan, Jia Wenjuan, Liu Cheng, Liu Jian, Luo Xiaopeng, Boy Luethje, Meng Quan, Shen Yuan, Wang Kan, Wang Ning, Wang Shifu, Xu Xiaohong, Yuan Jun, and Zhou Gang. I owe special thanks to Liang Guowei and Tian Miao for their assistance in the research presented in chapter 5. Additionally, I thank Anthony Spires and the faculty of the sociology department at Chinese University of Hong Kong for hosting me while I conducted archival research at the Universities Service Centre.

Outside of Berkeley, I have benefited greatly from the feedback and support of many people, including Joel Andreas, Mark Anner, Jennifer Chun, Sun Wook

Chung, Manfred Elfstrom, Louis Hyman, Kjeld Jakobsen, Sarosh Kuruvilla, Chun-yi Lee, Jamie McCallum, and Mark Selden. In particular, Hao Zhang has not only provided top-notch research assistance but has also been an important intellectual interlocutor. I also thank Tom Kochan and Jeff Sallaz for inviting me to present my research at MIT and the University of Arizona, respectively. I received excellent feedback at each of these events, which helped shape the final manuscript.

Without the efforts of Fran Benson at Cornell University Press this book would never have seen the light of day. I thank her and the editorial staff for all of their work.

While conducting fieldwork I received generous support from the University of California's Pacific Rim Research Program as well as the Labor and Employment Research Fund. My time at Chinese University of Hong Kong was supported by the Global Scholarship Programme for Research Excellence—CNOOC Grant.

My wife, Julia Chang, gave me unconditional love and support throughout many months of overseas fieldwork—and then through the much longer process of turning that research into a book. The acknowledgment section of a book is an awkward place to formally recognize the profundity of a spousal relationship. Nonetheless, I love her deeply and have counted on her for emotional and intellectual inspiration time and time again.

And then there are my parents, Ellen and Stuart, who have probably set some sort of record for direct contribution to a child's research. For the first several months of my fieldwork (undoubtedly the most personally challenging part of the project) I lived in an apartment with them on the campus of Sun Yat-sen University in Guangzhou. They of course fed me and listened to me gripe about the challenges of studying labor politics in China but also engaged in substantive daily conversations about the research that profoundly shaped the development of the project. While it is perhaps customary to dedicate a first book to one's parents, mine have actually earned it in spades. I love them very much and dedicate this book to them.

Abbreviations

ACFIC	All China Federation of Industry and Commerce
ACFTU	All China Federation of Trade Unions
CCP	Chinese Communist Party
CEC-CEDA	China Enterprise Confederation-China Enterprise Directors Association
CFL	Chinese Federation of Labor
DPP	Democratic Progressive Party
FDI	foreign direct investment
FKTU	Federation of Korean Trade Unions
GDFTU	Guangdong Federation of Trade Unions
GZFTU	Guangzhou Federation of Trade Unions
KMT	Kuomintang (Nationalist Party)
PRC	People's Republic of China
RAFTU	Rui'an Federation of Trade Unions
RMB	renminbi
SEZ	special economic zone
SHFTU	Shanghai Federation of Trade Unions
SOE	state-owned enterprise
VGCL	Vietnam General Confederation of Labor
WCC	wage-only collective contract

INSURGENCY TRAP

LABOR POLITICS AND CAPITALIST INDUSTRIALIZATION

On the night of June 6, 2011, migrant workers rioted in the southern Chinese town of Guxiang. The protesters were furious over an incident in which a fellow worker had been violently attacked while seeking back wages. On June 1, Xiong Hanjiang, a nineteen-year-old migrant from Sichuan province, went to demand 2,000 yuan in back pay from the ceramics factory where he was employed. Rather than give him his wages, some of the bosses' relatives attacked Xiong with knives, cutting tendons in his hands and feet. Between June 3 and June 6, workers demanding justice for the victim protested in front of the municipal and township government offices, as well as at police headquarters. Protesters vandalized the government buildings, and a number of police were hospitalized with injuries. On the night of the sixth, the workers originally surrounded the Guxiang government offices to continue to press their demands for harsh punishment for the attackers and fair compensation for Xiong. Things quickly escalated as physical confrontations took place with police, leaving dozens injured. Witnesses claimed that more than one hundred cars were smashed, though the official number was just nineteen. Widespread violence between migrants and locals ensued, with one migrant saying, "If you couldn't speak Chaoshan dialect [the local language], they would beat you."[1] Riot police were called in to put down the unrest, and the town was placed under martial law for several days.

While the extreme brutality of the attack on Xiong was shocking, this type of lawlessness was nothing new to migrant workers in Guxiang. A migrant with years of experience in the area would later recount how the government was an active partner in these regularly occurring acts of violence: "The first factory

I worked in here was an [enterprise with strong government connections]. One of my colleagues was arguing with the boss over something, and the boss just placed a call and people from public security came by, tied him up, and beat him good. Around here, this kind of thing is a regular occurrence....I'd say that the primary function of public security is to help bosses deal with workers."[2] Workers in Guxiang experienced many of the problems typical of migrants throughout China—low wages, long hours, few or no benefits, no contracts, and frequent nonpayment of wages. With the government firmly behind management and nowhere else to turn, many migrants joined mafia-like "hometown associations." For a fee, these groups would help members try to resolve workplace grievances—often meeting the threat of police violence with more violence. It later appeared that Xiong Hanjiang was a member of a just such an organization, as a Sichuan hometown association played a major role in the subsequent mobilization. Thus, while the original grievance was rooted in a seemingly straightforward labor rights violation, the June 6 protest quickly escalated into a major confrontation between migrants on one side and the police and local vigilante groups on the other.

Hu Jintao had surely hoped a different method for resolving labor disputes would be in place nearly a decade into his term. Shortly after assuming Party leadership in late 2002, Hu had quickly—if subtly—moved to reorient the state away from the single-minded pursuit of growth that had characterized the administrations of Deng Xiaoping and Jiang Zemin. Over the course of his first year and a half in office, he unveiled the key slogans that would be associated with his tenure: "scientific development view," "putting people first," and most famously, "harmonious society." Though each was imbued with a slightly different shade of meaning, in sum these slogans were meant to indicate that the state would no longer be *exclusively* concerned with GDP growth as an end in itself. Under this new approach to development, the state was to pay greater attention to environmental protection, reducing inequality, expanding the social welfare system, and enhancing rule of law. In short, Hu wanted to take steps to soften the edges of the bare-knuckle capitalism that, while leading to many consecutive years of high growth, had resulted in stark class polarization, ecological destruction, and rapidly expanding social conflict.

And indeed, over the next several years there were strong indications that the central government was backing away from full-throttle marketization and reorienting its growth strategy away from one highly dependent on wage repression and export-oriented manufacturing. Although calls for a shift away from exports grew significantly following the global economic crisis of 2008, the central government had been advocating an increase of domestic consumption since at least 2004.[3] In part responding to massive protests among laid-off workers in the late 1990s and early 2000s, the high wave of privatization of state-owned enterprises (SOE) subsided. It became clear that the public sector was going to continue to play a large role in the economy, particularly in key industries such as energy, arms, transportation, finance, and education. Scholars and media commentators began to refer to the phenomenon of "advance of the state, private retreat" (*guo jin min tui*) to refer to the process of renationalization happening in several sectors. A series of prolabor (in intent, if not necessarily in effect) policies and laws were implemented, culminating in the landmark Labor Contract Law approved in 2007.[4] Additionally, the government took a number of steps to reform the discriminatory *hukou* (household registration) system (Wang Fei-Ling 2010) and increase social insurance coverage of migrant workers, and it raised minimum wages. Most significantly for this discussion, the All China Federation of Trade Unions (ACFTU) appeared to be more aggressive in pushing for collective bargaining and unionizing private employers, as most clearly represented by the high-profile Walmart campaign in 2006 (Blecher 2008; A. Chan 2007, 2011b). Unions around the country began to talk more assertively about organizing migrant workers and negotiating better contracts for their members to promote "harmonious labor relations."

It appeared as if years of high levels of social unrest—chief among which was labor conflict—had taken a toll on the state, and the central government was ready for compromise. For some scholars, it seemed that the state had embraced decommodification and a reembedding of the economy in response to the chaos of the market, just as theorized by Karl Polanyi in *The Great Transformation* (1944). Indeed, Wang Shaoguang (2008) argued that by the late 1990s, "the golden tablet (jinzi zhaopan) of market reform toppled, shattering the seeming consensus on the efficacy of market forces.... [Those hurt by marketization] felt that Chinese economic reform had gone astray, and they longed for harmony between the economy and society. This initiated the protective countermovement to re-embed the economy into the society" (21). In Wang's view, by 2008 the central government's change in direction was successful: "By using state power, the redistribution breaks the market chain and reconnects everyone. These are the changes China has been experiencing recently" (22).

It now appears that Wang's optimistic prognosis was premature—or at least only partially realized. Particularly for migrant workers—rural residents who are formally second-class citizens once they move to the city—the market nexus largely continues to mediate needs. Managerial autonomy remains essentially uncompromised, and workplaces are subject to endemic legal violations. And workers are not satisfied. Indeed, for the duration of the Hu-Wen administration (2002–12), the volume, and seemingly the intensity, of labor conflict increased dramatically. Officially adjudicated disputes rose continuously until 2007 and spiked sharply in 2008 because of the economic crisis and the passage of new labor laws. While the number of disputes declined somewhat following the resumption of rapid growth in 2009, they increased again in 2012 and remain incredibly high in absolute terms (see figure 1). Autonomously organized strikes, road blockades, riots, and worker suicides continue to upend social order. In at least two high-profile cases, workers who murdered their bosses were widely hailed as heroes on the Internet.[5] Just one week after the Guxiang riot, an even more spectacular worker insurrection took place in the Guangzhou suburb of Zengcheng. Workers blocked a national highway and set fire to a police station—and the unrest continued for days until the government deployed the military to quell the uprising. By 2012 the government was spending renminbi (RMB) 701.8 billion (US$111.4 billion) on internal security, significantly outpacing its national defense budget of RMB 670.3 billion.[6] Clearly, all was not peaceful in the People's Republic.

This book, then, seeks to address a problem of the political economy of early twenty-first-century China: Why is it that in the more than ten years since the central government began to shift away from full-fledged marketization, migrant

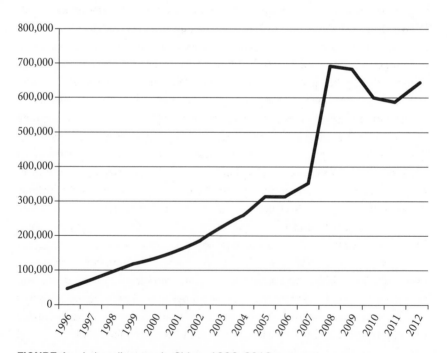

FIGURE 1.   Labor disputes in China, 1996–2012.
Source: Zhongguo laodong tongji nianjian (2012) [China labor statistical year-book 2012] (Beijing: Zhongguo tongji chubanshe).

worker unrest has continued to grow apace?[7] Why have the efforts of certain segments of the state to promote class compromise largely failed? Perhaps one might assume that the answer is simply that there has been collusion between the local state and capital, unions are weak, and therefore worker interests continue to be violated. Indeed, there is strong evidence that even if migrant workers' nominal wages increased in this period, the workers did not experience significant increases in real wages, and their wages relative to those of urban workers steadily declined (Golley and Meng 2011). But if this is the case, a second question immediately arises: Why is it that labor is strong enough to win concessions at the national and sometimes provincial or municipal level but not strong enough to allow migrant workers to significantly benefit from these victories or gain their recognition? In broad terms, I am interested in identifying what is particular about the labor politics of capitalist industrialization in a postsocialist political environment. In order to answer these questions, I focus on the state-controlled unions under the umbrella of the ACFTU and their relationship to migrant workers, capital, and other state agencies.

Insurgency Trap

My central argument is that the dynamics of working class representation in postsocialist China have confounded institutionalization of class compromise. ACFTU-subordinate unions are weak at the enterprise level and are therefore unable to overcome endemic collusion between capital and local governments. Because unions in China are part of the state, they have good access to policy-makers but are highly illegitimate among their own membership—that is, they are strong at the top but weak at the bottom. Labor's impotence within enterprises means that potentially prolabor laws and collective agreements frequently go unenforced—and since these unions are generally controlled by management, they are often *uninterested* in strict enforcement. Workers are therefore forced to take radical autonomous action in order to have their grievances addressed, often in direct opposition to union representatives. This means that when workers secure marginal material improvements, the legitimacy of the union is not enhanced, leaving the working class unincorporated within the polity. Expanding worker insurgency does strengthen the hand of unions at the national (and potentially provincial and even municipal) level, but it fails to produce a durable realignment of power at the point of production that is able to enforce laws. The one method likely to reduce conflict—developing an independent countervailing force at the point of production—remains off the table as far as the central state is concerned; hence there is an "insurgency trap."[8] The central state is "trapped" in the sense that it is unable to realize its own goals because of *self-imposed* political constraints.

Through an analysis of several most-likely cases in Guangdong and Zhejiang provinces, I empirically demonstrate the problems generated by monopoly representation and attempt to discern under what conditions insurgency trap might be undone. We will see that the ACFTU, despite being an exemplar of rigid oligarchy, *is* attempting to promote decommodification and gain recognition from its constituency in response to worker insurgency. I analyze how the union negotiates the tension between the impetus to respond to intensifying worker resistance on the one hand and structural oligarchy and heteronomy on the other. How then does the union try to ameliorate labor conflict given existing institutional parameters? What sorts of internal organizational changes are taking place? Given the failure of legal reforms to effectively incorporate workers into the state as individuals, can the union guide rebellious workers into rationalized legal channels? And can such legalized mechanisms resolve conflict? Although in general Chinese unions have not been able to decommodify and incorporate labor, there are some cases where they have been *relatively* successful. Even if such cases remain exceptional, the processes that produced a degree of institutionalization are worthy of investigation.

There are important implications for theory that follow from this empirical investigation. The mechanistic theory of the double movement as outlined by Polanyi at first glance seems sufficient to explain the movement between commodifying and decommodifying policies coming out of Beijing over the past thirty years. However, the countermovement is not simply a policy response but also a social response to market dislocations. When we look at ongoing lawlessness in private enterprise and expanding worker unrest, it is clear that the countermovement in China is "incomplete" from a Polanyian perspective. As a result, I argue that countermovements must be broken down into two constituent but intertwined "moments": the "insurgent moment," which consists of spontaneous resistance to the market, and the "institutional moment," when class compromise is established in the economic and political spheres. This allows me to break with a teleological conception of the countermovement that assumes a pendular swing toward decommodification and reembedding of the economy. By reconfiguring the theory of the countermovement, I gain conceptual clarity on the relationship between spontaneous resistance to the market and institutionalization of class compromise. Specifically, we see how rejection of the market is merely a tendency and that the institutionalization of countermovements is always contingent on politics. Before detailing my conceptual framework at greater length, it will first be necessary to explain something about social and economic policy in contemporary China.

Commodification and Harmonious Society

If China's command economy of the 1950s to the 1970s failed to result in the liberation of the working class, it certainly brought about a profound decommodification of land, labor, and money. With the implementation of the *hukou* system and the construction of the *danwei* (urban work unit) and rural communes, labor markets were controlled administratively by the state. While there were certainly implications for worker democracy and autonomy, this system also meant that the state (or more precisely state-controlled work units) provided workers and their families with education, health care, and housing. Wage labor was greatly reduced or eliminated, and markets to provide for most human needs disappeared or were tightly constrained. Although there was ongoing abject poverty during this period, to the extent that people's needs *were* met, this occurred through nonmarketized mechanisms.

Marketization was initiated in 1978 but deepened dramatically between 1992 and 2002. But during 2002–12 the state began to shift tack and increased social spending and prolabor legislation under the banner of "harmonious society." The year 2002 should not be thought of as a rigid demarcation, but we will see that many important national policies began to shift in a seemingly decommodifying direction around that time. As argued by Wang Shaoguang (2008), this could be seen as evidence that the Chinese state is doing precisely what Polanyian theory would have us expect and moving to decommodify the provision of various needs in response to social dislocations brought about by the free market. Although this shift began as early as 2002, "common prosperity" received even greater emphasis in the eleventh five-year plan adopted in 2006 (Fan 2006). Perhaps this shift in direction is most directly reflected in new labor legislation passed during this period. But I am also interested in how provision for the core human needs of health care, education, and pensions changed, as the removal of these items from the market also serves to decommodify labor.

While an in-depth overview of commodification of labor in reform-era China is impossible here, a few things are worth pointing out. To begin with, the implementation of the *danwei* and *hukou* systems in the late 1950s effectively blocked rural-urban migration and closed the labor market. Until the reforms began in the late 1970s, there were essentially no opportunities to engage in wage labor. Early private industry in the 1980s and 1990s was almost wholly unregulated, and while labor was certainly commodified, the wage labor relationship was generally not formalized in contracts. The state began taking steps toward formalizing capitalist labor relations with the passage of the Labor Law in 1994, but migrant workers continued to be subjected to an essentially laissez faire labor market.

The Labor Contract Law of 2008 was seen by many as an attempt to both formalize wage labor and provide some better protections to employees. Of particular relevance to the question of labor commodification were the stipulations on signing open-ended contracts—not surprisingly the feature of the law that employers resisted most vociferously. Although the intention of the law was to provide workers with greater protections, there is now evidence that capital responded to the new law by massively increasing use of "dispatch" (outsourced) and other forms of precarious labor. According to an ACFTU investigation, between the implementation of the law in January 2008 and the end of 2010, the number of dispatch workers leaped from 20 million to 60 million.[9] A broad array of industries and ownership types (state-owned, domestic private, foreign private) were increasingly using outsourcing to skirt legal obligations and social insurance payments. In fact, the state subsequently revised the law in an attempt to rein in the explosive growth in such contract labor. So even if the intent of the central government was to provide better protection to employees, it is not clear that this has necessarily been the case in practice. This is a clear example of how employers and local governments can circumvent laws intended to enhance the economic standing of workers.

Perhaps the welfare issue that has generated the most vocal dissatisfaction within China has been the transformation of the health care system. Previously, urban workers received medical care through the *danwei* system at little or no cost, while 90 percent of rural residents were insured by the mid-1970s (Yuanli Liu 2004, 159). In the 1980s, however, the government began to move toward a market-oriented approach to health care, which led to the collapse of the collective medical system in rural areas (Liu, Hsaio, Li, and Liu 1995). By 1993, the number of rural residents covered by medical insurance was down to 12.8 percent, falling yet further to 9.5 percent by 1998 (Yuanli Liu 2004, 159). Throughout this period, out-of-pocket expenses increased dramatically for individuals. But as can been seen quite clearly in figure 2, out-of-pocket expenses as a share of total health care spending began to decrease quite significantly starting in 2001. And in 2002, the government unveiled the New Cooperative Medical System in an effort to increase insurance coverage in the countryside (Brown and Huff 2011).

Similarly dramatic changes took place in the provision of education. Putting aside questions of quality, education under the command economy was provided by the state (broadly conceived) with minimal or nonexistent tuition. Starting in the mid-1980s, the central government moved to decentralize both control over curriculum and responsibility for operating costs (Hawkins 2000). One consequence of this has been the widespread adoption of various fees in public schools (Chan and Mok 2001) as well as rapid growth of private schools

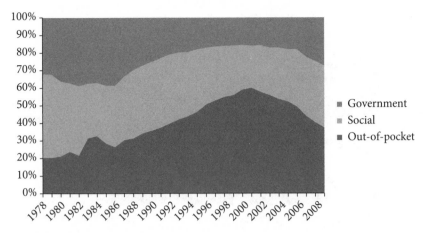

FIGURE 2.   Health care spending in China, 1978–2009.
Source: Zhongguo tongji nianjian (2011) [China statistical yearbook 2011]
(Beijing: China Statistics Press).

(Lin 2007). Marketization was not limited to secondary and primary school but also had a profound impact on higher education (Mok 2000). Additionally, and quite significantly for this study, migrant workers' children face enormous obstacles (financial, administrative, social) to enrolling in public schools in the city, and so they are often relegated to a much inferior system of private schooling (Chen and Liang 2007; Kwong 2004).

The shift to increased government spending on education occurred somewhat later than was the case for health care. And yet by 2005, individual expenditures on education began to decline as state expenditures expanded (see figure 3). In 2006, the central government required that provincial governments eliminate the random "fees" in rural schools that had grown rapidly since the 1980s, and it provided increased funding to the localities to ensure that this would happen (Brock 2009). The central government's renewed emphasis on education is reflected in the increase of expenditures as a share of GDP, particularly after 2005 (see figure 4). Of course, this increased funding has not dealt with the problem of segregated schools in urban China, and profound class and regional inequality persists (Mok, Wong, and Zhang 2009; Qian and Amyth 2008).

The pattern with pensions is somewhat more complex but follows a similar trajectory. Under the *danwei* system, worker pensions were provided and managed by the enterprise. If there was unevenness in the generousness of the pensions across enterprises, everyone was guaranteed some sort of protection in insurance by virtue of his or her position. The state did not provide pensions to rural residents, who had to rely on family and the commune/collective.

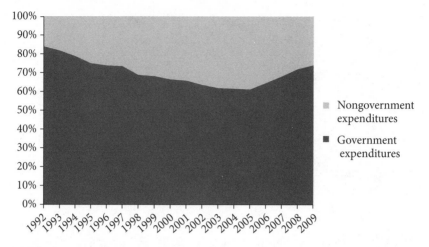

FIGURE 3. Education expenditures, 1992–2009.
Source: *Zhongguo tongji nianjian* (2011) [China statistical yearbook 2011]
(Beijing: China Statistics Press).

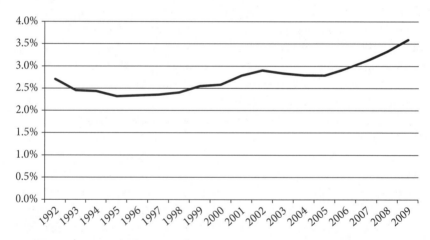

FIGURE 4. Government expenditures on education as a share of GDP,
1992–2009.
Source: *Zhongguo tongji nianjian* (2011) [China statistical yearbook 2011]
(Beijing: China Statistics Press).

The process of marketization of pensions was really a subsidiary feature of the process of "smashing the iron rice bowl," or the privatization and mass layoffs of the state-owned sector, which accelerated in 1997. This process resulted in widespread bankruptcies, as well as outright theft of pension funds, leaving many aggrieved workers with little means for subsistence (F. Chen 2000). However, as

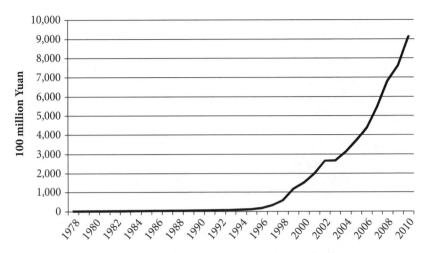

FIGURE 5. Government expenditures on social security and employment, 1978–2010.
Source: Zhongguo tongji nianjian (2001–2011) [China statistical yearbook 2001–2011] (Beijing: China Statistics Press).
Note: "Employment" refers to training and services related to reemployment. Unfortunately disaggregated data are not available.

Mark Frazier (2010) has shown, state spending increased significantly, largely in response to widespread unrest among laid-off workers (see figure 5). This increase in spending looks more dramatic than it actually is because it does not account for the rapid decline in spending by state-owned companies. Nonetheless, the five-year plan unveiled in 2006 called for 49 million more urban residents to be provided with retirement insurance (Fan 2006, 710). And in 2009 the government initiated a plan to expand social pensions to rural residents, with the intention that 50 percent of them would be covered by the end of 2012 (Shen and Williamson 2010, 242).

Although the preceding account is far too brief and leaves many problems untouched, it is clear that the central government began to back away from the hypercommodification that characterized the 1990s and early 2000s in terms of labor market regulation and welfare provision. But an analysis of aggregate social spending and policy directives fails to capture ongoing power asymmetries in society, profound lawlessness, and the ongoing existence of social groups systematically excluded from increased spending. Chief among these groups were migrant workers, as expanded social welfare was largely directed either at urban or rural residents but not those in between. According to a national survey of 6,232 migrant workers conducted by the State Council, in 2009 migrant participation in workplace injury insurance, basic medical insurance, and basic pension

TABLE 1.   2012 insurance participation rates among migrant workers

Pensions	Workplace injury	Medical	Unemployment	Maternal leave
14.3%	24%	16.9%	8.4%	6.1%

Source: "2012 quanguo nongmingong jiance diaocha baogao" [2012 National investigative report on migrant workers] Beijing: National Bureau of Statistics.

programs was only 24.3 percent, 18.8 percent, and 11.5 percent, respectively (Li Wei 2011, 198). A different survey conducted by the National Bureau of Statistics found slightly different, but still very low, numbers for insurance participation rates in 2012 (see table 1). The 2009 survey found that the top two reasons migrants were interested in getting urban *hukou* were "good education for children" and "high levels of social insurance" (Li Wei, 129) While a large majority listed "wages" as their primary existing dissatisfaction, the next biggest concerns were "living conditions," "social insurance," and "health care" (128). It is precisely these sorts of issues that trade unions have frequently fought for in the process of capitalist industrialization. Without such representation, workers have been taking matters into their own hands.

Worker Unrest in China

At present, there is significant literature on how this process of commodification has generated worker unrest in China, but as yet there are no comprehensive studies on how the state and union are responding. The destruction of the *danwei* system that had previously integrated urban workers into state structures during state socialism (Walder 1983, 1984) resulted in a loss of direct control over urban workers (Lau 2001; Solinger 1995), and there were massive revolts in the late 1990s and early 2000s (Cai 2002; Hurst 2009). Although many of these laid-off workers have suffered immensely in the reform era and have had little success finding reemployment in the private sector, municipal governments have greatly expanded social insurance coverage for them (Frazier 2010). But migrant workers, from the very beginning existing in a precarious economic position and with ambiguous legal status once in the city, have emerged as a new social class without an institutionalized channel for integration of collective demands into legalized mechanisms. The first wave of scholarship on migrants identified their legal and economic precariousness (Solinger 1999) and the frequently brutal employment conditions they have been subjected to (Chan 2001; Choi 2003). Subsequent studies have focused on the volume and character of worker resistance, which has remained largely focused on economic demands. But though migrant workers are not explicitly political in their demands, there is an important debate in the field focused on the question of class formation and subjectivity. Ching Kwan Lee (2007) has a relatively pessimistic perspective, arguing that legal reforms have given rise to a highly legalistic mode of resistance and that the state's project of individualizing labor conflict has been actively supported by unions and nongovernmental organizations (NGOs) alike (Friedman and Lee 2010). She argues that worker resistance in China is characterized by "cellular activism," in which insurgents are unable to construct durable organization or articulate political demands. On the other hand, Pun Ngai (2005) maintains that the category of *dagongmei/zai* (working girl/boy) represents a potentially subversive discursive formation, one that could serve as the symbolic foundation for more broad-based mobilization. And indeed, she has found evidence of strikes spreading beyond single factories, a phenomenon she sees as an indication of heightened worker consciousness (Chan and Pun 2009). Despite his relative optimism about class formation in China, Chris Chan's (2010) key phrase of "class struggle without class organization" (16) is an implicit recognition of current limits. Regardless of such different interpretations of working class subjectivity, there is consensus that capitalist development generated resistance that has been rapidly expanding in scope since the early 1990s and that this represents a major political challenge for the regime.

My primary aim, however, is not to describe the dynamics of worker resistance but rather to provide an analysis of how the state, through the auspices of the unions, is responding to this conflict. Dorothy Solinger (2009) deals with this issue in her comparative work on labor politics under neoliberalism in China, France, and Mexico. We are in full agreement that a primary reason that worker unrest has been so persistent in China is the weakness of unions. However, her research analyzes how the state increased social spending to placate laid-off SOE workers. At the moment of exit, the state did not need to worry about the political issue of incorporation, as is the case for the still-emergent migrant working class. In other words, Solinger's focus is the politics of the unmaking of a class, while I am focused on the politics of a class in formation. As noted by Ching Kwan Lee (2007), the expansion in legal rights for workers has been a primary thrust of the state's attempt to deal with increasing unrest.[10] This response—which culminated in the 2007 passage of the Labor Contract Law—is an effort to integrate workers into the structure of the state as atomized individuals. In this sense we can see strong parallels with Hagen Koo's (2001) characterization of the relationship between state and worker in other export-oriented economies in East Asia.[11] But as argued by Feng Chen (2007), the extension of individual rights in the absence of collective rights has failed to reduce labor conflict. The focus of this book is how the union responds to generalized worker insurgency by attempting—within given political parameters—to incorporate workers and potentially advance decommodification. These issues are particularly pressing for the "new" working class—the 250 million rural migrants who have powered the Chinese economic miracle.

Migrant and Urban Workers

"Migrant workers" refers to people working in cities with nonlocal *hukou*. *Hukou* is an intergenerational system of formally tiered citizenship, in which the provision of social services is tied to a specific locality. People with nonlocal *hukou* do not have guaranteed access to public services such as health care, education, pensions, and subsidized housing and suffer various forms of political and social discrimination. The consequence of this is that migrants are formally second-class citizens when they leave their place of *hukou* registration and go to work in the city. This system has allowed urban employers to pay less than the full cost of labor as the costs of reproduction are borne in the countryside. Although some local governments have experimented with liberalizing *hukou* requirements, the system still results in major administrative obstacles for migrants wishing to make a decent life in the city (Chan and Buckingham 2008; K. W. Chan 2010). Despite these ongoing challenges, there are now 250 million migrants living in China's urban areas.[12]

In this book I focus on migrant workers rather than their urban-resident counterparts because migrants now constitute the most important section of the working class, not just numerically but also politically and economically. Economically, the highly commodified and precarious position of migrants is indicative of the overall tendency of the working class—that is, conditions for urban workers from old SOEs have converged downward. And politically, although it is difficult to determine with great confidence migrants' share of total labor unrest, anecdotal evidence suggests that they are the primary actors in contemporary insurgency—and in this sense they are less politically incorporated. Without a doubt, migrants are the central actors in posing *offensive* demands, while resistance among urban SOE workers has largely been defensive in nature. Politically, then, migrants represent the future of the working class. This is not to suggest that workers with urban *hukou* are without grievances—and as indicated above, there is much evidence to suggest that with advancing marketization, their concerns are increasingly similar to those of migrants. But the kind of widespread (defensive) militancy witnessed during the major privatization push in the late 1990s and early 2000s has subsided, if not wholly disappeared. To the extent that urban workers engage in overt resistance, it is likely to look increasingly like migrant-style unrest, as the old *danwei* system of incorporation is increasingly inoperable. While I suspect that the framework developed here will also be useful in explaining the politics of urban worker unrest, I do not address this issue empirically in this book.

Why China Is Different and Why It Matters

In considering which features of China's labor politics are peculiar and which general, it is useful to consider the historical interplay between marketization and labor politics globally. In updating Polanyi, Burawoy (2008) delineates three historical waves of marketization, each generating a countermovement for social protection. The first wave led to the development of radical labor movements in the West, causing theorists such as Karl Marx to predict the imminent collapse of capitalism. But this prediction was of course wrong, and second wave marketization emerged in the interwar period. Once again, this resulted in labor militancy, but by this time the state response was distinct from that of its nineteenth-century counterparts. Thus, in the countermovement under the second wave, the state established a set of institutional protections from the vagaries of the free market, though this appeared in very different forms around the world—fascist, state-socialist, and various types of welfarism. While each type of state had a very different approach, in general labor movements were legalized and integrated into the structures of the state. We have been in the neoliberal (third) wave of marketization since the 1970s, during which time many of the institutional protections established by the state in response to the second wave have been undone. This includes social welfare provisions as well as a weakening of labor unions.

China's experiences in these successive waves have been shaped by its confrontation with imperialism and the construction of state socialism. Beginning in the mid-nineteenth century, China was subject to imperialist aggression from Britain and other European powers, which eventually played a central role in the fall of the Qing Dynasty. Marketization in the interwar period was inseparable from imperial projects—now emanating from Japan as well as from Europe. As we will see in the following chapter, this meant that the response of both the Communist Party and much of the labor movement to second-wave marketization was marked by the colonial encounter. ACFTU unions played a crucial role in early anti-imperialist mobilizations, and national interests were more central to their politics than were class interests. In the postwar era, the most important institution for decommodifying and incorporating labor was the *danwei*, which provided the urban working class with permanent jobs and a wealth of cradle-to-grave social services (Perry and Lu 1997; Walder 1983). Under this system, the role of the unions was largely to administer the distribution of welfare to workers in the *danwei*. And marketization in China since the late 1970s has largely eliminated the protections afforded to the old working class while simultaneously producing a new working class composed of rural migrants. But up to the present, the Chinese state has been attempting to use institutions constructed during second-wave marketization to respond to the social dislocations brought about by contemporary marketization.

In other words, the Chinese state is using state-socialist institutions to deal with the eminently (if not exclusively)[13] capitalist problem of proletarian unrest—hence the *postsocialist* character of China's labor politics. But not all forms of postsocialism are the same, as China is remarkably different from former Soviet and Warsaw Pact countries in two respects. First, despite the persistence of state-socialist–era union organizations in many countries in Eastern Europe (Clarke and Pringle 2009; Crowley and Ost 2001), a relatively liberal political environment (compared with that of China) means that there is greater pluralism in labor representation. Second and perhaps more important is distinct growth trajectories. While Eastern Europe was relatively industrialized in the 1980s, China was still an overwhelmingly agricultural society—and a poor one at that. If China's postsocialist experience is marked by explosive growth and the formation of a new working class, Russia experienced astonishing "involution" during this period (Burawoy 1996). Although the worst of post-shock therapy has passed in Russia, and other Eastern European countries have not fared as poorly, this region has not experienced anything like the capitalist dynamism that has taken place in China. Nor has Eastern Europe had anywhere near the levels of labor unrest that China has experienced over the past two decades. Thus Chinese postsocialism is remarkably different from the post-Soviet variant.

There are some parallels between Chinese labor politics and those of other countries in East Asia. The "Asian Tigers" of Taiwan, South Korea, Singapore, and Hong Kong maintained greater political exclusion of labor than was the case in other regions (Deyo 1987, 1989). With the possible exception of South Korea (Koo 2001), workers were less militant than their counterparts in the West or Latin America had been at a similar stage of industrialization. Perhaps the closest analogue is Vietnam with its Leninist system of trade unions and high levels of worker unrest. Limited research suggests that the Vietnamese state is more tolerant of worker unrest, and as a result labor protest is somewhat more coordinated than is the case in China (A. Chan 2011a; Clarke 2006; Pringle and Clarke 2011). Although political exclusion is, at the most general level, common to all these countries in the early phase of capitalist industrialization, the Chinese state is unusual in both its dedication to maintaining a monopoly on representation of labor and its coercive capacity to enforce this.

At a very general level, there is nothing surprising about the fact that unregulated capitalist industrialization has generated worker unrest in China—such dynamics have appeared in countries around the world for nearly two centuries. But the specificity of postsocialist politics requires a somewhat different approach to studying this phenomenon in China. Whereas under second-wave marketization states had to decide whether/how to integrate worker representatives into the structures of the state, in China *incorporation* (see below for an elaborated definition) is the state's struggle to integrate atomized workers *into the union,* thereby rendering their struggles intelligible. Without legitimate representation—a potential means for co-optation—such a procedure encounters difficulty. If under second-wave marketization, the key site of analysis was between unions (as relatively unproblematized representatives of workers) and the state, the particular conditions in contemporary China imply that the focus must shift to the relationship between dispersed insurgent workers and unions. Although the theory of the countermovement is able to account for high levels of unrest and legislative efforts of the central government to ameliorate conflict, it fails to account for the politics of institutionalization in contemporary China.

Finally, it is worth noting that labor politics in China hold profound consequences for the future of global capitalism. China occupies an increasingly central position in the global economy (Arrighi 2007a, 2007b; Hung 2009; Li Minqi 2009), and the nation's leaders have lofty geopolitical ambitions. China's transition to capitalism has already fundamentally reconfigured the structures of the global economy. It is the world's largest exporter,[14] one of the top recipients of foreign direct investment (FDI),[15] the second-largest national economy, and it increasingly dominates the production of all sorts of goods, from the very low-end and labor intensive to high-end and capital-intensive. Given the high degree of concentration of the globe's manufacturing, a shift in the country's mode of accumulation will reverberate internationally. Additionally, although China is of course dependent on the markets of wealthy nations, it is not politically or militarily subordinate to the United States in the way that Japan, South Korea, Taiwan, and any number of Latin American countries have been. China will increasingly be in a position where it is less bound by external constraints than has been the case for many newly industrialized countries. The consequence is that if pushed in a prolabor direction by worker insurgency, China may be in a position to lead a decommodifying restructuring of global capitalism (Arrighi 2007a). As noted by Peter Evans (2008, 2010), any adequate response to neoliberal globalization must itself be global in nature, and China is the most important single country in this regard. While the emergence of a globally oriented counterhegemonic labor movement in China seems remote at present, such a development would have far reaching consequences.

Countermovements and Appropriated Representation

Just as Polanyi (1944) studied the great transformation of nineteenth- and early twentieth-century Britain, I am concerned here with similar tectonic social and political shifts that derive from capitalist industrialization in contemporary China. Polanyi's theory of the "double movement" held that the commodification of land, labor, and money would, if left unchecked, result in the destruction of society and the ecosystem. However, he argued that commodification generated a countermovement for social protection from various classes in society that would result in decommodification of labor (as well as land and money, but labor is most relevant for this discussion) and a reembedding of markets. One of his key examples of a successful countermovement was the American New Deal.

Scholars have criticized Polanyi's conception of countermovements as being deterministic[16] and functionalist (Munck 2004, 253; Dale 2012, 9–10). As Burawoy (2003) has argued, "Polanyi gives us a signpost to an architecture of counterhegemony even as he fails to appreciate the obstacles it must face" (231), which is to say he does a poor job of accounting for *politics* (Hwa-Jen Liu 2011, 22). This is because in the original formulation of the countermovement, social resistance to commodification is conflated with actual institutionalized class compromise such as that which characterized the postwar political economy of North America, Western Europe, and Japan.[17] If we were to uncritically apply this teleological framework to contemporary China, we would be unable to explain the persistence of worker unrest in the face of major policy change from the center.

I make several adjustments to the Polanyian theory of countermovements to account for this difficulty. As discussed above, the seeming inclination of the Chinese central government toward class compromise has not resulted in a reduction in migrant worker insurgency, as labor remains highly commodified and labor conflicts often cannot be resolved by unions or through other legal means. Theoretically, this allows us to see that countermovements against commodification must be broken down into two distinct, if dialectically intertwined, moments: the insurgent moment, in which social groups marginalized in the process of capitalist development engage in disorganized and ephemeral resistance to commodification; and the institutional moment, when durable class compromise is established in the political and economic spheres.[18] It is important to stress that these moments refer both to particular events and to an aspect or instance of a broader tendency (in this case the countermovement). But I am not suggesting a strictly linear temporal progression from one moment to the next—empirically speaking, they will coexist as insurgency may generate an institutional response, and new institutions may create new forms of resistance.

I conceive of migrant worker resistance in China as an insurgency rather than a social movement. "Social movements" as conceived of in classic works by political process theorists (McAdam 1982; McAdam, Tarrow, and Tilly 2001; Tarrow 1998) generally display the following characteristics: (1) relatively coherent political program and well-articulated goals; (2) a preponderance of formal "social movement organizations," which are necessary in articulating said goals (Burstein and Linton 2002);[19] (3) targeting of the state; (4) exploitation of political space that is available in liberal democracies (e.g., through public marches, media outreach, political lobbying, etc.). These scholars of course acknowledge that there are all sorts of noninstitutionalized politics that are *not* social movements, as indicated by the more general concept of "contentious politics" (Tilly and Tarrow 2007). However, I follow Ching Kwan Lee in adopting Guha's (1983a, 1983b) more specific term of "insurgency." Worker unrest in China is cellular (Lee 2007), dispersed, fractured, and ephemeral; that is, worker organization is not durable across space or time. This resistance addresses only immediate economic grievances and therefore appears apolitical. But when viewed in the aggregate (either from the perspective of the central state or analytically), seemingly apolitical eruptions of insurgency are responding to relatively uniform structural conditions,[20] which is to say this resistance *is* eminently political. The unstated logic unifying disparate acts of insurgency is that of the countermovement, which while lacking a coherent and rationally articulated set of demands is a tendency toward rejecting commodification of social life.[21] Without legitimate representatives that could develop rationally articulated policy proposals, the state is faced with a complex challenge: rather than responding reactively to rationally articulated demands (as is the case for states facing a challenge from a social movement), it must respond unilaterally and rationally in response to "irrational" insurgency that has posed no political demands. These are the political dynamics of insurgency that sharply differentiate it from a traditional social movement.

In my formulation, the institutional moment refers to the establishment of class compromise in durable organizational forms that grant economic and political power to subordinate social groups. I take decommodification of labor as an indicator of the emergence of the institutional moment in the economic sphere; decommodification is defined as *social action that lessens the extent to which workers are immediately compelled to submit the satisfaction of their needs to the logic of the market.* Things such as guaranteed health care, pensions, job security, increased wages, and having a say in how the labor process is organized all contribute to decommodification. The political aspect of the institutional moment is represented by incorporation of the working class. This means that workers have substantive representation both on the shop floor (relationship to capital) and in giving the working class a voice in policymaking (relationship to the state). If workers are able to resolve collective problems and contend with capital within rationalized, legal channels (especially collective bargaining) and if they recognize the legitimacy of their legal union representatives, this serves as evidence of incorporation.

Decommodification and incorporation are based on existing concepts, both of which I modify for the Chinese context. For Polanyi, "decommodification" remains vague and hardly an analytical term at all. But theorists of the welfare state, most notably Esping-Andersen (1990) have refined the concept in focusing on national policies that remove the provision of basic human needs (e.g., health care, pensions, education, housing) from the market. The key difference between my conception of decommodification and that of Esping-Andersen is that he analyzes national-level policies while I insist on determining whether potentially decommodifying policies/collective bargaining agreements are implemented on the ground. This is because one of the primary obstacles to decommodification in China is the strong alliance between the lowest levels of the state and capital. Potentially prolabor legislation and collective contracts often go unenforced with the implicit or explicit approval of precisely those officials who are supposed to enforce them. Thus it is necessary to enter the workplace to study decommodification in China.

It is also worth clarifying my normative assessment of the term, as some may assume that decommodification is an unalloyed good from the perspective of workers. While this is certainly true in a number of cases, I am using the term in a strictly analytical sense to refer to the diminution of the extent to which labor power is bought and sold according to market principles. So for example, bonded labor is highly decommodified since there is no free exchange, but few would hold this up as a normative ideal. And decommodification may be pursued not only by workers but also by state and capital—one of Polanyi's major insights is that the self-regulating market creates chaos in *society*, not just for one particular class (even if the chaos is unevenly distributed). Perhaps Polanyi's greatest normative concern was whether decommodification and reembedding would be exclusive (e.g., fascist) or inclusive (e.g., socialist) in nature.

As for incorporation, China once again calls for a reconfiguration of the concept as it has traditionally been used. Political scientists Collier and Collier (1991) conceive of incorporation in their influential work as follows: "State control of the working class ceased to be principally the responsibility of the police or the army but rather was achieved at least in part through the legalization and institutionalization of a labor movement sanctioned and regulated by the state" (3) In both this work and other studies of Europe and Latin America, the question is how states deal with incorporating unions that developed independently (and that often had highly developed political agendas). Chief among these unions' political demands were official recognition and collective bargaining rights.

But Chinese unions are already granted official recognition, collective bargaining rights are enshrined in law, the constitution guarantees freedom of association, and workers have quite strong job protections on paper (e.g., working hours, vacation time, job security, health and safety). As with decommodification, the question cannot be one of the existence of potentially incorporating formal rights and administrative arrangements. Rather, verification of incorporation must be done at the microlevel. Do workers recognize the legitimacy of union representatives? Do workers resolve collective grievances through rationalized official procedures? Do collective bargaining mechanisms allow for rationalized negotiation over pay and workplace conditions? In short, we must see whether formal state and union interventions (laws and collective contracts) are able to effectively regulate labor relations or whether workers continue to engage in extralegal activities to defend/advance their rights and interests.

Decommodification and political incorporation are mutually reinforcing trends: to the extent that workers have greater collective voice in the state and workplace, their economic standing is likely to improve, and improvements in economic standing are likely to increase the legitimacy of union representatives and collective bargaining mechanisms. In China, the state and union were for a long time largely unconcerned with the economic problem, as evidenced by their presiding over a program of radical labor commodification since the late 1970s (Gallagher 2004, 2005; Kuruvilla, Lee, and Gallagher 2011). But over the course of the Hu administration, certain segments of the state (notably the central government) became increasingly interested in expanding workers' ability to consume to promote economic "rebalancing." And the state has long been concerned with the political problem of incorporation, as it fears the instability that may result from expanding labor unrest. But since the political and economic are intimately linked, some degree of decommodification will likely be necessary in order to attain incorporation. Additionally, strengthened representation in the workplace—especially mobilizational capacity—could increase the power of union representatives within the state.

A schematic of my reformulation of countermovements (figure 6) appears below.

In these terms, then, my question is: Why did the countermovement in China stall at the insurgent moment? Why did high levels of resistance among migrant workers result in legislative, regulatory, and symbolic[22] victories but did not

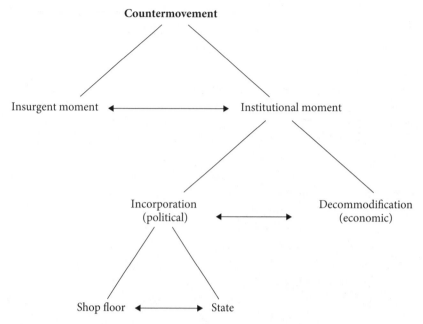

FIGURE 6.   Schematic of countermovements.

translate into incorporation or significant decommodification? My claim is that the transition from insurgency to the institutionalization of the countermovement (i.e., class compromise) that we would expect based on Polanyian theory was confounded because the new class of migrant workers in China emerged under conditions of *appropriated representation*. This monopolistic setup resulted in the illegitimate political representation of workers by the ACFTU.

"Appropriated representation" is a term originally used by Max Weber (1978, 292), which he juxtaposed to the radically democratic "instructed representation" (293) but which he did not develop at any length. I have adopted and reconfigured the term to refer to a situation in which *the state unilaterally grants exclusive rights of political representation of an entire class to a particular organization in the absence of substantive or formalistic delegation from membership.* Historically, unions in many other countries undergoing capitalist industrialization have played a crucial role in channeling insurgent worker energy into the construction of collective power capable of winning compromise from the state and capital. But in the Chinese case, the ACFTU did not mobilize or actively involve itself in the lives of migrant workers as they emerged as a new class,[23] as it maintains the state's goal of reducing labor unrest. Under conditions of appropriated representation, dispersed worker insurgency strengthens the hand of union representatives at the national level (since the state fears instability and may be willing to promote legislative reform) but simultaneously results in weak, illegitimate unions on the shop floor, which are generally incapable of enforcing laws and collective agreements.

Appropriated representation may recall earlier definitions of corporatism, or more specifically "state corporatism" (Schmitter 1974, 103). Indeed, the corporatist framework has been popular in describing labor politics in China (A. Chan 1993; Unger and Chan 1995), with some even arguing that China has shifted toward "social representation" (Yunqiu Zhang 1997). But why is appropriated representation a more appropriate concept for China's contemporary labor politics than corporatism (or one of its many variants)? The first reason is quite simply that corporatism implies that the group in question has been more or less *incorporated* into state structures. This may have been an apt description of the relationship between the working class and the state during the Mao era but clearly no longer is. A primary purpose of this book is to determine whether and under what particular conditions it may be possible to incorporate workers, a change that has certainly not yet occurred at the class level. A second and related reason is that corporatism (for labor) refers to a historically specific arrangement in which the working class was forced to abandon political goals in exchange for economic benefits. Whether in the fascist, state-socialist, or welfare state variant, corporatism implied that the state would preside over a regime of relatively decommodified labor (as well as frequently providing representatives with material and symbolic benefits) in exchange for acquiescence to "national interests."[24] The Chinese Communist Party has not been nearly so benevolent toward migrant workers, which means that the new working class is not dependent on the state in the way that workers in many Latin American countries were (Cohen 1982). Third, corporatism frequently implied that independent, mobilized, and perhaps militant trade unions where to be tamed, co-opted, and integrated into the state, a situation clearly at odds with practices in contemporary China. Even in previous instances in which the state created new labor organizations to serve corporatist goals, few if any states have been able to police their labor monopoly as tightly as China. In other words, much as corporatism is a historically specific political arrangement (associated with second-wave marketization), appropriated representation is dependent on highly developed and competent state apparatus that can effectively crush alternative forms of political representation. State corporatism may accurately describe the relationship between the state and urban working class during the Mao era—but the institutions developed under this arrangement have not been able to incorporate the new working class. Empirically, this situation is no longer captured by corporatism.

It is also worth addressing the much-discussed topic of union oligarchy, a line of inquiry first established by Robert Michels (1962) and carried into the

American context by Seymour Lipset and others (Lipset, Trow, and Coleman 1956; Jacobs 1963). I do not conceive of oligarchy primarily as a union that fails to pursue the interests of membership (since "interests" are always the object of symbolic struggle) but rather in process-based terms. Unions are democratic rather than oligarchic to the extent that membership is actively engaged and mobilized in the determination of organizational ends of action and the pursuit of those ends. In other words, do workers have a say in what the union will do? And once organizational goals have been established, are workers involved in pursuing these goals? ACFTU unions are de jure subject to control by the Party from the national to the district level[25] while remaining de facto subordinate to capital at the firm level. I do not, however, take a static perspective on union oligarchy but rather assume that it can be subject to challenge and revision (Voss and Sherman 2000). And yet the relationship between the ACFTU and migrant workers is quite distinct from earlier instances of oligarchic unions. While some unions in the West were able to remain relatively democratic because of specific qualities of leadership or internal opposition (Stepan-Norris and Zeitlin 1995, 1996; Stepan-Norris 1997), the general tendency was for unions to begin quite democratic and to ossify over time into increasing oligarchy. However, the ACFTU was re-created in toto by the state, once in 1948 and again in 1978. It is this specific (Leninist) historical trajectory in the relationship between union, state, and working class that I refer to as appropriated representation and that puts the ACFTU in a different category than other unions. In my conceptualization, unions can be expected to behave "oligarchicly" under conditions of appropriated representation (i.e., they will respond to the wishes of state and capital while members will be excluded from practical activities). Whereas appropriated representation refers to the general processes of political representation, oligarchy (as juxtaposed to democracy) refers to the union's practical organizational activity. To put it another way, appropriated representation refers to the ACFTU's relationship to state and workers at the *class level,* while its relationship to specific workers *on the shop floor* is characterized by oligarchic behavior.

The tension between the insurgent and institutional moments of the countermovement can be best analyzed at the point where the state is now attempting to incorporate rebellious workers: the trade union structure. To put things concretely, I am interested in how the state, through the auspices of highly oligarchic unions, deals with the problem of labor conflict in the process of capitalist industrialization and attempts to integrate workers into legalized channels of contention. This analysis requires an investigation into not just the relationship between workers and union (although this is the primary focus) but also these two groups' respective relationships to state and capital.

Studying Chinese Unions

Gaining access to Chinese unions is a significant challenge, and studying how unions respond to the crisis of worker resistance only compounds the problem. However, I had the good fortune to serve as an interpreter for prominent American labor leaders on several exchanges held with national leaders from the ACFTU as well as the Shanghai Federation of Trade Unions. Given this friendly introduction, I was able to meet people, conduct interviews, and gain access to information that I would not have otherwise. Additionally, while serving as a lecturer at Sun Yat-sen University in Guangzhou, my mother developed a close working relationship with the chairman of the Guangzhou Federation of Trade Unions, Chen Weiguang. Although certain activities of the unions remained highly opaque, the access I did secure would not have been possible without these personal connections.

This book is based on ethnographic data collected during one and a half years of fieldwork in China. I spent approximately ten months in Guangzhou, with the remaining time divided up between Zhejiang province, Shanghai, Hong Kong, and Beijing (in descending order). My respondents include union and government officials, workers, and enterprise managers. As anyone who has conducted qualitative research on sensitive topics in China will attest, such work requires a high degree of flexibility in approaches to data collection. Sometimes I was able to conduct formal, semistructured interviews; other times, I would not be afforded an interview but would be allowed to "chat." I attended numerous formal meetings between foreign and Chinese union officials and an equal number of formal meals. These meetings mostly took place during four separate multiday trips by Chinese and American delegations in 2007 and 2008, two each in the United States and China. As I befriended some of the younger staff of various unions, I would sometimes meet up with them for lunch or tea. With workers and managers, my methods were similarly diverse. Sometimes I would have several hours to conduct a formal interview, or perhaps I would chat with a worker while playing a game of pool. Additionally, much of the data in chapter 6 comes from supervised interviews conducted by research assistants.

In addition to interview data, I rely on media reports and historical documents. Although the media's ability to report on labor issues in China is constrained, it is not uncommon for strikes or other labor conflicts to be reported. In several instances, I found out about some incident in the media and then would conduct follow-up interviews with workers to gain a greater depth of understanding about the case. The historical data in chapter 3 come largely from collections of official documents stored at the Universities Service Centre at the Chinese University of Hong Kong.

Since the working hypothesis is that conditions of appropriated representation serve as a significant impediment to decommodification and incorporation, this book focuses on several most-likely cases. By analyzing the most proactive attempts of Chinese unions to advance the interests of their membership, I aim to identify the conditions under which the countermovement might be institutionalized. These cases, exceptional though they may be, reveal underlying dynamics that hold implications for the entirety of the trade union system in China. I look at how three general factors impact possibilities for institutionalization of the countermovement: (1) internal organizational factors (prolabor leadership); (2) external economic factors (model of development and shifts in global economic conditions); and (3) external political factors (center-local relations and specific incidents of worker insurgency).

Finally, I would like to emphasize that data triangulation was very important in this project. I decided to study the ACFTU at a time when many in the West were under the impression that Chinese unions were in a period of significant reform. On the basis of what I had heard from many Chinese union officials during exchanges in 2007, I began my research expecting to find unions that were playing a key role in advancing decommodification and winning recognition from membership. However, I found time and time again that union officials' claims about what was happening in the workplace were not verified by interviews with workers and managers. Thus, I frequently employ a method of contrasting union officials' representation of a particular reality with the lived experience of workers and managers. This allows us to understand what sort of a model of labor relations the unions *want* and how structural and organizational impediments frequently prevent them from realizing such ideals.

Stages of the Argument

Before moving to an analysis of contemporary postsocialist labor politics, it is important to understand the historical evolution of the ACFTU in order to grasp how appropriated representation was established in China. The argument spelled out in chapter 2 is that the ACFTU is not simply a union that is deeply integrated into state structures and severed from its membership (like many other unions around the world). In fact, given that the union was founded in the context of semicolonialism, it has *always* maintained the interrelated goals of realizing ethnonational autonomy and increasing productive capacity. Through an analysis of the historical development of the union federation, I show how relations of appropriated representation were established at the class level and how union activity can therefore be understood as derived from an internal organizational logic rather than simply imposed by external Party control. This background helps us to understand the postsocialist political and institutional context within which migrant workers emerged as a class and how their relationship to the state differs from urban workers who had been incorporated through the *danwei*.

The subsequent three chapters empirically assess the dynamics of migrant worker-union interactions in the contemporary era. In particular, the chapters focus on how union activities are influenced by (1) prolabor leadership at the municipal level; (2) a regional model of development; and (3) center-local relations and the evolving dynamics of worker resistance. Respectively these represent internal organizational, external economic, and external political factors.

In chapter 3 I ask the question, Can prolabor leadership at the municipal level advance decommodification and incorporation of labor? It is frequently suggested by union practitioners (and some scholars) in China that leadership can make a very large difference in outcomes, since laws and regulations are often fuzzy and hence subject to interpretation in implementation. Since the working hypothesis has been that ACFTU-subordinate unions have *not* played a decisive role in actively bringing about decommodification and incorporation, I began this book by investigating the places *most* likely to provide some counterevidence. Hence, chapter 3 looks at the Guangzhou Federation of Trade Unions (GZFTU), chaired by Chen Weiguang—the man widely considered by scholars and practitioners alike to be the most consistently prolabor union leader in China. The findings on the effects of leadership are inconclusive, though there is significant evidence that leadership is in general not able to overcome structural oligarchy and that a "passive repressive" approach to dealing with worker insurgency persists.

Based on a comparison of sectoral unions in Guangzhou and southeast Zhejiang, chapter 4 turns to an analysis of the impact of regional political economy on organizational form and innovation. In particular, unions in Zhejiang have been much more successful in engaging in sectoral-level collective bargaining, a development that I argue stems from the region's particular approach to economic development. However, these top-down negotiated contracts still encounter severe institutional obstacles to enforcement, as will be made clear in the case of the Rui'an Eyeglass Union. In showing how regional models of development impact municipal unions' ability to engage in sectoral-level bargaining, I argue that the existing literature has focused excessively on the issue of external Party control, thereby overlooking the impact of external economic conditions on union activity.

Chapter 5 turns to look at how unions respond to particular instances of worker resistance and how these responses evolved in 2007–10 (bookending the main period of research). Between the strike at Ascendant Elevator (pseudonym) in late

2007 and the strike wave of spring-summer 2010 sparked by workers at Nanhai Honda, major political and economic events had taken place. After the strike wave, some leaders began to make public calls for legalization of strikes, particularly in Guangdong but in other regions of China as well.[26] This chapter provides a clear example of the insurgent-institutional dialectic at work over the course of two and a half years in which major political and economic changes took place. Even if unions continued to fail to incorporate workers in the aftermath of the strike wave, we can see that the pressure generated by worker resistance is forcing continual adjustments, fixes, and occasional compromises. Such a dynamic will continue to be an ongoing feature of China's process of capitalist industrialization.

In chapter 6 I ask, How does China differ from other East Asian countries that maintained similar levels of repression against independent union organizing during capitalist industrialization? What impact will labor politics in China have on the global political economy? And how might the dynamics of insurgency trap develop in the future? First of all, Chinese workers are much more rebellious than their counterparts in Taiwan, Hong Kong, Singapore, or postwar Japan (again, South Korea is somewhat different). Additionally, the state in China appears to have both greater dedication and greater capacity to use repression against independent labor organizing. We will also see that the spatial and social dynamics of capitalist development in China are distinct from those of smaller countries. I close by stressing the incredible importance of labor politics in China's economic "rebalancing," drawing some conclusions about implications for the world system, and proposing some future paths of development—some liberating and some potentially catastrophic.

THE HISTORY AND STRUCTURE OF THE ACFTU

The headquarters of the Guangdong Federation of Trade Unions (GDFTU)—the most important provincial-level union organization in China—is situated directly between two buildings, each respectively imbued with profound and seemingly diametrically opposed symbolic values. On the left is the East Garden, the building that housed the *shenggang* (Guangdong-Hong Kong) strike committee during the revolutionary upsurge of 1925–27. Initiated in June of 1925, the *shenggang* strike remains the longest continuous general strike in history, and it played a crucial role in the development of the Chinese revolution. Today the site is closed to the public, although there is a small commemorative plaque to the side of the guarded entrance. To the right of the union headquarters (indeed, located within the same building complex) is the Guangdong Union Hotel. This hotel is wholly owned by the union federation but operates just as a normal hotel would and is used for generating profit. In early 2009, management fired an activist in the hotel after she pushed for expanded health insurance, housing subsidies, and overtime pay for low-paid migrant employees. After this incident of retaliation, the union federation that owned the hotel stated that it would "not take sides" in the dispute. Thus we have two materially objectified symbols of radically opposed modes of political action. On the left we have the ACFTU's past—organization, mobilization, and confrontation; and on the right we have its present—atomization, acquiescence, and heteronomy.

And yet, as we will see in this chapter, if the methods have changed dramatically, there is a coherent logic that connects the past and present of the ACFTU. Founded in Guangzhou just one month before the initiation of the *shenggang* strike in 1925, the ACFTU actively organized and mobilized the working class to engage in militant actions, including strikes, marches, and armed pickets (Kwan 1997; Perry 1993, 69–87). However, even at this time, mobilization was primarily directed toward defeating imperialism rather than destroying capitalism (Smith 2002). Before final military victory in 1949, ACFTU unions began working to maintain workplace harmony and increase efficiency and output. With marketization and the emergence of a new class of migrant workers in the 1980s and 1990s, this basic setup did not change. But it was the conditions under which the ACFTU was first constituted that defined a persistent internal logic—one that is quite different from the orienting logic of unions in capitalist states.

In this chapter, I aim to accomplish four things. First, I provide an empirical account of the activities of the ACFTU from its founding in 1925 until the early 2000s. Second, I delineate major changes in trade union structure. Of crucial importance in this regard is the dynamic relationship between union, Party, capital, and working class. Related to this is the third point, which is an analysis of the emergence of "appropriated representation" that was solidified in the post-revolutionary period. Finally, I argue that on the whole, working-class organization in China has since the 1920s accepted the goals of promoting ethnonational autonomy and increasing productive forces. Although the *danwei* system effectively incorporated and decommodified labor during the era of the command economy (Lau 2001; Walder 1983, 1984), the organizational logic of unions was and is that of the state. As the goals of the state and those of the working class increasingly diverged beginning in the 1980s (though not in a linear manner), this presented new challenges for the union. Even if contemporary worker demands look quite similar to those of their counterparts in other regions and historical time periods, we will see that the ACFTU does not see increasing the material and political standing of its membership as an end in itself—and in this sense it challenges commonly held notions of what constitutes a "union."

The Revolutionary Years—Mobilization

The emergence of labor activism among the ACFTU and its subordinate trade unions cannot be viewed in isolation from the development of the Chinese Communist Party (CCP) and the struggle against foreign imperialism. Prior to the Kuomintang (KMT) purge and massacre of Communists in April of 1927, the CCP had been following Marxist-Leninist orthodoxy by focusing its organizing efforts on the urban working class. While much analysis of the Chinese revolution has focused on the Communists' mobilization of peasants (Bianco and Bell 1971; Hinton 1966; Skocpol 1979), most of their pre-1927 energies were devoted to building industrial unions and a national union federation, the ACFTU. As the revolutionaries became painfully aware of later, the Chinese urban proletariat in the 1920s was still quite small. Although the extractive and transportation industries were somewhat developed in many places in the country, modern industrial manufacturing was concentrated in two places: Shanghai and Guangdong province. There the ACFTU and Communist-affiliated unions actively sought to organize and mobilize workers, sometimes in defense of immediate economic rights and sometimes for broader political struggles.

One of the ACFTU's official histories, *A Concise History of Chinese Trade Unions* (Wang, He, and Cao 2005), provides an account of the activism of Communist-affiliated unions in the 1920s. Even before the official establishment of the Communist Party, the prominent Chinese Communist Chen Duxiu argued in August of 1920 that most unions in Shanghai were controlled by bosses and were therefore useless. Chen claimed that "10,000 of these [yellow] unions could be formed and it wouldn't matter," and that workers should "unite and organize real worker groups!" (9). Shortly after the formation of the CCP and the establishment of the Party's Labor Secretariat, there was a strike wave throughout the country between January 1922 and February 1923. During this time, the Secretariat was actively involved in protesting against the official ban on strikes and organizing strikes in which a total of three hundred thousand workers participated nationwide (14). These strident prolabor activities and proclamations surely helped solidify the position of Communist unions among the working class. However, in response to a strike of workers on the Beijing-Hankou railroad, the ruling warlords launched a vicious nationwide crackdown on organized labor. Dozens of railroad workers were killed and imprisoned, and Communist labor organizations around the country went underground.

This low tide of revolutionary labor activity did not last long. By 1925 more favorable political conditions prevailed in certain regions, and Communist labor activists began regrouping in Shanghai and Guangzhou. Though the Communists and Nationalists were operating under the "united front" policy, right-wing Nationalist labor activists boycotted the second National Labor Conference, which commenced on May 1, 1925. This boycott allowed the Communists to avoid the confrontations and gridlock that had plagued the first national conference and to realize their goal of formally establishing a national labor federation under their control: the ACFTU (L. Lee 1986, 8).

Just weeks after the ACFTU was established, the federation and its subordinate industrial unions were to receive a series of opportunities to mobilize and increase their credibility among Chinese workers. The Communist-controlled Japanese Cotton Mills Union began a series of strikes in 1925. On May 15, the union activist Gu Zhenghong was killed by a Japanese manager, stoking both nationalist and class-based outrage (Perry 1993, 80). Gu instantly became a martyr of the anticolonial and class struggle, and his memorial service was attended by thousands of workers. A reporter at the event, which was presided over by the Cotton Mills Union chair Liu Hua, commented, "I daresay that this sort of grand proletarian gathering is unprecedented in Shanghai. Nine out of ten participants were workers"(80). On May 30, there was a huge solidarity protest in which workers from a wide variety of industries gathered to express their dismay over the murder of their fellow countryman and worker. But this protest was not to end peacefully: the British authorities opened fire on some of the protesters, eventually killing thirteen workers. Then, on May 31 the just-established Shanghai Federation of Trade Unions (SHFTU) called for a general strike, which was to last several months. This revolutionary event was crucial in establishing the SHFTU as a worker-representative organization and in giving coherence to the Shanghai working class: "After the [Shanghai] General Union had gradually been deserted by its allies, it had done a tremendous job of organization during July and August, and had given the working masses of Shanghai a unity and a crusading spirit they had never known before" (Chesneaux 1968, 269). Additionally, the union federation very quickly gained recognition in the political field, as indicated by its hosting of a delegation of Soviet trade unionists and increased consultation with the Beijing government on pending labor laws. Between the start of the strike in May and September of the same year, SHFTU-subordinate unions increased in number from 20 to 127, and their membership grew from 20,000 to 220,000, a phenomenon that was not limited to Shanghai: "[During the summer of 1925] regional union federations and national industrial unions were set up under the leadership of the ACFTU one after another" (Wang, He, and Cao 2005, 20) The so-called May thirtieth incident became a rallying cry for the emerging *wuzhou* movement, which immediately thereafter burst on the scene not just in Shanghai but throughout China.

The labor movement in Guangdong was not to be left out. With some political protection coming from the Communist-Nationalist united front policy (Li Guofang 2001), a general strike in Guangdong and Hong Kong was initiated in late June of 1925. The ACFTU and Communist activists were able to gain control over the strike committee, though some Nationalist sympathizers were also involved. As was the case with the labor upsurge in Shanghai, the *shenggang* strike was propelled by anticolonialism. After Communist-influenced unions in Hong Kong initiated widespread strikes starting in mid-June of 1925, the ACFTU called for solidarity action among workers in Guangzhou. On June 23 French and British soldiers attacked protesting workers and students just outside Shamian, a foreign concession in Guangzhou. The "Shaji Incident" left 52 people dead and 117 wounded and led to great outrage among people throughout the province and the country. Approximately 250,000 workers in Hong Kong and Guangdong began a general strike, which stretched out over many months (Wang, He, and Cao 2005, 21).

The Primacy of Anti-Imperialism

As has already been alluded to, both the ACFTU and the Party were primarily concerned with the anti-imperialist struggle during the mid-late 1920s. I follow S.A. Smith's (2002) characterization of labor struggles in this period as "class-inflected anti-imperialist nationalism" (190). Although anti-imperialism was the dominant discursive frame, Communist unions in particular occasionally wove class-based analyses into their rhetoric. In a sense, anti-imperialism frequently coincided with class struggle, given the large number of foreign-owned enterprises in Shanghai and Guangdong. That the institutional foundations of the Communist union federations were constituted largely in opposition to imperialism rather than capital was to have important consequences for the development of labor politics in China.

Through the revolutionary upsurge of 1925–27, union leadership frequently employed the language of *minzu* when speaking of the need for liberation. The term *minzu*—which can be alternately translated as "nation" or "ethnic group"—was first used by nationalists in the late nineteenth and early twentieth century in political rhetoric (D. Wu 1991, 161) and was an attempt to sharply differentiate Chinese from foreign. In open letters from ACFTU leadership to workers involved in the *shenggang* general strike, the need for national liberation was always paramount. In one such letter from July 1925, the second month of the strike, union leadership said: "We must safeguard the national [*minzu*] movement and workers' movement in Guangdong and Hong Kong in order to safeguard China. We should unite with all the people of Shanghai, and workers, and all oppressed people in the nation in order to resist the imperialist offensive." (*Zhongguo gonghui lishi wenxian* 1958, 93). In a separate letter from the same week, the ACFTU very clearly lays out its argument for the importance of the general strike: "Workers! Why do we strike? We strike to win the freedom of the nation [*minzu*]. Who stole our nation's freedom? It was stolen by the imperialist" (94).

As revealed in these letters, union and Party leadership primarily viewed the *shenggang* general strike as a means to eliminate foreign aggression in China. When the ACFTU announced the formation of the *shenggang* strike committee in June of 1925, this sentiment was unequivocal: "Compatriots from Guangdong and Hong Kong are implementing an allied strike because of their hatred of British and Japanese imperialist massacres in Shanghai, Hankou, Qingdao, and other places" (*Shenggang da bagong ziliao* 1980, 149) Deng Zhongxia, an early ACFTU leader and one of the central organizers of the *shenggang* strike, was quite direct in his assessment of the movement's goals: "This national strike of the working class is originally not an economic struggle to 'increase wages,' or 'reduce hours,' but rather is a political struggle to 'oppose imperialism and liberate the nation'" (150). Since foreigners were highly dependent on the labor of Chinese workers, particularly in Shanghai, Hong Kong, and Guangzhou, the strike exacted a high economic toll on their profits.

Despite the refrain from union leadership that "the entire country has a common enemy,"[1] more traditional class-based Marxist language occasionally appeared in official speeches. In particular, the commemoration of the hundredth meeting of the *shenggang* strike committee in March 1926, nearly one year into the strike, was marked by specifically class-based rhetoric and mention of the liberation of the working class rather than the nation. Deng Zhongxia (who in 1925 said that the goal of the strike was to oppose imperialism) stated the following in his address to the assembly:

> If the working class wants to achieve full liberation, it will only come after the working class has seized state power. If the working class tries to implement peaceful and reformist policies before the capitalist system has been eliminated, that is to say under the rule of the capitalist class's government, then liberation will never be realized. The working class can only rely on its own class organization and exercise continuous and absolute state power to eliminate all previous forms of the state, before full liberation will be possible. The Paris commune represented the first historical step in this direction, and Russia's Soviet government is the second step. (*Shenggang da bagong ziliao* 1980, 187)

And although "the enemy" remains undefined in this official union statement from April 1926, the implication seems to be that it is capital in general rather than specifically foreign capital:

> In order for the oppressed working class to liberate itself, it must unite across all boundaries and increase its own strength and defeat the enemy. Workers must manage production by themselves. Policies of compromise or reconciliation either intentionally or unintentionally help the enemy and bring our working class into a realm where they will never be able to achieve liberation. (*Zhongguo gonghui lishi wenxian*, 1958, 197)

Additionally, many union demands during the *wuzhou* movement and *shenggang* strike focused on bread-and-butter workplace issues, such as limiting the working day, increasing the minimum wage, and the provision of benefits such as housing and education for workers.

It is unclear why such class-based analysis occasionally appears in the official record of the strike, even if it is certainly less emphasized than ethnonational unity. There likely were intense debate and negotiations among workers and intellectuals as to whether an anticapitalist or an anti-imperialist frame was most appropriate for the Chinese labor movement. Additionally, changes in rhetoric may be related to the ongoing fight between the Communists and the KMT for control over the movement. In the struggle between the right wing of the KMT and the Communist Party, perhaps the ACFTU was encouraged to emphasize class rhetoric as a means of differentiation.

And yet such strong class-based language was clearly the exception in this period. Deng Zhongxia, in a separate address at the very same conference where he claimed that the working class could never attain liberation without destroying the capitalist state, had this to say while ticking off the victories of the *shenggang* strike:

> Another victory has been economic development in Guangdong.... Since the *shenggang* strike, the Central Bank has been fortified. Previously, Guangzhou was flooded with Western currency, and even in the villages, Western currency was "better than gold." But since the strike, there has been a boycott of Western currency while only using Central Bank currency, so now Central Bank currency is "better than gold." The Central Bank has not only been fortified but has expanded, establishing branches in various places. The Central Bank now has more credit than foreign banks. (*Shenggang da bagong ziliao* 1980, 214).

Not only was there economic nationalism, but union leadership directly and explicitly sought assistance from Chinese capital in furthering the anti-imperialist struggle. For example, in March of 1926, the ACFTU wrote a letter to the Shantou Chamber of Commerce explaining its position on a cross-class alliance: "[Unions] should call on normal civic organizations to establish a common front to attack the enemy, and should establish a national representative assembly to seize political power" (*Zhongguo gonghui lishi wenxian* 1958, 182). "Normal civic organizations" in this case refers to employer associations.

In Shanghai, the SHFTU also sought cooperation with the local bourgeoisie as well as with organized crime. After the May thirtieth massacre, the local Chinese Chamber of Commerce was the largest contributor to the union's strike fund (Perry 1993, 82). The petite bourgeoisie was organized to participate in the general strike, although union leadership later expressed disappointment at this group's lack of commitment. And SHFTU chair Li Lisan, as well as other union activists, had extensive ties with Shanghai crime syndicates, something deemed necessary in order to mobilize the proletariat. In SHFTU documents from the summer of 1925, aggression is clearly (and justifiably) directed toward Japanese cotton mill owners and the foreign police that committed the massacre of protesters.

But perhaps it is in the closing slogans of union communiqués that the primarily anti-imperialist slant is most evident. Below is a sampling of such slogans from the revolutionary upsurge of 1925–27:

- From an open letter from the ACFTU to *shenggang* strikers: "Workers! Keep struggling till the end! Eliminate the unequal treaties! Defeat imperialism! Long live the victory of the national revolution!" (*Zhongguo gonghui lishi wenxian* 1958, 95)
- From the closing of the Guangzhou Workers' Assembly, April 1926: "Our slogans are: Protect the national government! Support the Northern Expedition![2] Protect the *shenggang* strike! Defeat the imperialists and their running dogs! Long live the victorious national revolution! Long live the world revolution!" (200)
- From ACFTU secretary Liu Shaoqi's remarks at the opening ceremony of the Labor Institute in June 1926: "Workers, peasants, business, and students unite! Defeat imperialism! Defeat reactionaries! Establish the revolutionary foundation!" (247)

Reaction and Retreat

The period of revolutionary activity starting after the May thirtieth massacre witnessed some of the most significant working-class mobilization of the twentieth century. Massive general strikes in Shanghai and in Guangdong-Hong Kong had been organized by newly established union organizations and had given the working class a coherence that had not existed previously. And yet the anti-imperialist struggles of the ACFTU and its subordinate unions ended in defeat when the right wing of the KMT undertook a series of attacks on the Communists, thereby decisively ending the fragile alliance and driving much labor organization underground.

The beginning of reaction was signaled by Chiang Kai-shek's coup in Guangzhou on March 20, 1926. During the initial stage of the *shenggang* strike, KMT leaders had publicly expressed support for the workers, though they were careful to emphasize the national rather than class-based character of the movement.

Communist leaders had failed to grasp the growing threat from the right wing of the KMT and so were completely unprepared when Chiang seized power in March (Kwan 1997, 164). However, immediately after the coup (which involved confrontation with both Chinese and Soviet Party officials), Chiang quickly engaged in damage control. Rhetorically at least, he attempted to maintain his favor with the left wing of the KMT and continued to pledge allegiance to the national revolution. His political maneuvering was at least somewhat successful as he received a warm reception at the ACFTU's third national congress in May of that year (Wu Tien-Wei 1968, 592).

Although the Communists and Chiang were able to paper over the growing rift revealed after the March 20 coup, no such détente would be possible just thirteen months later. After the KMT captured Shanghai in March 1927, Chiang quickly moved to establish an alliance with the city's powerful organized crime syndicates and leaders of industry (Smith 2000, 190). And although the general strike and armed insurrection led by the SHFTU on March 21 had played a decisive role in the KMT's capture of Shanghai, Chiang showed little gratitude toward the Communist activists. Early in the morning of April 12, armed groups of thugs began a systematic attack on union offices throughout the city, killing scores and arresting many high-ranking labor leaders. The following day, a group of more than one hundred thousand workers stopped work and went to protest against the military commander in the northern part of the city. With the full support of the foreign powers, the military opened fire on the protesters, killing one hundred and wounding hundreds more (Chesneaux 1968, 3370). Similar attacks against Communist labor organizations took place in many of the other cities under control of the newly emboldened right wing of the KMT. By the end of April, the strength of these unions had been greatly diminished.

Even if Communist labor activism was not completely eliminated in the cities (Stranahan 1998), space for leftist political activity was extremely limited. With the left wing of the KMT holed up in Wuhan and Chiang's reactionary forces dominating the central and southeastern parts of the country, the Communists had little room for maneuver. Retreating from the city, they reconvened in relatively remote Jiangxi province, where they led a brief takeover of the capital Nanchang in August 1927. Although they did not hold the city for long, many Communists retreated to the rural areas of the province and began laying the organizational groundwork for the Jiangxi soviet. The success with rural organizing in Jiangxi was crucial in the emergence of Mao Zedong's rural strategy (Averill 1987, 280). With the initiation of the Long March, Mao's ascendancy in the Party, and the eventual establishment of a base in Yan'an, it was clear that the working class was not going to be the primary revolutionary agent. The ACFTU fell into disuse at this time and would not be resurrected until military victory neared in 1948.

Socialist Trade Unionism—Appropriating Representation

Postrevolutionary trade unionism was to be very different from the unionism of the revolutionary years of the anti-imperialist struggle. As the Communist military victory neared, the ACFTU was rehabilitated, although under political conditions remarkably different from those of the mid-1920s. With the defeat of the Japanese and the turning of the tide in the civil war, large swaths of the country were firmly under control of the Communists. As a result, the role of the union federation was inevitably going to change dramatically from what it had been in the anti-imperialist mobilizations in Shanghai and Guangzhou. Starting in the late 1940s, the ACFTU and its subordinate unions were primarily interested in encouraging workers to increase efficiency and production. Advocating for the particular interests of the working class came to be denounced as economistic, and the Party successfully undermined attempts at greater operational autonomy for the union. This resulted in the establishment of appropriated representation at the class level. Despite becoming politically defanged, the urban working class was effectively incorporated into the state through the *danwei*—a highly institutionalized system that eventually ensured nearly complete decommodification of labor.

The key figure in the postwar development of the ACFTU is Li Lisan. Li, who had been one of the leaders of the Shanghai labor movement in the 1920s, remained a powerful figure in the Party until 1930. After the split between the KMT and the CCP, the "Li Lisan Line," which called for armed insurrection in the cities, gained prominence in the Party. However, these uprisings were ultimately not successful, most notably the ones in Nanchang. Li's "extremist" politics fell into disfavor, and he was banished to Moscow for fifteen years.

But by 1948 labor organization was back on top of the Party's agenda, while Li had already admitted his past mistakes and had returned to a position of power. In March of 1949, the CCP Central Labor Movement Committee announced a conference to be held in Harbin in June, the goal of which was to establish a Liberated Areas Worker Association. However, as planning was under way for this conference, the KMT held a conference in April that they claimed was organized by the ACFTU (despite the fact that the ACFTU had always been a Communist organization). In order to combat what was seen as an attempt to divide the labor movement, the Communists canceled the June conference and on May 1 announced that they would be convening the sixth national labor congress, at which time they would reassert *their* rights to the name ACFTU. The congress attracted representatives from unions with 2.83 million members, and the delegates ratified a new constitution for the union federation and passed resolutions to fight the KMT and American imperialism (Li and Liu 2005, 294). Although Chen Yun was formally the chairman of the revived union federation, Li was elected first deputy chair and assumed effective leadership over day-to-day operations.

Even before the formal reestablishment of the ACFTU, the question emerged as to what precisely unions in areas under Communist control would do. Clearly, their activities would be quite different than they had been during the massive strike mobilization of the 1920s. The general direction was definitively established in a 1948 report by Chen Yun in which he proclaimed a policy of "developing production, making the economy prosper, caring for both public and private, benefiting labor and capital" for trade unions in liberated areas. Of central importance to the Party was the rehabilitation of production in areas under its control in order to have sufficient supplies for the ongoing civil war against the KMT. In order to do this, union leadership exhorted the working class to distinguish between "short-term" and "long-term" interests—that is, to sacrifice immediate economic and political advancement for the good of the nation.

It became clear that increasing production was to be the top priority for the union, and cooperation with private capital was therefore encouraged. In a trade union handbook from the immediate postrevolutionary period, it was explicitly stated that "the major criterion of judging a trade union was the production record of its enterprise" (L. Lee 1984, 19) Unions were also exhorted to increase their leadership in promoting "labor competitions," which were seen as a means to increase the productivity and efficiency of workers (All China Federation of Trade Unions 1988, 379; L. Lee 1984). Li Lisan wrote a very important article published in *People's Daily* on May Day, 1949, in which the union's position on the issue was expounded at length. He started by pointing out that Chairman Mao supported the principle of "benefiting labor and capital," and that there were consequences that followed for the appropriate resolution of labor conflicts in private enterprises: "Hence, 'developing production and benefits for labor and capital' should be the starting place for the resolution of all problems within private enterprises."[3] Union leadership also made the argument that because China was no longer a capitalist country, the character of labor conflicts had necessarily changed (even if ownership was still private) (All China Federation of Trade Unions 1988, 407).

When it came to the possibility of worker-controlled production, Li was unequivocally opposed. He argued that while rural land could be expropriated and operated collectively, the same was not true for industrial production:

> The property of the capitalist is a factory, and a factory cannot be divided. If it is divided, there can be no production. For instance, if a factory was broken up and given to workers, you would get one wheel, he would get one driving belt, and all of the machinery and the entire factory would be destroyed. Then will there still be production?...So, workers absolutely must not divide capitalists' factories, but must do precisely the opposite: work hard to protect the factory and increase production, and this is necessary for workers to receive a benefit.[4]

Li went on to address concerns that workers might have, particularly as related to immediate workplace issues. However, he claimed that, "in this historical period, [exploitation] is impossible to eliminate, it will require patience....The working class needs to have the spirit of eating bitterness first and enjoying life later, to labor hard and set an example for the entire nation."[5] He even went so far as to claim that the interests of labor and capital were, as far as an expansion in production was concerned, identical: "If we took all the money that private enterprises earn and used it to improve workers' lives, may we ask how we would have capital accumulation to expand production and develop industry?...An appropriate amount will serve as profit for the capitalist, to make the capitalist interested in expanding production. So on this point, the interests of capital and labor can be identical."[6] The interrelatedness of the twin goals of increasing production and ethnonational autonomy were neatly summarized by the following line: "Without great development of industry, not only will socialism be out of the question, the Chinese nation's economic independence from imperialism will be out of the question."[7]

The sometimes contradictory imperatives to increase production and represent workers tended to be resolved in favor of the former. This was the case not only in state-owned enterprises but in private ones as well. As described in the *Workers' Daily* in early 1951:

> In private enterprises, there are a few trade union cadres who not only are not good at giving consideration to the interests of the working masses, but who even take the place of the capitalists in carrying out "firing workers and lowering wages," and who openly speak on the capitalists' behalf. Because of this, in some trade unions the phenomenon of the masses' not trusting the trade union and the trade union being divorced from the masses has appeared.[8]

But if union leadership and cadres frequently proclaimed support for the Party-dictated policy of nonconfrontation with capital, workers were less accommodating. As was the case for workers in the early twenty-first century, workers in the immediate post-'49 era often criticized union officials for their "bureaucratism, isolation from rank and file, a preference for coercive or commandist methods, failure to trust in the workers, arrogance and high-handedness, formalism, and a lack of democracy within enterprises and in the trade unions" (Sheehan 1998, 14). As argued by Paul Harper (1969), workers' expectations were raised by the success of the revolution, and they were not necessarily willing to accept the wage reductions and increased workload that union leadership frequently encouraged them to accept.

As a result of this increasing pressure from below, national leadership began to shift away from unconditional support for management toward support for worker demands. Starting in late 1950 there was a union rectification campaign that aimed to make union cadres more accountable to their membership. Even in state-owned factories, many cadres argued that the interests of the working class and Party were not identical. And Li Lisan attempted to increase centralization of power within the ACFTU such that lower-level trade unions were more vertically integrated and less subject to the power of horizontally connected Party units.

It should be noted that Li Lisan's position on the relationship between the union, Party, and enterprise management is remarkably inconsistent in existing documents, a fact that perhaps is indicative of the rapidly and constantly changing political environment of the time. For instance, in July 1949, at the very same time he was saying that the interests of labor and capital were frequently identical, he also argued for greater union autonomy: "The management committee is an administrative organization, the trade union is a mass organization, the Communist Party is a Party organization. These three organizations are independent and none of them can command any of the others." (Li and Liu 2005, 318) This autonomy was necessary precisely because, as argued in June 1949, "This contradiction between public and individual interests must be reflected in the relationship between the administration [of a factory] and the union. The location and environment of the administration will inevitably lead to it representing public interests more, and it is very difficult for them to be concerned with every person's day-to-day interests" (317). And yet in March 1951 he would directly contradict this earlier statement: "The administration and union are part of an organic whole, and we should be clear that the union is for helping the administration complete tasks.... The interests of the administration and the union are basically identical, and there are not any contradictions at all. If there are some contradictions, it is just the result of bad temperaments" (318).

The relevant point is that there was a constant back-and-forth in the early years of the PRC as the ACFTU was frequently tugged in opposite directions by membership and the Party.

Official pronouncements aside, by the end of 1951 the Party had decided that Li had pushed too far with constructing greater union autonomy. In December of that year, the ACFTU's Party organization held a meeting at which it passed a resolution condemning him for "errors of principle," including economism, formalism, and syndicalism. Li was forced to step down from his position in early 1952, and a broad critique of the former chair spread throughout the union structure.

The fear of being singled out for excessive focus on the particular interests of workers once again put union cadres in a position where they were squeezed between workers with increased expectations and the Party, which was focused on increasing production. This led to more distrust between workers and their representatives: "From this [critique of Li] union officers were afraid of committing economism or syndicalism and so they dared not speak out on behalf of the interests of workers. This caused the union to become lifeless, and to occupy a nonessential position, leading to the problems of the Party committee handling everything and separation from the masses" (Tang 1989, 191).

The problem of "separation from the masses" became increasingly apparent with an uptick in strike activity among workers in the first half of 1953. In July of that year, the ACFTU submitted a report to the Party's Central Committee in which it detailed these problems at length. In particular, the report was concerned that "these [strikes] reflect that the union cannot connect with the masses, and that union cadres do not have the trust of the masses" (All China Federation of Trade Unions 1988, 174). Just as this worker activism was expanding, the ACFTU's seventh congress in May 1953 was used to firmly reestablish Party control over the union organization (Sheehan 1989, 13).

Despite unequivocal subordination of the union to the Party, from 1953 to 1956 the state seesawed between a focus on trying to increase workers' participation in factories on the one hand and unremitting pursuit of production on the other. The "three anti and five anti" movements attempted to address problems among the state/union bureaucracies and the capitalist class, respectively. While autonomy from the Party was still forbidden, union cadres were encouraged to mobilize the masses for greater say in the functioning of the enterprises. This was thought to be necessary in private enterprises in order to eventually make the transition to full nationalization. However, by 1955 the state had experienced enough of mass mobilization and once again returned to an exclusive focus on increasing production. This included a strong reassertion of managerial prerogative, particularly in SOEs.

Chinese workers, now deemed the "masters of the enterprise" in the official rhetoric, were not pleased with the new Soviet-inspired centralization of authority within the workplace. This increased focus on worker discipline and efficiency was a major factor in the emergence of a strike wave in the country starting in the latter half of 1956. This series of strikes, though not coordinated by any national-level organization, affected major swaths of Chinese industry. The unrest was particularly acute in Shanghai in early 1957, at which time there was more widespread labor unrest than even in the revolutionary years of the republican period (Perry 1994). Having coincided with an outbreak of student strikes, the central government became quite concerned that an uprising such as had taken place in Hungary that same year could develop in China.

In March 1957, the Party's Central Committee issued a document entitled "Directive on Handling of Student and Worker Strikes." It placed blame for the social disturbances squarely on the shoulders of state officials: "These [worker and student strikes] have occurred primarily because we have not done our work well, and especially because of bureaucratism by officials" (*Jianguo Yilai Zhonggong Zhongyang Guanyu Gongren Yundong Wenjian Xuanbian* 1988, 508). If bureaucratism was the cause of the strikes, then more democracy in the workplace (and schools) was seen by the Party as the antidote: "In order to prevent the appearance of student and worker strikes...the most important [method] is to overcome bureaucratism and expand democracy" (509). While there were certainly no calls for union independence from the Party, once again the pendulum appeared to be swinging back toward greater accountability for officials.

Not coincidentally, the Party had launched the Hundred Flowers Movement in 1956, at which time various sectors of society were invited to openly criticize the Party and other officials. Certain elements within the ACFTU took quite liberal positions, likely in response to the upsurge in independent worker organizing that had materialized with the strike wave. Chairman Lai Ruoyu, originally brought in during 1952 because of his lack of experience within the trade union (and therefore supposed allegiance to the Party), began arguing that the union should side with workers under all circumstances. This of course was a marked change from the previous rhetoric of unions working hand in glove with factory administration. Gao Yuan, another high-level official in the ACFTU, went as far as to say that workers should be allowed to set up independent organizations. This was a truly exceptional moment in ACFTU history.

But just as before, this loosening at the top was quickly met with a harsh response from the Party, this time in the form of the Anti-Rightist Movement launched in the summer of 1957. While much of the literature on the Hundred Flowers Movement and its aftermath has focused on intellectuals (Goldman 1962; MacFarquhar 1960), workers and supportive union officials were also active participants in the outpouring of criticism of the Party that emerged in this period. Chairman Lai Ruoyu was criticized after his death in 1958, and other union leaders throughout the organization were purged. Once again, insurgent and autonomous worker activity had pushed union leadership toward greater liberalization, only to be ultimately foiled by a nervous Party leadership.

This awkward balancing act between trying to maintain legitimacy with insurgent workers and at the same time not disrupting the relationship with the Party has been a defining characteristic of the ACFTU in the People's Republic. During the course of the Cultural Revolution, the dynamics changed somewhat, as popular mobilization became officially sanctioned from the top, and all sorts of autonomous worker organization became prevalent. Indeed, the ACFTU ceased to function for all intents and purposes during this time period, failing to hold any national congresses. The details of labor organization during the Cultural Revolution are too complex and exceptional to go into here. However, it is worth mentioning one last major struggle for greater union independence that was once again crushed: the one that took place in the spring of 1989.

The ACFTU in 1989

At the ACFTU congress in 1978, the first one held since the 1960s, Deng Xiaoping blamed Lin Biao and the Gang of Four for the "paralysis" suffered by the union federation during the Cultural Revolution (Wang Hong 1990, 3). Furthermore, class struggle was off the table, and the union's role was to encourage market-oriented reforms: "The Center believes that various union federations will deeply enter the masses to do propaganda work so that enterprises can smoothly enact these reforms. This will be for the interest of socialism and the interest of the Four Modernizations, and the working class will play a vanguard function of considering the public and denying the individual" (5). The union federation was being resurrected completely on the Party's terms, quite explicitly to serve goals that were understood as not being in the "short-term" interests of the working class.

As before, the loosening of the political environment in the late 1980s caused some in the ACFTU to begin to take limited yet significant steps toward greater accountability to its membership. The clearest example of this tendency was in the "Basic Plan for Union Reform," a resolution passed by the ACFTU executive committee in October 1988. This document said that previously, "leftist" thinking had incorrectly led to union leaders' being accused of economism and syndicalism.

The assessment in 1988 was both that the working class had distinct interests and that this would require greater independence for the unions:

> For a long time, there was an excessive emphasis on the unity of social interests and high levels of centralization of leadership, with no distinction between the functions of Party, state, and social organizations. This caused the union to be unable to embody its role as a mass organization and it did not function according to the role it is supposed to have. In reality, the union became a work department of the Party committee or a subordinate organ of the administration. (Li and Chen 1989, 325)

As far as the relationship to the Party was concerned, the resolution said that horizontally located Party committees should "respect the organizational independence of the union and the democratic system of the union, and support the local union in independently, autonomously, and creatively carrying out its work" (328). It went on to argue that the existing system of appointing rather than electing cadres should be reformed.

While it is not difficult to find official boilerplate about promoting democracy throughout the history of the ACFTU, the rhetoric in late 1988 and early 1989 was noticeably more strident. In this sense it echoed previous calls for reform from the 1950s. When students and workers began taking to the streets en masse in Beijing and other cities in April and May of 1989, it is likely that an internal debate within the union arose, much as was taking place in the Party. But it is unlikely that union officials were prepared for the very direct threat they faced, as represented by the formation of independent worker organizations.

Although student activists were the main focus of the media and subsequent scholarly work on the 1989 protests (Gold 1990; Zhao 1998, 2001), workers played a key role, particularly in Beijing. As the movement in that city grew in late April, dozens of worker activists began meeting up in Tiananmen Square to discuss politics and potential forms of organization. Because they understood that their own participation was riskier than the students', the existence of the newly formed Beijing Workers' Autonomous Federation was not made public until student hunger strikers took over the square on May 13 (Walder and Gong 1993, 6). Staking out a much more radical position than most of the students, the workers' organization openly rejected the leadership of the Party and official unions and called for direct worker supervision of production. Unsurprisingly, workers eventually suffered more severe state violence and repression than did the students.

How did the ACFTU respond to this political crisis? To some extent, the worker protest enhanced the position of union officials as they officially represented the interests of the working class within the state bureaucracy. Anita Chan (1993) relates a story from this period in which the mayor and deputy mayor of Shanghai went to the union offices (an unusual reversal of protocol), and union officials successfully put forth a number of proposals for improving workers' conditions. Chan concludes that "[trade unions] were expanding their corporatist power by laying claims to representation of a restive social force" (56). Back in Beijing, ACFTU officials had occasionally expressed support for the students, even going so far as to make a large donation to support hunger strikers in the square (Walder 1991, 485). Of course there were limits to what was possible: when members of the Beijing Workers Autonomous Federation asked the ACFTU for help in formally registering, they were rejected.

Any sympathy union leaders may have felt for the protesters was quickly brushed back under the rug with the incursion of the military and the subsequent massacre on June 4. With the hardliners acting decisively to end the standoff, it was clear that political liberalization was now off the table. Reformists within the ACFTU got the message, and talk of independent worker organization or even a more assertive role for the official unions ended abruptly.

As if the state's actions in the street were not clear enough, in December of 1989 the Party released a wide-ranging documented entitled "Notice on Strengthening and Improving Party Leadership of the Trade Union, Youth League, and Women's Federation." The Party's deep concern about the emergence of independent trade unionism is quite apparent:

> Currently, the tasks of rectifying governance and deepening reform are incredibly formidable. Foreign and domestic enemy forces have used our temporary difficulties to try to change our forward direction....Party organizations at various levels must enforce unified leadership over the trade union, youth league, and women's federation according to the Party line, such that these organizations will maintain the correct political direction. (Wang Jian 2002, 196)

Of particular importance for union activities in the reform era was the strong reassertion of the authority of Party organizations. Unions were warned to "guard against and prevent any tendencies toward throwing off or weakening the leadership of the Party, guard against and prevent some people with ulterior motives from destroying stability and unity" (197). Additionally, there was a rhetorical shift away from recognizing the "particular" interests of the working class, and back toward consideration of the "national interests." In an October 1988 address to the ACFTU's national congress, Party Secretary Zhao Ziyang had argued, "In the past, the union's protection of workers' specific interests has been overlooked, which has brought a negative influence to union construction which should not exist" (Li and Chen 1988, 295). But in the aftermath of June 4, the tone from the Party was markedly different: "At the same time [as protecting particular interests] in the practical operations workers, youth, and women should be led to self-consciously subordinate individual interests to the nation's interests, subordinate particular interests to general interests, subordinate short-term interests to long-term interests" (Wang 2002, 199). Additionally, the Party's single-minded pursuit of economic growth was reaffirmed as a common goal for the union: "In our current period of governance rectification and deepening of reform, [trade unions] should educate workers to understand and make allowances for the nation's difficulty, and work hard to increase production and economize, increase income and reduce expenses, and continuously increase economic benefits" (201). After the release of this Party notice, ACFTU leadership distributed an "advice" throughout the trade union structure on how to interpret the new marching orders. Of paramount importance was the unions' role as first line of defense in crushing independent worker organizations:

> When worker organizations are discovered that oppose the four basic principles[9] and that harm state power, unions must immediately inform same-level Party organizations and higher levels of the trade union. Additionally, they must be resolutely exposed and disintegrated, and the government should be asked to ban them according to law. As for spontaneous worker organizations that arise for reasons of economic interests, trade unions should convince and lead them to disperse and stop their activities. (251)

In addition to reaffirming the commitment to oppose independent organizations, ACFTU leadership nearly went so far as to claim that workers' particular interests were irrelevant:

> When the union protects the legal rights and interests of workers and participates in interest mediation, it must begin with benefiting social stability and developing the productive forces. [Unions] must conduct their work according to the law and relevant policies, and actively lead workers to self-consciously subordinate individual interests to national interests, subordinate partial interests to general interests, subordinate short-term interests to long-term interests. (254)

In the space of less than one year, ACFTU leadership had gone from openly calling for greater reform and for the promotion of distinct interests of the working class to full submission to the authority of the Party and a renewed focus on increasing economic growth at all costs.

The fallout from 1989 was to have profound implications for the activities of the ACFTU and its subordinate unions as marketization in China accelerated over the next two decades. When the state determined that pursuit of national interests required reform of the state-owned sector, unions stood to the side as innumerable millions of workers were laid off (Solinger 2001), had their pensions stolen by corrupt officials, or were forced to accept lower wages, longer hours, and reduced job security. At the same time, a new class of migrant workers was taking shape in the export zones of the southeast. Although these workers were subject to high rates of exploitation, long hours, and dangerous working conditions, the official union structure had essentially no presence in these privately owned factories. With a strengthening of the alliance between state and capital at the local level, unions—even those that might have *wanted* to take a more aggressive position—were left with few means for actively taking up demands from below.

1989–Present—Postsocialist Trade Unionism

The period following 1989 is when the constitutive elements of postsocialist labor politics came into existence: the destruction of the *danwei* system of incorporation and decommodification and the birth of the economically precarious and politically unincorporated migrant working class. Particularly after 1992, the central leadership advocated increased openness to foreign investment, the development of private enterprise, and privatization of state-owned enterprises. Despite these changes, unions were not allowed to actively organize workers, lead strikes, or confront employers in any meaningful sense. The period from 1989 to the present has not been marked by any of the power struggles or internal pushes for reform that characterized the 1950s. Many of these activities will be elucidated in subsequent chapters, but it is worth highlighting here a few prominent trends. First, the union has been deeply subordinated to Party control and has focused its energies on pursuing new legislation and guiding (mostly) individual workers into the legal system of mediation, arbitration, and litigation. More recently, union leadership has pursued "collective negotiation," though as we will see later, this project has faced immense challenges. Finally, in 2003 the ACFTU officially recognized migrant workers as part of the working class, thereby indicating that they were now within the union federation's jurisdiction. All these activities have been predicated on the assumption that labor conflicts are purely economic in nature and therefore can be dealt with administratively and apolitically.

Coinciding with China's general promotion of the rule of law in the reform era, the ACFTU focused on consolidating a new legal framework for labor relations during the 1990s and 2000s. The Labor Law of 1994 and the Trade Union Law, first enacted in 1992 and then revised in 2001, gave the ACFTU the right to represent workers in employment relationships and in signing collective agreements. As the Chinese state moved from a "social contract to a legal (or no) contract" (Friedman and Lee 2010, 508), this legally sanctioned role was crucial in the determination of employment relations in the market economy. But throughout the 2000s, many employees continued to work without any sort of contract or with very short-term contracts, and legal violations were endemic (Cooney 2007; Cooney, Biddulph, Li, and Zhu, 2007). Given ongoing political constraints, lobbying for yet more legislation was the natural response of the ACFTU. Thus, in 2006 a sometimes heated process of political jockeying took place in which the union federation and the Ministry of Labor and Social Security (renamed the Ministry of Human Resources and Social Security in 2009) produced distinct draft laws. The ACFTU's version of the law was widely seen by experts as being more prolabor, and once it was made available for public comment, it elicited a harsh response from private capital. The American Chamber of Commerce-Shanghai, as well as the EU Chamber of Commerce, directly threatened the state, saying the passage of the law would result in capital flight. While there remain questions about how beneficial the law has been for workers (J. Chan 2009), the eventual passage in 2007 was seen as victory for the ACFTU and an indication of its increased power within the state.

One of the ACFTU's primary motivations in promoting the Labor Contract Law was to ensure that all employees were actually granted an individual labor contract, as the official dispute resolution mechanism cannot accept a case otherwise. Particularly in the 2000s, union federations around the country began to increase their legal aid capacity in the hopes of channeling labor conflicts into the system of mediation, arbitration, and litigation. As can be seen in table 2, the number of people employed in these legal aid centers tripled from 2003 to 2007, an astonishing increase in capacity. Despite workers' frequent "disenchantment" with the failure of such systems to resolve their grievances (Gallagher 2006), the number of officially mediated disputes skyrocketed throughout this period (see figure 1 in chapter 1). A generous interpretation of unions' increased focus on legal mobilization is that leadership saw it as a practical way to address grievances, given existing constraints (Chen 2004). A more skeptical perspective is that this was a conscious effort by the state and union to individualize and depoliticize labor conflict—and the data reveal that there was a marked decline in the number of workers per dispute from 1996 to 2009 (see figure 7). There is also evidence that courts and unions have been consciously splitting collective grievances into individual cases in an attempt to reduce the likelihood of social unrest (Chen and Xu 2012).

TABLE 2. Legal activities of unions, 2002–2007

	2002	2003	2004	2005	2006	2007
No. of union organizations with legal aid center	N/A	2,393	2,990	3,856	5,335	6,178
No. of employees in union legal aid centers	7,600	6,048	9,976	11,059	16,695	18,433
No. of cases received by union legal aid centers	17,030	31,775	39,879	30,755	46,783	46,354
No. of cases resolved by union legal aid centers	10,850	20,573	19,915	16,657	31,291	29,410

Source: Zhongguo gonghui tongji nianjian (2003–2008) [China union statistical yearbook (2003–2008)] (Beijing: Zhongguo tongji chubanshe).

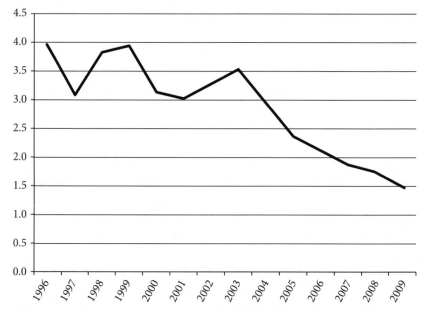

FIGURE 7. Number of workers per dispute, 1996–2009.
Source: Zhongguo laodong tongji nianjian (1996–2010) [China Labor Statistical Yearbook 1996–2010] (Beijing: China Statistics Press).

More recently, union federations around the country have been promoting "collective negotiation" at both the enterprise and sectoral level. For many years, union officialdom preferred the term "collective negotiation" (*jiti xieshang*) to "collective bargaining" (*jiti tanpan*) because the former presumes coincidental interests between labor and capital, while the latter is predicated on antagonism.

But in 2008, Shenzhen was the first municipality in the country to use the term "collective bargaining" in a legal document when it promulgated its "implementation guide" for the Trade Union Law. At the national level, the ACFTU announced in summer 2010 that 60 percent of all enterprises should be covered by collective contracts by the end of the year and that 80 percent should be covered by the end of 2011.[10] Certain localities have been even more aggressive in pursuing collective contracts, especially heavily industrialized coastal areas with high levels of labor unrest. These collective agreements have focused almost exclusively on wages, with other workplace issues wholly unaddressed. As we will see in subsequent chapters, these initiatives around collective negotiation/bargaining have, with a few exceptions, excluded membership from participation in formulating and attempting to realize a particular set of demands. The consequence of this top-down and administrative approach to negotiation is that collective agreements are generally ignored by management.

Finally, and perhaps of greatest relevance for this discussion, the ACFTU officially recognized migrant workers as part of the working class in 2003. Previously only urban workers, the majority of which were employed in state-owned enterprises, were considered within the union's jurisdiction. Migrant workers, or "peasant workers" (*nongmingong*) as they are referred to in Chinese, were wholly outside the formal system of employment for many years. But as these migrants came to constitute an increasing portion of China's workforce, and particularly as worker unrest began to spread, the ACFTU was forced into giving this new group official recognition. The consequence is that migrant workers are now an officially recognized constituency of the ACFTU. This may seem self-evident to people outside China, but this was the first time in the history of the PRC that the union federation explicitly acknowledged responsibility for representing the interests of workers who were not urban residents. When Wang Zhaoguo made this proclamation in 2003, it did not come about as a result of a process of delegation from migrant workers themselves. In this sense, we can identify with great specificity the moment in which the ACFTU appropriated representation of this new class of workers. This symbolic shift is particularly important to my discussion in this book, since I focus on the relationship between migrants and unions.

There are clear organizational consequences of having representative power arrogated to the ACFTU by the state rather than through delegation by membership. The salient point is that in the socialist period and up to the present, the working class has been subjected to conditions of appropriated representation where the Party unilaterally assigned the ACFTU a monopoly on representation. Given this monopoly, ACFTU subordinate unions have continually excluded workers from participation. Union heteronomy combined with the Party's single-minded pursuit of economic development resulted in an ongoing crisis of legitimacy. This was not such a pressing problem in a period in which labor was highly decommodified. But with the transition to capitalism and the birth of a new and increasingly restive working class, this setup has resulted in serious political problems for the regime. In order to better grasp how the ACFTU has failed to incorporate workers in the reform era, we now turn to a more detailed explanation of the organizational form of the Chinese trade union system.

The Structure of the Trade Union System in Contemporary China

Unions in China are officially referred to as "mass organizations," putting them in the same category as the Youth League and the Women's Federation. Officially, the function of these organizations is to link the Party to various social group-ings in society (workers, youth, and women, respectively). Following the Leninst conception, the union structure is conceived of as a "transmission belt" to carry information back and forth between the Party and workers (Unger and Chan 1995, 37). The ACFTU claimed a membership of 258 million in 2012,[11] which if true would make it the largest national union federation in the world by an extremely large margin. In this section, we will see quite clearly how the union's legitimacy derives from the state, often times at the expense of the relationship to workers.

National Organization and Relationship to the Party

At every level of the union hierarchy, union organizations are subject to "dual control." The first and primary form of control comes from the horizontally located Party organization if one exists. Party organizations do exist for all regionally based union federations, in state-owned enterprises, and in many large private enterprises. Second, union organizations are subordinate to the immedi-ately superior trade union organization (see figure 8). The primacy of Party con-trol was strongly reasserted after the 1989 political crisis, when it was announced that unions at various levels could "listen to the advice" of hierarchically superior union bodies (Wang 2002, 198) but that final decisions must be made by the Party organization. Such an arrangement has not been questioned since, and for a union official to do so publicly would certainly lead to severe consequences.

The original logic behind this arrangement was that with the successful realiza-tion of the dictatorship of the proletariat, independent labor organizations such as exist in capitalist societies were no longer necessary. Since the Party represents the interests of the nation *as a whole*, there can be no antagonism between the working class and the Party. As was argued in each successive moment when unions attempted greater autonomy, confrontational independent worker struggles run counter to the national and long-term interest.

Trade union leaders are quick to point out that what they lack in independence they make up for in access to state power. When visiting American unionists beam with envy over the rapidly burgeoning membership of the ACFTU, their Chinese counterparts frequently take the opportunity to describe how the Party can bring enormous pressure to bear on recalcitrant employers. Perhaps most important, the union at various levels has direct access to the state's legislative bodies. When labor laws are being considered, it is necessary protocol to consult with the unions, in not an entirely pro forma way. The most prominent recent example of the ACFTU mobilizing its political strength in legislation was the passage of the 2008 Labor Contract Law over the objections of the more conservative Ministry of Human Resources and Social Security.

But even if unions claim high levels of access to state power, their relative status within the state is still quite low. As a mass organization, the union does not wield the same power as a government ministry. Although union cadres claim that their status has been on the rise over the past decade, the union system has typically not even outranked the Youth League, the organization from which Hu Jintao originally hails. To the extent that their power has increased in recent years, union officials are explicit that this is because the problem of labor unrest has become more acute.

Although the ACFTU is not formally a government body, ACFTU-subordinate unions *are* part of the state to a degree rarely matched in any historical setting (including earlier corporatist arrangements). Nowhere is this fact more apparent than in the method of cadre recruitment and leadership selection.

Union Leadership

The most significant way that the Party keeps control over the union (and not coincidentally, alienated from workers) is through tight control over union leadership. Although formally subjected to "internal democracy," the selection of union federation chairs at all levels is a fully nontransparent procedure[12] and is almost certainly dictated by the Party. In order to win any position of power within the union system, an official must be a Party member and have a track record of allegiance to Party-determined goals. While there are exceptions, the rule is for high-level leaders *not* to be drawn from within the ranks of cadres who have worked their way up through the union but rather to be rotated in from other mass organizations or government agencies. This is to prevent leadership from developing broad-based support from within the ranks of the union, a scenario that could potentially lead to a power struggle at the top. Because of this policy, union leaders at every level are likely to have much stronger allegiance to those who gave them their positions than to their own membership.

This frequently makes for career trajectories for union leaders that differ significantly from those in most other countries, as it is not at all unusual for people with no experience whatsoever in trade unionism to be appointed to very high-level positions. For instance, before he became ACFTU chair in 2002, Wang Zhaoguo's longest official appointment was in the Taiwan Affairs Department, where he served from 1990 to 1997. Wang Yupu, appointed first ACFTU deputy chair and Party organization secretary in 2010, was an executive and Party committee member at the Daqing Oilfield Company from 1999 until 2003, after which he served as CEO and general manager until 2009.[13] Another former ACFTU deputy chair, Xu Deming (the man personally responsible for bargaining the first collective contract in a Chinese Wal-Mart), previously served as the director of Liaoning province's Mines and Geology Department. Upon leaving the ACFTU in 2008, Xu was appointed director of the State Bureau of Surveying and Mapping.[14] The consequence of such a career structure within the union is that leadership is frequently unfamiliar with, and often uninterested in, labor issues.

Another reason that union leaders are often unconcerned with their role as representatives of the working class is the system of joint appointments. Union chairs of regional federations, from the municipal level all the way to the national, have in recent years been given joint appointments as deputy directors of the standing committees of the relevant People's Congress (the legislative body of the Chinese state). So for instance, Chen Weiguang served as both the chairman of the Guangzhou Federation of Trade Unions and the deputy director of the standing committee of the Guangzhou Municipal People's Congress. The logic behind such an arrangement is that the trade union will have a greater say in legislative affairs at all levels of the state. While this is certainly true to some extent, it also means that many trade union chairs are much more concerned with their position in the People's Congress and are consequently less fully engaged in union work.

In addition to these steps aimed at controlling union leadership, the state has also taken extensive measures to ensure the allegiance of regular union cadres. While it is not required that lower-level officers be Party members, it is certainly welcomed (and is necessary for long-term career advancement). Union cadres must pass the same civil service exam that other government officers take. In the 1990s the state changed the rules dictating pay and benefits for union cadres, such that they are now the same as those for government officials at an equal level of the hierarchy. Additionally, unions have recently been pursuing "professionalization," which implies recruiting more university graduates rather than recruiting internally (see chapter 3).

Although some have argued that union cadres are thus subjected to a "double identity" (F. Chen 2003)—as both worker representatives and agents of the state—my research supports Raymond Lau's (2003) contention that these officials think of themselves as, and behave like, government officials. Lau relies on the Bourdieusian concept of *habitus,* which is defined as "not only a structuring structure, which organizes practices and the perception of practices, but also a structured structure" (Bourdieu 1984, 170). The *habitus* of union officials is *structured* by the same set of institutional parameters as those of government officials, and it therefore generates (i.e., structures) similar social practices. That union officials have a state *habitus* is of course a difficult proposition to prove, but there is much evidence to support such a claim. As has been discussed, they undergo the process of selection and socialization that is entailed by gaining Party membership. They are subject to the direct and unquestioned domination of horizontally located Party organizations and higher-level union organizations. Many of them have extensive formal experience as government and Party officials. And from a practical standpoint, they have much in common with formal agents of the state. Whether it is their diction and reliance on official slogans, hosting lavish dinners, being chauffeured around in black luxury cars with tinted windows, the stiffness and formality of interaction, or their professed enthusiasm for national events (e.g., Beijing Olympics, Shanghai World Expo), the practices of union officials are clearly structured by the same *habitus* as that of government officials.

But where this practical alignment is most obvious and perhaps most problematic is in dealing with labor conflicts. Union officers' first response to strikes is that of an agent of the state: intervene, "rationally" encourage dialogue, convince the workers to make "reasonable" demands (i.e., generally not in excess of legal requirements), and perhaps try to persuade management (through noncoercive means) to meet some of the workers' demands. And this practical activity is produced by a set of institutional parameters: the Trade Union Law states in article 27 that "[in the event of a work stoppage] the union should assist the enterprise or work unit in completing their tasks, and in resuming production and work order as quickly as possible."[15] Until major changes in 2010 (discussed in chapter 6), union officials' primary concern when discussing strikes had always been how to avoid them altogether. In general, union officers believe that the best way to avoid labor conflict is through legislation and administration. The parallels with the state's "logic of practice" are apparent enough.

Regional, Industrial, Sectoral, and Enterprise Unions

The primary form of organization within the ACFTU-controlled hierarchy is the regional federation. These federations officially represent all the other union organizations (industrial, sectoral, enterprise) within their given jurisdiction. At the apex of this hierarchy is the ACFTU, followed by union federations at the provincial, municipal, and—depending on particular jurisdictional arrangements—district (*qu*), county (*xian*), township (*zhen*), and street (*jiedao*) levels. They participate in labor-related legislation, are first responders to major labor conflicts, and—particularly at the municipal level—experiment with new forms of union organization and coordinate unionization drives. Regionally based federations have attained the most power within the union hierarchy, in part because they strictly mirror the organization of the Party (and therefore are seen as relatively safe).

Parallel to this geographically based structure is the system of industrial unions. There are ten industrial unions within the ACFTU, including the Educational, Scientific, Cultural, Health, and Sports Workers' Union; Seamen and Construction Workers' Union; Energy and Chemical Workers' Union; Machinery, Metallurgical, and Building Material Workers' Union; Defense Industry, Postal, and Telecommunications Workers' Union; Financial, Commercial, Light Industry, Textile, and Tobacco Workers' Union; Agricultural Forestry and Water Conservancy Workers' Union; Railway Workers' Union; Aviation Workers' Union; and Financial Workers' Union.[16] These unions are subject to dual control, first by the horizontally located, geographically based union federation and second by the immediately superior entity within the industrial union. In addition to the national-level organizations, they are generally established at the provincial and municipal levels but not below. These unions are relatively weak and indeed were specifically undermined by the Party in the 1950s for fear that they would seek greater autonomy. They do not sign collective contracts on behalf of workers or seek to organize new members but rather engage in legislative activities, consultation with government agencies, and interactions with large companies in the relevant industries.

In recent years, "sectoral unions" (*hangye gonghui*) have become increasingly widespread in China. These unions, generally organized by municipal-level union federations, seek to organize all the employees in a given industry (e.g., construction, shoes, eyeglasses, hotels) within the municipality. The aim of such an organization varies somewhat depending on the industry, but the general intention is to attempt to set some standards that apply to all employers within the specific geographic region. The most common practice is to try to establish unified pay rates, although we will see that there are immense challenges in actually implementing sectoral wage agreements (chapter 4). The ability to represent workers in signing collective contracts is what distinguishes sectoral unions most clearly from the industrial unions. Additionally, they are not directly integrated into national-level hierarchies. They are generally staffed, financed, and controlled by municipal union federations. For a variety of reasons that will be discussed in later chapters, this organizational form has become heavily promoted by many different levels of the union structure.

Finally, there are the "grassroots" (*jiceng*) or enterprise-level unions. It is within these organizations that workers directly encounter the union. The enterprise-level union activities include collecting dues, conducting various forms of entertainment activities (including birthday and holiday parties, field trips, etc.), distributing gifts of cooking oil, mooncakes, and sometimes cash at holidays, running "sending warmth" activities (providing assistance to workers facing severe economic difficulties), mediating labor disputes, and perhaps most important, representing workers in collective negotiations. In many enterprises few (if any) of these activities actually take place, and the union exists on paper only. But in many industries in China, a workplace-based system of industrial relations is emerging, so these enterprise-level unions continue to be of great potential importance.

Workers' relationship to both sectoral and enterprise unions is worth clarifying somewhat. If a worker is going to become a union member, he or she becomes a member of the enterprise-level union. These unions are also legally empowered to represent workers in engaging in collective negotiations and in signing collective contracts. However, sectoral unions are also legally empowered to sign collective contracts on behalf of employees in any number of enterprises as long as they are within their geographic jurisdiction. To complicate things a bit, it is possible to have an enterprise that is party to a collective agreement at the sectoral level even if it does not have an enterprise-level union organization. I have found that municipal union federations often hope that setting up sectoral unions will aid them in establishing new enterprise-level unions. One key distinction between enterprise and sectoral unions is that the latter do not maintain the welfare functions of the former.

Relationship to Management

Even if union federations have gained better access to state power at the national and regional level, union organizations in the workplace remain weak and incapable of ensuring even basic legal enforcement (Chen 2009). Whereas the autonomy of higher-level unions is deeply circumscribed by the Party, at the enterprise level it is management that dominates the union (see figure 8). In

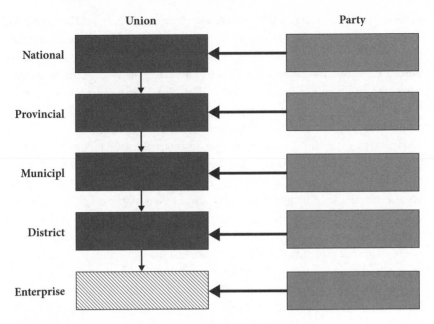

FIGURE 8. Union organization and the system of "dual control."
Note: The thicker horizontal lines represent the primary form of control, while the thinner vertical lines represent the secondary form of control. The enterprise-level union is striped to indicate control by management.

most cases, management's control of the enterprise union is completely transparent, as it is quite common to have human resource managers or the enterprise owner serve as union chairs. For example, in 2009 the GZFTU revealed that more than 50 percent of union chairs in private enterprises were from management.[17] This was particularly alarming because the announcement came more than a year after Guangzhou had passed a new regulation specifically banning the practice. A 2004 nationwide survey by Hishida, Kojima, Ishii, and Qiao (2010) of 1,811 enterprise-level trade union chairs revealed similar trends. Most immediately significant was the finding that only 3.7 percent of those surveyed listed "staff and worker" as the position held immediately prior to assuming the post of union chair (121). But even in the event that a union chair is elected (or appointed) who *is* interested in confronting management, his or her ability to do so is highly constrained by organizational factors. Unions are financed primarily by a 2 percent payroll tax paid by the enterprise rather than by membership dues. All employees of an enterprise are allowed to be members, including upper management. Most important, the wages for enterprise union chairs are paid directly by the enterprise. There are countless examples of activist union chairs being summarily fired for antagonizing management, with few (if any) repercussions for such retaliatory behavior. The consequence is that enterprise-level unions' capacity to make demands on capital in collective negotiation and other spheres is severely curtailed (Clarke, Lee, and Li 2004).

There have been some exceptional cases in which workers have been allowed to directly elect their own union chairs at the enterprise level. In at least two cases such elections came about as a result of pressure from foreign brands (A. Chan 2008; Yu Xiaomin 2008), while in others, activists had the support of higher levels of the trade union (A. Chan 2007). The ACFTU has been interested in conducting experiments with direct elections in various places around the country, but so far there is little evidence of long-term success (Howell 2008). As we will see subsequently, in the rare instances when activist union chairs are elected, they are continually hamstrung by threats of retaliation from management and higher levels of the union. Thus, while much of the criticism of Chinese unions focuses on their lack of independence from the Party-state, lack of independence from capital is an equally vexing problem.

In this chapter we have traced the trajectory of the ACFTU from its revolutionary beginnings in the 1920s up to the present. The common theme uniting each of the seemingly very different iterations of the ACFTU has been the interrelated goals of securing ethnonational autonomy and expanding production. During the general strikes in 1925–27, unions mobilized the working class in an attempt to resist foreign imperialism and to advance the national revolution. While class-based demands were certainly included at this time, they were secondary to anti-imperialism. During the Maoist era, union leadership occasionally pushed for greater autonomy, but each time Party dominance was strongly reasserted. Operating under the theory that socialization of the relations of production would result in a liberation of the forces of production, labor in this period came to be highly decommodified as industry was nationalized and the "iron rice bowl" was institutionalized. As market reforms began in the 1980s, there was a push from within the ACFTU for organizational reform; however, this was quickly crushed in the aftermath of the Tiananmen Square massacre. There is basic consensus among scholars that Chinese unions of today are part of the formal state apparatus and share the state's logic of practice.

The union's orienting principles have been indelibly marked by the encounter with imperialism and the relationship to the Party. At various critical junctures, the Party and the ACFTU were mobilized against potentially existential foreign threats—beginning with colonial incursions of major European powers, then full-scale Japanese invasion, and finally the danger posed by Cold War tensions with the United States and then the Soviet Union. In such an environment, it is easy to understand how many people in China would come to see national interests as taking precedence over class interests. In the early years of the PRC the Party used state power to decommodify and incorporate labor through the *danwei* system, and unions had relatively little impetus or space to represent working class interests qua working class interests. Under these conditions, the revolution and early processes of state formation produced a socialist union structure that is quite distinct from its counterparts in liberal democracies.

The question of postsocialist labor politics, then, is, What happens when a monopolistic union oriented to ethnonationalistic ends is thrust into a situation in which labor is increasingly employed by private capital? In an era when a new working class is fully unincorporated and engaged in widespread extralegal resistance, what is the response of a union that was designed in a different historical moment for particular political purposes? As a practical matter, now that worker demands from below are no longer related to ethnonational autonomy but rather directed toward securing better wages and benefits (among other demands that are antagonistic to capital), what will the union do? If it was never the job of the union to politically incorporate the working class under state socialism—this was largely handled by the *danwei*—how will the ACFTU deal with the political problem of expanding worker insurgency? These are the central dilemmas of postsocialist trade unionism in an increasingly capitalist economy. When we turn to the case of contemporary Guangzhou, we will see that even in the most likely cases, the unions' ability to institutionalize compromise between labor and capital is highly circumscribed.

GUANGZHOU
At the Forefront of Union Reform?

We now shift our focus from the historical development of the ACFTU to its current activities in Guangdong's capital of Guangzhou. This metropolis of over 12 million[1] anchors the Pearl River Delta, the most significant manufacturing center in China and indeed the world. There are a number of good reasons to believe that this city would be most likely to experience the emergence of the institutional moment of the countermovement: its relatively long experience with marketization, high levels of worker insurgency, self-professed openness to international cultural and intellectual currents, and most important, the prolabor inclinations of the leadership of the municipal union federation, the GZFTU.

By 1980, three of China's four special economic zones (SEZs) were located in Guangdong province. Guangzhou itself was subsequently designated a "coastal open city" in 1984, allowing for the large inflows of FDI and private enterprise that emerged a few years earlier in the SEZs. Guangdong quickly became the country's premier destination for FDI (Chen, Chang, and Zhang 1995, 694) and private enterprise more broadly. As many Chinese trade unionists now openly proclaim, the old model of regulating labor relations through the "iron rice bowl" and *danwei* system is inoperable in private enterprises where the workforce is made up largely of migrant labor. In other words, one might reasonably expect there to be great impetus for unions to play a role in representing workers in places where commodification is the most advanced.

It has been a key argument thus far that unions and states do not pursue decommodification and incorporation of labor out of any necessary or mechanical response to commodification but rather because continual accumulation is threatened by worker insurgency. And just as one would expect from Polanyian theory, as the place with the highest levels of capitalist industrialization, Guangdong has also experienced the highest levels of worker resistance (Chan and Hui 2012; C. K.-C. Chan 2010; Friedman 2013; Leung and Pun 2009; Pun, Chan, and Chan 2009). The province accounted for more than 17 percent of all labor disputes in the country in 2009 with 118,155, well above the 74,637 cases in second-place Jiangsu.[2] This instability in labor relations is a major concern for union and government officials who are preoccupied with reducing such conflicts. Thus we see that the insurgent moment of the countermovement is pushing union officials to respond with the existing institutional machinery they have at their disposal.

Finally, we might expect unions in Guangzhou to be more prolabor because of the unusual political disposition of the city's preeminent labor leader, Chen Weiguang. There is significant literature on unions both in China (M. Liu 2009) and in the West (Stepan-Norris and Zeitlin 1991, 1995, 2002; Kay 2010), which suggests that the particular qualities and political commitments of leadership can have a significant impact on outcomes.[3] What's more, there is reason to believe that in China, specific leadership qualities could have an even greater impact than in liberal democracies. Despite the Chinese state's propagation of "rule of law" (*fazhi*) in the post-Mao era (Keith 1991, 1994; Lubman 1999), it is popularly believed that China remains a country "ruled by people" (*renzhi*). That is to say, laws are not universally applied by an impartial judiciary, but rather their proper application is adjudicated in each particular instance by what Weber might call the "cultivated man" (1946, 243).[4] To the extent that administrative decisions in the union are not being made according to Weberian principles of instrumental rationality, there is the possibility for an increase in the autonomy of the individual officer (though of course the flip side to this is that any given officers cannot count on *their* subordinates to rationally carry out orders). In any event, GZFTU chair Chen Weiguang is a truly exceptional character within the ACFTU-controlled union structure, and his outspoken prolabor positions have helped him gain prominence within China as well as internationally. If the political outlook of leadership can in fact have a significant impact on unions' role in institutionalizing decommodification and incorporation of labor in China, then the workplaces within Chen Weiguang's jurisdiction would be the most likely spots to witness such a phenomenon.

Since it is likely that all ACFTU officials would self-identify as "prolabor," it is worth clarifying what this term means analytically. I use the term to refer to the pursuit of working-class interests as an end in itself, without regard to the interests of capital or the nation. In any given context the content of working-class interests is the object of intense symbolic struggle. While recognizing the diverse ways in which workers and others have understood these interests in different national and historical settings, for the sake of brevity I am going to elide this debate.[5] I assume that working-class interests are being served to the extent that workers' material well-being and autonomous political capacity are enhanced, regardless of whether this impinges on the interests of other social groups. According to this definition, the ACFTU has never been a fully prolabor organization in the sense that it sees working-class interests as a subset of national interests. To the extent that working-class interests coincide with national interests, the union has been able to pursue prolabor positions—but the ACFTU's primary organizational logic is not oriented to working-class interests as such. But though this is the situation at the organizational level, there is diversity among particular union officials.

In this chapter we begin with an extended introduction to Chen Weiguang. We see that his rise to power is in itself an indication of tentative first steps toward class compromise, as is the series of prolabor policies that were adopted under his guidance. This account allows us to identify the extent to which internal organizational conditions present opportunities and limits to greater decommodification and incorporation of labor—and Guangzhou is a clear "most likely" case. However, when we analyze labor conditions in the enterprise with supposedly the best union in Guangzhou, Hitachi Elevator, we find that the limited levels of decommodification that have been secured came as a result of state action rather than from the union acting as worker representative. Oligarchy within the union prevents more encompassing decommodification, as is most clearly evidenced by the continual prevalence of highly contingent intern workers. Since workers were not involved at any point in advancing decommodification, the union has failed to secure recognition and incorporation is tenuous. On the other hand, when there is bottom-up initiative to use enterprise unions to advance worker interests, we find that the leadership of the GZFTU maintains a "passive repressive" position when grassroots activists are subject to unchecked managerial retaliation. This continual resistance to bottom-up initiative is clearly demonstrated in the case of Liu Yongyi, the union chair from the Guangdong Union Hotel—wholly owned by the Guangdong Federation of Trade Unions. We see that there *are* attempts to secure decommodification within the auspices of the union structure—however, we also see that there are severe limitations as to what can be accomplished given highly durable union oligarchy.

Chen Weiguang—Maverick Labor Leader

I first met GZFTU chair Chen Weiguang in late 2007, when—in a highly unusual violation of protocol for an official of his stature—Chen came to my family's apartment for dinner. At the time, my parents had been working as visiting lecturers at Sun Yat-sen University in Guangzhou. My mother, a longtime labor activist in the United States, had first communicated with the GZFTU via contacts in Hong Kong. That he was so willing to meet and engage in substantive dialogue with foreigners is quite exceptional among Chinese union leaders, particularly in instances when there is no symbolic payoff (which is certainly the case for an informal dinner at home). Chen arrived that evening with the director of the GZFTU's international department, as well as his official translator.

My previous experience with ACFTU officials had been in highly scripted interactions with union leaders in Beijing and Shanghai. The informality with which Chen spoke was the first noticeable marker of difference. What's more, he was engaged and interested in discussing labor politics in China and internationally, and he ended up staying for nearly five hours. During this time, conversation ranged across a number of topics, and I was taken aback by his obvious dedication to his work and his highly forthcoming critique of the existing setup. Although I came to understand the limitations of Chen's political position as the research project advanced, he certainly lived up to his reputation as the most prolabor union leader in China.

His dedication to union work, while not totally unique, set him apart from most union leaders. Zhou Ling (pseudonym), a staff member of a union federation in a major industrial city on China's east coast,[6] compared Chen quite favorably with the chair of her own union. Ms. Zhou confirmed that most union chairs are selected from the Party and government rather than starting as workers and moving up. In her view, the chairman of her union federation had felt "sidelined" when he failed to win a more prestigious post in city government, and he maintained a resentful attitude toward union work.[7] Another worker-activist who had dealings with unions in China's interior before coming to Guangzhou commented that most union chairs rarely come to the union offices (preferring to spend time at the People's Congress, where most of them hold joint appointments) and that they will show up only for important meetings. This activist thought that Chen was more dedicated to his work because he spent the majority of his time at the union headquarters, even though he also held a more prestigious position as deputy chair of the standing committee of the Guangzhou Municipal People's Congress.[8]

Chen's views on labor politics were shaped by his experiences as a young worker in a state-owned textile factory during the 1970s. With a hint of nostalgia he recalled the social bonds and lack of disparities between workers and managers in the factory where he worked as a youth. Even though workers earned only RMB 30 a month, the director's salary was RMB 50, which meant that "the interpersonal relationships were good, and we could talk about anything with the managers."[9] His career trajectory, in which he began as a regular worker and ended as the top labor leader in one of China's largest cities (and perhaps most important in terms of industry and manufacturing), is unusual within the ACFTU. While experience as a worker is certainly no guarantee against oligarchic behavior once in office, in Chen's case he continued to draw on this past for inspiration about how to effect change in the present.

Chen referred to himself as a "resolute socialist"[10] (with no mention of "Chinese characteristics"), an identity that most government officials in today's China embrace awkwardly at best.[11] For him, the realization of socialism was more important even than following the leadership of the Party. Indeed, he once commented that he would leave the Party if it ever turned its back on socialism, though he conspicuously failed to explain how he would be able to recognize such an event if it came to pass. Having come of age in the era of state socialism, he continued to hope that the Party could guide society toward a more just and equitable future. However, in a meeting in 2009 he could not suppress a trace of melancholy in noting that there was a real danger that the "socialist road" might cease to have any meaning.[12]

There are of course limits to how far any union leader can go in criticizing the ACFTU and other subordinate unions. That being said, Chairman Chen was more vocal in his criticism of the ineffectualness of Chinese unions than any other official in the country. One of the most notable of such instances was when he openly differed with ACFTU chair Wang Zhaoguo at the union federation's fifteenth congress in Beijing during the fall of 2008. Wang had given a speech where he claimed that "Western"[13] and Chinese unions share some "common ground" but that their "essence" (*benzhi*) is different. Chen took issue with this characterization, and in a speech at the very same congress rejected the views of his superior, claiming that the essence of unions in both places is to "organize and provide solidarity to workers in order to protect their interests." Rather, it is merely the methods employed that are different, and this is due to different national conditions and the political and social systems. Perhaps in part because of such comments, other municipal union leaders at the congress chided Chen for being "too much like a Western union [leader]."[14]

Not infrequently, Chen's critique of the status quo and calls for reform were even more explicit. In a meeting with instructors from Sun Yat-sen University, he outlined what he thought the primary problems were in what he termed "officially run" (*guanban*) unions: "administrativeness [*xingzhenghua*], bureaucratism, and separation from the masses." His solution to these problems was for reform and "more independence," and that "we can't completely follow the Western model, but we can't *not* reform."[15] Though it is not unusual to hear union leaders use the word "reform," Chen spoke of changing union practices with greater conviction, and as we will see shortly, actively advocated changing existing laws and regulations in an attempt to hasten such a process.

As may be evident from his critique of officially run unions, Chen was at the forefront in calling for greater union accountability to its members, as well as for expanded grassroots strength and worker involvement in the union. In his view, "The union is there to represent the workers but the union doesn't have any strength unless the workers are strong too."[16] And in a highly surprising move for a one-party state such as China, he was quoted in the media as saying that legal action should be taken against derelict cadres: "When an enterprise violates the rights and interests of employees and the union chair doesn't do anything about it but takes the opposite side from the workers and represents the enterprise in legal cases against workers, how can such a union chair protect the rights and interests of workers? I support workers in suing this kind of union chair."[17] After the publication of this article he encountered some blowback, but a year later he continued to hold his ground: "I was quoted as saying that if union cadres in Guangzhou are not doing what the workers want them to and are being too bureaucratic, the workers should sue the cadres. I got a lot of pressure for this, and many cadres were very worried about being sued. But it's important to make them represent the workers."[18] He additionally expressed opprobrium for the method of establishing unions through purely administrative means, arguing, "We just want to let workers organize trade unions by themselves."[19]

This support—on the rhetorical level, at least—for worker initiative in union activity was paired with a relative willingness to compromise the interests of capital. Chen not infrequently would maintain that improving conditions for workers could result in the win-win outcomes advocated by ACFTU leadership. But he also talked about forcing concessions from capital if necessary. When questioned by a group of American unionists about fears of capital flight resulting from passing prolabor legislation, he responded that companies that were just searching for the lowest-cost labor were not contributing to the economy, and if they wanted to "move to Vietnam," that was fine with him.[20] While in the thick of a campaign to establish unions in all Fortune 500 companies operating in Guangzhou, Chen remarked that the current unionization drive was different from previous ones for two reasons. The first was that GZFTU leadership did not care if GDP growth was negatively affected, and the second was that they did not care whether the employers wanted a union: "I've said in the media that we don't need the agreement of employers to organize trade unions."[21] This lack of concern for protecting GDP growth is of course in part due to the fact that Guangzhou is one of the wealthiest cities in China. However, many union leaders in other developed regions of China highlight economic growth and strength in attracting investment just as much as if not more than their union achievements.

For instance, in a meeting between visiting U.S. trade unionists and the leadership of the union federation in Shanghai's Pudong district (one of the wealthiest areas in the entire country), the deputy chair spoke for nearly half an hour about economic growth and then added a few comments about labor rights almost as an afterthought. Chen did not feel that capital's success within his district was something worth highlighting to visiting foreign trade unionists, and he was open in discussing overcoming resistance from employers in defense of worker rights.

If his willingness to criticize employers and other trade unionists is surprising in the context of an authoritarian state, his open interrogation of the appropriate relationship between Party and union is even more remarkable. Chen was always careful to establish that the Party exercises leadership over the union and that this relationship is just and appropriate. But he openly questioned what the precise content of such a relationship should be. After a presentation he made to an industrial social work class at Sun Yat-sen University, one student bluntly asked him to detail the main factors inhibiting union reform.[22] As part of his response, Chen referred to the metaphor of a nanny teaching a baby to walk in order to describe what sort of leadership the Party should exercise over the union. The argument was that whereas in China nannies always hold children's hands to prevent them from falling, in the West they allow children to try to walk on their own. Even if babies in the West sometimes fall, they can learn from the experience.[23] The straightforward implication was that Chinese unions should be able to walk by themselves even if it meant that the nanny was still watching over them.

Chen's view of strikes—one of the most politically sensitive topics in China—was more accepting than any other union leader in the country. As the number of conflicts and strikes in China skyrocketed throughout the 2000s, most trade unionists tried to ignore the problem or attribute it to unreasonable behavior on the part of workers. Legal strikes were seen as Western and not in line with purported Asian values of harmony and nonconfrontation. On the very first night I met Chen, he argued that while some strikes are illegitimate, "many strikes are reasonable and the workers are just trying to get their rights. Actually, I'm secretly happy when workers go on strike and I support it, because it gives more pressure to the government. I think when workers go on strike for good reasons we can take an open attitude in dealing with it." In nearly every meeting I attended, he would speak directly and frankly about the question of strikes, never attempting to gloss over the expanding discontent among Guangzhou's working class. There were limits to his support of strikes, and he was explicit that he could not accept them when strikers turned violent or when explicitly political action was taken. But even before the watershed auto industry strikes in the spring of 2010 (discussed in chapter 5), Chen believed that some forms of strike action should be legalized.

Finally, Chen was very open to interactions with foreign activists, though he stopped short of coordinating cross-border solidarity actions. In November 2007, when nearly all international union exchanges were quite limited in scope and channeled through the national leadership (though there were some exchanges with the Shanghai Federation of Trade Unions), my mother was afforded the incredibly rare opportunity to attend the GZFTU congress, held once every five years. This was one of the few times that a foreigner has been allowed to attend such a high-level union congress in the post-Mao era. In somewhat of a violation of protocol, which holds that national-level foreign unions should be funneled through Beijing, Chen hosted the Service Employees International Union president Andy Stern in August of 2008. With a slight chuckle, Chen noted that ACFTU leadership was "surprised" to learn of this exchange.[24] Additionally, in December 2008, the GZFTU established a formal relationship with the San Francisco Labor Council, one of the first such agreements with an American union federation. Finally, this book would not have been possible had Chen not, completely of his own accord, invited me to Guangzhou to conduct research.

In sum, Chairman Chen has been quite an exceptional figure in the world of Chinese union politics. Especially when he is compared with the typical leaders who see union work as just one step in advancing their political careers, Chen's dedication to the work and his willingness to confront capital, engage with foreign activists, and even openly criticize colleagues and the state set him apart. Additionally, he rejects the essentialist—and empirically false—position of much of union and state officialdom that sees confrontation as a Western behavior.[25] In all these regards, we might reasonably expect that a union under the command of such a chair might be more active in fighting for the interests of its membership and more likely to win the allegiance of these workers, thereby advancing the institutional moment of the countermovement. But before we descend to the shop floor to analyze the lives of Guangzhou's workers, let's first look at the organizational context of the GZFTU as well as some of the policies that Chen was successful in pushing for.

GZFTU at the Forefront of Reform?

Before getting to specific policy initiatives, it is first important to explain something about the political character of the union federation as a whole. One failing of my own research is that I was never able to get a satisfactory answer to the question of how Chen became union chair. When I asked him directly, he merely responded that the union has internal democratic procedures and that he was elected according to these procedures. Other officers attributed his position to a meritocratic selection process, saying that his performance as a lower-level officer was commendable and therefore he continued to rise through the ranks. Given the preponderance of career politicians with little interest in labor politics who end up as union leaders (including those within the GZFTU, as we will see immediately), the meritocratic and democratic explanations do not seem sufficient. An alternative explanation is that Guangzhou is more economically developed and has more acute class conflict than other places in China, and so the Party leadership saw Chen as more likely to effect some degree of compromise. If this were the case, then Chen's election could be seen as an institutional response to insurgency. But other municipalities with similar levels of development and worker unrest such as Shanghai and Dongguan have the conservative union leadership (in the sense that they do not see the working class as having distinct and potentially antagonistic interests to capital and/or the state) typical of ACFTU unions, so there must be some political factors at play as well. Given the lack of transparency in Chinese unions, it will likely remain difficult to gain greater insight into the process of leadership selection.

Chen's ascension was certainly not due to prevailing prolabor tendencies among other leaders within the union federation. As Mingwei Liu (2009) has noted, national leadership had criticized the GZFTU in 2000 for its general ineffectualness. At that time ACFTU chair Wei Jianxing had pushed the unions in Guangdong to reform in order to better handle rising labor conflicts, and Chen's election in 2003 may have been related to this effort. Chen's experience as a factory worker remained unusual in the federation, and in 2010 only two of the six deputy chairs had similar working experience (and significantly these were the two oldest members). But though Chen had some minor success at bringing in more overtly prolabor officers, such people were still generally confined to union headquarters and were not engaged in actual worker organizing.

Under Chen's leadership the GZFTU had made a concerted effort to bring in younger, highly educated officers. One such officer spoke excellent English and had studied abroad but had no interest in, or experience with, labor issues prior to coming to the union. When asked why he came to the GZFTU, he mentioned that he had a friend who had worked there previously and that "I must find a job and the union will [need to] employ somebody. And so I tried, and I got in."[26] Another young officer wanted to come to Guangzhou because her boyfriend had found work there. When asked why she wanted to work for the union, she responded, "because I met their conditions"[27] but nothing more. These staff members certainly brought additional cultural capital and a greater worldliness into the organization, but they were neither experienced with, nor necessarily interested in, union work.

There was one instance in which Chen took something of a risk to bring in a staff member who had exhibited strong organizing skills in earlier union work. Gao Haitao had been hailed in the national media as the most capable organizer to emerge in the ACFTU-directed Walmart campaign of 2006. While studying for the legal exam, Gao had taken on a job at a Walmart store in Nanchang, capital of Jiangxi province, to cover living expenses. Once the campaign in Nanchang got off the ground (against strident opposition from management), he quickly came to be recognized as having strong leadership and organizing skills and played a crucial role in the successful establishment of the store-level union in Nanchang. In the relatively democratic elections that followed, he received the overwhelming support of his colleagues and was elected union chair. Over the subsequent months, Gao was fearless in pushing hard for the interests of the rank and file, and he successfully outmaneuvered management on several occasions. However, he eventually pushed the envelope a bit too far, which led to "some divergence with the higher levels of the union,"[28] as he put it, and he was forced out of office.

At this point, Gao had received national and even international attention. But his departure from the position as union chair clearly signaled that he had lost the support of the leadership in Beijing that he had previously enjoyed. In early 2009, a foreign labor scholar approached Chairman Chen to see if he would consider hiring Gao, as Chen had expressed interest in recruiting officers with more organizing experience.[29] Much to the surprise of Gao and others, Chen decided to take him on as a staff member in one of the union's street-level legal clinics (offices where workers can drop in for advice on resolving workplace grievances). While Gao's position was not a particularly prominent one, it is still highly indicative of Chen's willingness to take some risks in pushing reform within the GZFTU.

Despite these efforts, most GZFTU officers maintained the highly conservative dispositions typical of other union officials. Many were hardly interested in labor issues at all and would stick to official slogans such as "harmonious labor relations," "win-win labor relations," or "scientific development" when talking about union business. Leadership sometimes expressed neoliberal economic views, including that "[unions] cannot interfere with the objective operation of the market." One of the younger staff members argued that the "most important thing is development. Maybe during the development some people or some organizations will pay a price, but the most important thing is development. Once we've reached a step when we've developed enough ... everybody can eat the cake. Then everybody can eat the cake together, but the cake must be big enough."[30] Another young officer claimed that China has a "Marxist government and so they can mediate between the two groups on equal ground." She continued by saying,

"If we want to do union work well, we need to develop the enterprise...to allow the workers to have a good life."[31] The director of international affairs for the federation was even more blunt in his assessment: "When we establish unions we aren't there to resist the boss; we are there to look after the interests of the enterprise."[32] The belief that economic growth and the health of the enterprise are both of immediate benefit to workers and therefore must be a central part of union activity is fundamental to the ideology of ACFTU unions, and the GZFTU is no exception.

But though Chen's efforts at recruiting more overtly prolabor officers failed to produce a sea change within the federation's personnel, he could sometimes use his authority to affect policies at the municipal level. One indication of his success in this regard was Guangzhou's relatively high minimum wage. By 2010, Guangzhou had the second-highest minimum wage in the country at RMB 1100 per month, behind only Shanghai where the wage standard was an additional RMB 20 a month (a difference of USD $3). When the global economic crisis intensified in late 2008, many top officials called for a freeze or temporary suspension of the minimum wage. Chen, on the other hand, said, "We are unwilling to accept the [central] government's announcement of temporarily putting off raises in the minimum wage....I believe we still need to raise the minimum wage to get through the economic crisis."[33] It is true that after a 10 percent increase of the minimum wage in Guangzhou in spring 2008 the Guangzhou Labor Department announced that there would be no such raise in 2009, though it rebuffed calls to eliminate the wage standard.[34] However, it had been the practice for many years previously to raise the minimum wage only once every two years, and levels were once again increased in 2010, this time by nearly 30 percent. It is impossible to assess with any great precision how important the role of Chairman Chen or the GZFTU was in such a process. However, unions are consulted in the determination of minimum wages, and we do know that he consistently expressed strong support for increasing minimum wages.

Perhaps the clearest example of the GZFTU's being at the forefront of union reform was in its attempts to win greater autonomy—from management, not from the state—for enterprise union chairs. Chen had frequently expressed frustration with the fact that the norm was for such officers, crucial as they are for union work, to come from high-level management and the human resources department rather than from the rank and file. Indeed, according to the publicly announced results of a 2009 survey conducted by the GZFTU, more than 50 percent of all private enterprise union chairs were concurrently held by someone from management.[35] An additional problem Chen (and others) identified was that those chairs that *did* try to fight on behalf of membership were subject to unchecked retaliation by management.

In an attempt to address these problems, in December 2007 the union announced that it would be enacting the "Guangzhou Municipality Measures for the Implementation of the 'People's Republic of China Trade Union Law.'"[36] The first and most important feature of this measure was to explicitly ban enterprise managers, human resources officers, other mid- to high-level managers, and any of their relatives from serving as chairs or deputy chairs of the enterprise-level unions. Managers who were already serving as union chairs would not be removed from office but would not be able to serve an additional term (most of which last for three years). Additionally, the measure required that higher levels of the trade union (most likely the district union federation) be consulted before any trade union chairs could be dismissed prior to the end of their terms. This was seen as a method for reducing the likelihood of retaliation by management against activist union chairs.

A year and a half later, the GZFTU felt that the measures for implementation had not gone far enough, and it passed a new resolution in July 2009. The "GZFTU Resolution on Advancing Union Reform and Construction" aimed to reinforce the earlier commitment to eliminate managers from enterprise union leadership and to further protect union activists who suffered from retaliation. The union aimed to "resolve the problem of enterprise leaders holding concurrent posts as union chairs within three years."[37] Of course, the need to reaffirm such a commitment was an implicit recognition of the fact that the measures for implementation from a year and a half prior had in fact *not* resolved the issue of management's controlling enterprise unions. But such a public reaffirmation was directed both at managers and at other officers within the union, to let them know that this was something the leadership was taking quite seriously. An additional feature of this 2009 resolution provided that the union was to start a fund to support union chairs who had been fired in retaliation for their activism. But this fund was seen as a stopgap measure to control the relatively lawless environment in which activist union chairs faced essentially unchecked retaliation. Chairman Chen was quoted in the newspaper as saying, "National laws and Guangzhou municipal laws clearly protect the rights of union chairs. If [union chairs] are pushed out or fired, this is only a short-term behavior. Once the union finds out about such activities, it will intervene and handle the matter to protect the rights of the union chair."[38] This implied that the long-term intention was to ensure that union chairs were not fired in the first place, rather than have them rely on the union support fund.

Once the government's worst fears about the economic crisis passed, the union again went on the offensive. In the spring of 2010, GZFTU deputy chair Liu Xiaogang submitted a draft regulation to the Guangzhou Municipal People's Congress in his capacity as a congressional representative. The draft, entitled "Guangzhou

Municipal Labor Relations and Collective Negotiation Regulations," sought to address difficulties the union federation had experienced in the course of collective negotiations. As stated in the official introduction, failures in collective bargaining had resulted in negative consequences for Guangzhou's workforce: "Increases in workers' wages have not been ideal. From 2003 to 2007, workers' wages did not develop along with the economy and society; they did not grow along with GDP."[39] In the hopes of overcoming the issue of frequent management recalcitrance, the new regulations called for a fine of up to RMB 20,000 for failure to respond to a request for collective negotiations within twenty days. However, the GZFTU legal department chair, Zhang Ruizhou, was explicit that management could not simply pay the fine to avoid negotiations: "The fine doesn't mean you don't have to negotiate; bargaining still has to take place as before."[40] While RMB 20,000 may not be a huge sum for most companies, the regulations were intended to send a clear message about the importance the union was attaching to promoting collective negotiations.

How, then, should we assess these moves by the GZFTU under Chen Weiguang's leadership? In particular, is it possible to detect the emergence of the institutional moment of the countermovement? One area in which Chen has had little success is in recruiting more union officers who have an interest in, and are dedicated to, advancing the interests of the working class. While there are a few exceptions, in general the move has been toward greater professionalization—that is, recruiting officers with advanced degrees and legal training but with little or no working or organizing experience. Part of the problem is simply that there is no social movement field in China, and so there are very few candidates. But the explicit decision to hire college grads rather than to recruit from among the rank and file of course has important implications for the political standpoint of union organization.

In some ways, the attempt to prohibit management from serving as union chairs was not a breakthrough at all. Indeed, in 2006 (more than one year before the measures for implementation were enacted), the ACFTU had inserted the following language into the national-level Enterprise Union Work Regulations: "Enterprise administrators, their partners, or close relatives cannot stand as union committee members in the enterprise."[41] Since enterprise union chairs are necessarily members of the union committee, this regulation would seem to ban the practice of having managers serve as union chairs. The Guangzhou regulation gives greater specificity as to which people count as "administrators" and expands the scope to include deputy managers and officers from human resources departments. Indeed, six months after the measures for implementation, the ACFTU issued a more detailed set of regulations on the "production of union chairs," which closely followed the example set in Guangzhou. But the most important difference is how the enactment of these regulations differed on a rhetorical level. China has many excellent laws and regulations—including the constitutional rights to freedom of association and speech—that officials never mention publicly and that are widely understood to be inoperable.[42] Agents of the state must leverage their symbolic power to summon such regulations into efficacy, something they are typically not inclined to do. Whereas the ACFTU quietly inserted its restriction (totaling one line) deep into a lengthy set of regulations, Chen Weiguang and other officers of the GZFTU made it a point to talk openly, forcefully, and frequently about the new ban. The resolution that was passed a year and a half later was in essence just another reassertion of the union's intention to enforce existing regulations. The regulations, measures, and resolutions passed in Guangzhou represent only marginal improvements on a formal level; it is the way in which they are talked about by those in power that lends them greater credence and that distinguishes Chen Weiguang's GZFTU from other municipal union federations.

These regulations, along with those to protect activist union chairs, were meant to ensure greater autonomy for enterprise-level unions from capital, if not from the state. Greater autonomy from capital would be necessary to make collective negotiation more meaningful, and the draft regulation from 2010 was meant to ensure that management could not refuse to bargain. The draft regulations on collective negotiation were subsequently tabled when the 2010 spring strike wave in the auto industry put collective negotiation high on the provincial and national agenda. However, that the GZFTU was considering such regulations even before the strike wave is an indication that on this issue it was ahead of other union federations.

At this point it should be clear that Chen Weiguang is a highly unusual character in the world of China's labor politics. He used his position of power within the GZFTU and Guangzhou's government to push for more prolabor policies and tried to force union cadres in his own jurisdiction to be more beholden to workers. But why was this raft of new legislation possible?

The Status of the Union

In interview after interview, union officials were nearly unanimous in their assessment that the status (*diwei*) of the union had improved significantly in recent years. As a mass organization, the union had historically occupied a marginalized position within the state structure. An assignment as a union official was not an auspicious sign for an ambitious politician, and the union's ability to affect state policy was limited. But as discussed in chapter 2, union officials have been given greater access to state power in recent years. As one union official in Shanghai put it, "the increase in union status is a good thing. Now when the union speaks, people listen."[43]

While one should be careful in overstating the absolute power of unions, the *relative* increase in status was clearly linked to expanding worker insurgency. A GZFTU official explained it thus: "The reason the status of the union has been increasing is that there have been more conflicts between labor and capital." As worker unrest expanded, the state turned to the union to deal with the problem of managerial intransigence. As a lower officer of the GZFTU recognized, "the government has thought of this problem [managers refusing to enforce laws], and so they are raising the status of the union."[44] As the political urgency of responding to worker insurgency increased, the status of the union within the state also increased.

But as argued in chapter 1, conditions of appropriated representation produce a situation in which worker insurgency enhances the union's access to state power even as workplace unions remain profoundly weak. As many union officials were painfully aware, their status had improved in the eyes of the state but not necessarily in the eyes of membership. An enterprise-level union chair in Guangzhou noted, "If you want to increase your status, you need to do some real things [for workers]."[45] The question now becomes, To what extent have this newfound status and its resultant prolabor policies been translated into decommodification and incorporation of labor? To answer this question, we must leave the halls of power and enter the workplace.

Hitachi—The Best Union in the Country?

From the perspective of Chen Weiguang and the GZFTU, the union at the Hitachi Elevator (China) plant in Dashi town was perhaps the best in the municipality. As we will see, the Hitachi union had been showered with praise from the GZFTU and was a showcase for visiting foreign trade unionists. Though conditions for many—but certainly not all—Hitachi employees were better than for most manufacturing workers in the Pearl River Delta, it is not clear that the enterprise union played a decisive role in bringing this about.

Hitachi Elevator (China) was established in 1995 as a joint venture between Hitachi and the state-owned Guangzhou Guangri. The initial investment was USD $90 million, with the Japanese holding a 70 percent stake in the company and the Chinese the remaining 30 percent.[46] The joint venture produces elevators, escalators, and moving sidewalks at production facilities in Guangzhou, Shanghai, and Tianjian. It has consistently been one of the top producers of elevators in the country.

I first had the opportunity to visit the Guangzhou Hitachi facilities while accompanying a delegation of visiting American trade unionists in December of 2008. We toured the incredibly clean and modern facilities on electric golf carts and then went to a conference room to hear about the union. We learned that the enterprise union had won a series of official accolades over the previous five years, including being deemed by the GZFTU as a "model workers' home" (*mofan zhigong zhi jia*), "superior trade union unit," and an "advanced trade union unit." Additionally, the Guangzhou Hitachi plant was one of only eight companies to be awarded the "AAA Harmonious Labor Relations Enterprise" rating by a committee consisting of the municipal labor department, the municipal employers' association, and the GZFTU. The Enterprise Party secretary and union chair Hu Feng (pseudonym) spoke in glowing terms about the accomplishments of the union and specifically mentioned that their union was better equipped to serve their membership than those of other joint ventures in Guangzhou. He was very proud of the collective contract the union had negotiated on behalf of workers and said that it required a huge amount of effort. This included seeking the advice of the rank and file and a series of challenging negotiations with management.

And there were reasons to believe that Hu Feng took his role as union chair reasonably seriously. Unlike many other union officials I encountered during my fieldwork, he was not only willing but quite enthusiastic to meet with me to discuss union work. Although I was invited to join him at a high-end seafood restaurant for the interview, he arrived wearing a production worker's outfit, adorned with a small hammer-and-sickle lapel pin. Hu's background was similar to Chen Weiguang's in that he had worked his way up from the shop floor through the union structure. Starting in 1979, he was a union committee member in the Chinese Navy, and in 1994 he switched to the state-owned elevator company, where he continued with union work. In sharp contrast to many enterprise-level union officials, he showed a keen interest in the labor politics of the United States and questioned me intensely during our lunch.

While not quite as politically astute as Chen Weiguang, he displayed eminently prolabor instincts and had only positive things to say about Chen's leadership. In particular, he thought that Chen had been effective in winning support from regular workers: "[Chen] has done some important things [for workers], and they have welcomed him....He is very easygoing with workers, and gets along with them. He is an outstanding representative of workers." Hu related a story in which leaders from the GZFTU asked him what the union's greatest accomplishment had been in recent years, and he responded, "It is that…the crisis had an influence on the company [in terms of reduced orders] but we didn't lay off workers." But perhaps most significantly, Hu was a supporter of (relative) independence from management. Mentioning that Chen had stated very clearly that enterprise union chairs cannot come from management, Hu said, "This method is correct.…If management is the union, how can this work? Your position won't be correct; it will be hard [to do your work]." Of course he did not advocate a hostile relationship to management, arguing that "in China, the union has to closely coordinate with the administration; it isn't antagonistic" and "the enterprise must develop a lot, and this depends on the workers." Additionally, he had high words of praise for the company president, with whom he had a close working relationship.[47]

But though the leadership of the Hitachi union was relatively prolabor, it had failed to make such an impression among the workforce. After my official introduction to Hitachi management and union officers, I returned to the district where the plant was located to meet workers independently from official channels. While not all workers had a negative impression of the union, they were hard-pressed to find something *positive* to say.

Many, but not all, workers were at least aware of the fact that they had a union, something that is not true in many unionized workplaces. Upon hiring, they received some introductory materials describing the union's work. But this introduction was unlikely to attract the interest or enthusiasm of the young men and women that made up the workforce, as union activities were described in the stiff and clichéd official language of the state. The employee handbook introduced the union as follows:

> As our nation's mass organization of the working class and the bridge and link between the Party and working masses, the basic task of the union in this new period is to lead the working masses in implementing "Three Represents" important thought. Representing China's advanced productive forces, representing China's advanced culture, and representing the basic interests of the broad masses cause us to more deeply clarify the basic responsibilities and other social functions of the union.…The union organization must fully implement its social role, and at the same time as upholding the general interests of the entire nation, express and uphold the specific interests of workers. This is to uphold the stable employment of the ranks of workers and to ensure political and social stability.

The document did go on to talk about union successes in improving health coverage, wage payments systems, and other benefits. It also claimed that "enterprise employees recognize the active function of the union in promoting occupational safety, labor protection, and worker benefits."[48]

And yet interviews with rank-and-file workers I met through nonofficial channels revealed quite a different perspective. First, and perhaps most crucial, was that none of these workers were aware that their employment was (theoretically) regulated by a collective contract. Workers did receive individual contracts, one of which was provided to me by a worker at my request. But there was no understanding that the enterprise union had played any role in negotiating the terms of employment. This stood in strong contrast to the claims of union leadership that membership had been contacted through the shop-floor organizations and their opinions solicited.

Even if workers were not active participants in the union, things for a certain portion of employees were *relatively* good when compared with the situation of other workers in the region. "Regular" workers (as opposed to the "interns," discussed below) could count on a degree of job security, wages above minimum wage, one day of rest a week, and some employer contributions to social insurance. Regular workers had to undergo a six-month trial period, during which time they received a reduced salary of RMB 1,000 (at the time, just above minimum wage). If they successfully made it past the trial period, they would receive a raise of RMB 400. With overtime, most workers were able to earn around RMB 2000 a month. The average monthly wages in Guangzhou in 2009 were RMB 922 for rural residents and 2,301 for urban residents (and since most Hitachi employees were from the countryside, this meant their wages were significantly higher than those of other migrant workers in the city).[49] Workers confirmed that they had always received their wages on the fifteenth of the month as stipulated in their contract. And it appeared as if the company was fulfilling its responsibilities in paying for social insurance. One worker who had suffered appendicitis said that he got time off from work and the company had paid for 60 percent of his operation, thereby greatly reducing the financial burden. Most regular workers characterized the benefits at Hitachi as "somewhat better" than those in other companies in Guangzhou.

But if things were reasonably good for the regular workers, the interns (*shixisheng*), who constituted up to half of the workforce in some workshops, were treated as flexible and highly exploitable labor. Following the trend of increasing use of contingent labor in both China (L. Zhang 2008) and Japan (Asano, Ito, and Kawaguchi 2011), Hitachi surrounded the core of regular workers with a cadre of interns hired from technical schools. Many of them were employed for periods of time exceeding the legal limit. Workers from the electronic equipment department claimed that nearly half of the employees in their shop were interns, who despite doing similar work received much lower pay (around minimum wage) and benefits than regular workers (also a legal violation) and enjoyed no job security. One such intern expressed great dismay at her continued informal status and was worried that even after she had worked for more than a year the company would not sign a formal contract with her. Additionally, since they were not regular employees, these interns were not allowed to join the union. When asked if the union could be of any help to her in trying to secure a regular contract, one long-term intern merely replied, "We employees haven't encountered them [the union]."[50] One worker who had made the transition from internship to a regular contract said, "I don't know if the union protects them [interns]....They just protect the regular workers." The only union functions interns were aware of were the "entertainment" activities, which included collective birthday parties and the occasional field trip to nearby attractions. When questioned about the union, one intern could only say, "I've heard that they take you to some fun places during holidays." Although union chair Hu had said that there were no layoffs during the financial crisis, he did admit that there were some "individual adjustments." It was not until I spoke with interns that I discovered that he was referring to firing interns (whereas "layoffs" would refer only to regular workers). In short, the interns at Hitachi were maintained as a reserve army of cheap and flexible labor to be disposed of at will, without any of the contractual or legal protections afforded to regular workers.

But even the contracts extended to the regular workers were, on a formal level, severely lacking in content. As has already been mentioned, regular workers were not aware of any collective contract, and the union denied my request to see such a document. Therefore, it is the individual contracts that are the only formal recourse workers have when involved in workplace disputes with management. The contract does very little to specify what sorts of conditions and benefits the workers are entitled to, and although it does list a monthly wage, there is no indication of how many hours are to be worked within a month. In nearly every section of the contract it is merely stated that "relevant laws and regulations" will be followed, without specifying what those are or how a worker might find out. Below are two such sections, in their entirety, which would seem to be crucial to any labor contract:

Section IV. Social Insurance

Party A [employer] and Party B [employee] will participate in and contribute to social insurance according to relevant national, provincial, and municipal laws and regulations. According to the law, Party B will enjoy the relevant social insurance benefits.

Section V. Labor Protection and Labor Conditions

1. Party A will, according to the work needs of Party B, establish the standard implemented work-time system.
2. Party A will implement relevant national, provincial, and municipal regulations on work, rest, vacations, and labor protection, and will provide Party B with labor conditions and safety equipment in accordance with national regulations.

Nowhere in the contract is any mention made of a collective contract, of the union representing the worker, or of how to receive information on relevant laws. Again, no mention is made of the union in the section on resolving labor disputes. Rather, the individualizing legal procedures are briefly outlined (first, informal negotiations; then filing with the enterprise level labor dispute committee; and finally filing for arbitration with the labor bureau) without providing any details about how to proceed with such a process. In general, the reference to unspecified legal standards, the vagueness of the contract, and the failure to mention the potential avenues for resolution of collective problems leave the individual worker—even one with a regular contract—in a highly precarious position even at the formal level.

This invisibility of the union qua collective voice of the workforce was reflected in workers' responses when asked how they went about resolving problems on the job. The temp workers were all unhappy with their unequal treatment, but none of them had considered seeking the help of the union. Some of these workers had no idea what a union was, with one of them stating, "I don't have any understanding of it," while responding with an emphatic "No!" when asked whether she had ever encountered a union officer. Another regular worker had a relatively positive response when initially asked about the union, saying, "The Hitachi union will protect your basic rights,"[51] pointing out that they always got their appropriate days of rest and were paid on time. But when pushed to provide some more details about how specifically the union had helped them, he said, "Most of us employees don't understand specific things about the union." As the conversation progressed, we began to discuss some specific grievances he had at work, most of which centered on an abusive manager, and the methods he had for resolving them:

> That manager was rather coercive, and I was dissatisfied with his management method, so I said something to higher leaders. [I said], "That manager has a big temper.... Lots of people are afraid of him." But the higher leaders said that they didn't have anything to say about this manager.... The union in the enterprise doesn't give us a lot of help.

The union doesn't have any use. In form it says that it will help us, but in reality there isn't any protection.[52]

While levels of satisfaction with their jobs varied for different workers, none of them said that they would seek the help of the union in resolving problems. If one of the core features of a trade union is to represent employees in resolving individual and collective issues in the workplace, the Hitachi union failed to accomplish such a task—and this failure was even more pronounced when the intern workers were taken into consideration.

In sum, overall conditions for regular workers at Hitachi were somewhat better than those for other manufacturing workers in Guangzhou and the Pearl River Delta more broadly. The extent to which labor was decommodified for these workers and the union's role in bringing this about will be addressed below. Regardless, the existence of internal labor market segmentation and the pervasive legal violations in long-term employment of interns represented a serious problem at Hitachi and is indicative of the inability or unwillingness of enterprise unions to think expansively about who makes up their constituency. Because both interns and regular workers regarded the union as illegitimate, they would not turn to it to resolve workplace problems. Thus, even though overall working conditions in the Hitachi factory were not as degraded as those at many other factories, the "model" union had failed to make a positive impression on its membership.

We will now turn to another "most likely" case in a different sector: the union-owned Guangdong Union Hotel.

The Union as Employer

One of the most noteworthy features of reform-era China's political economy—and something that distinguishes it sharply from liberal democracies—has been increasing demands for government agencies to generate revenue through market mechanisms rather than taxation (Duckett 2001). Perhaps the best-known example is the commercial empire built by the People's Liberation Army (Bickford 1994), though by the mid-1990s the Party had forced the military to spin many of their holdings off into private companies. Nonetheless, today union federations at various levels remain involved in commercial activity, especially hotel ownership. Such businesses are administratively distinct from state-owned enterprises, and thus far there is no scholarly research on labor relations in these enterprises. Unfortunately, the case of the union-owned Guangdong Union Hotel does not provide much hope that workers in these enterprises enjoy anything like the privileged position that SOE workers do.

I first came to understand the logic behind such state-owned businesses in a somewhat humorous moment while accompanying a delegation of American union leaders in Shanghai. While we were driving to a banquet with the leaders of the Shanghai Federation of Trade Unions, our guide—an officer in the international department of the SHFTU—was beaming with pride as he told us that we would be dining in the first union-owned five-star hotel in the country. One of the members of the U.S. delegation asked the guide why a union would own a hotel. Looking quite perplexed, the guide responded, "Why, to make money of course!" This was met with laughter from the Americans, but a profound point about the logic of government agencies was thus revealed.

There were several union-owned hotels in Guangzhou, though none as luxurious as those of the SHFTU. These hotels are open to the public, and, as was the case in Shanghai, they are used for generating profit according to market principles. Trivial though it may seem, one indication of the managerial logic applied in these businesses appeared in the form of a piece of calligraphy hanging in the restaurant of a GZFTU-owned hotel. Done in a traditional style, it read, "If you don't work hard today, you will work hard looking for a job tomorrow." (See figure 9.) The specific hotel we are concerned with here—the Guangdong Union Hotel (Guangdong gonghui dasha)—is wholly owned by the Guangdong Federation of Trade Unions and occupies the western side of the same building that houses the union headquarters. The seventy-five-room, three-star hotel is administered by the GDFTU's property management committee.

The central actor in the Guangdong Union Hotel case was a woman named Liu Yongyi, a fifty-two-year-old hotel employee and chair of the enterprise union. Liu began working in the hotel in 2000 and shortly thereafter was involved in establishing a union organization. She gained considerable support among other hotel employees and the following year was elected to a five-year term as union chair. Although it is unclear just how competitive and transparent the election process was, in 2006 she was reelected for another five-year term.

It was in the first year of her second term as chair that Liu began to attract the ire of hotel management. The company's policy had been to purchase medical insurance only for employees with a Guangzhou *hukou,* which meant that migrant workers in the hotel were on their own when it came to medical expenses.[53] Not coincidentally, the ten employees who had Guangzhou *hukou* were in management, meaning that all the other workers were without insurance. Liu brought this up with management and after several months won health insurance for all employees. The next struggle she took up centered on nonpayment of overtime wages. Management was refusing to pay employees the additional wages to which they were legally entitled for working extra shifts on weekends and holidays. Once again, Liu was successful in remedying this problem, and she gained

FIGURE 9. Translation: "If you don't work hard today, you will work hard looking for a job tomorrow." Photo by the author.

increased stature with her constituency as a result. Finally, in late 2007, a number of employees came to the union to complain about how increased rents in the city were creating financial hardship for them. Liu began a multimonth effort to establish a housing fund for employees, which ended victoriously the following spring. These three victories firmly established her reputation as a competent representative of the hotel's employees.

But while employees at the Guangdong Union Hotel were supportive of Liu's aggressiveness, management was increasingly frustrated. After a rapid succession of general managers at the hotel, Jiang Lingquan was brought in at the end of 2008. In December of that year, one of his first moves as general manager was to seal up Liu's office and notify her that she was not to discuss union business. As Liu fought this over the next few months, management decided to take more decisive action, and on April 1 it notified her that she was being dismissed at the end of the month. Losing her employment at the hotel also meant that she would not be able to continue to serve as union chair. Two other members of the union committee were also notified of their dismissal. Just over one week before her contract was to be terminated, the story blew up in the media, receiving extensive coverage both in Guangzhou and nationally.

After a number of articles sympathetic to the union chair's cause appeared, management went on the counteroffensive and held an emergency press conference. General manager Jiang's explanation for her dismissal focused on two main issues. On the one hand, he portrayed Liu as corrupt, having "problems with her character," and neglecting her work duties. But it was clear that dereliction of duty was not the only issue Jiang was concerned with. Rather, it became apparent that the difficulties Liu had created for management were a motivation: "[She] has created a negative environment here. She's had really bad relationships with the few prior general managers, and the cancellation of her contract was done according to the rules."[54] Becoming somewhat exasperated during the press conference, Jiang perhaps unwittingly revealed that Liu's dismissal was highly calculated and involved union leadership: "We the GDFTU should explain this to the Guangzhou media: last year when the Party organization sent me to this hotel, it was precisely because she had created such a bad environment."[55] Thus, while management tried to cast aspersions on Liu's character, it became clear that the primary motivation for the firing was related to her activism.

The general manager additionally invited the media to "come talk with our employees when you have time; many of them don't like her." But in a spurt of quite aggressive journalism, a number of reporters spoke with regular employees about their views of the union chair. Without exception, they supported Liu, with one worker saying, "She has a strong sense of justice, and won overtime and housing subsidies for us."[56] Additionally, employees believed that Liu's firing was directly related to her activities as union chair rather than any defect in character, with some describing her as "morally upright."[57]

Higher levels of the union refused to come out in support of the fired union chair as the district and municipal union federations remained silent on the matter. The provincial union federation deputy chair, Kong Xianghong, considered by some to be prolabor for his advocacy of reforms in collective bargaining laws, joined Jiang Lingquan at the press conference and declared that the GDFTU would "not side with either party."[58] Somewhat surprisingly, the most sympathetic union official was the GDFTU's property management committee chair, Wu Zhaoquan. Wu was quoted publicly as saying, "The union is originally a unit for helping workers protect their rights. Enterprises owned by the union should strictly follow the Labor Contract Law in employment relations."[59] He even went so far as to say, "The way the hotel handled the termination of the labor contract was clearly inappropriate."[60] But the reaction from people within the union who had the stature to change the outcome was decidedly less supportive.

The media, for its part, pushed the ambiguous borders of permissibility (Hassid 2008) and provided the public with highly critical coverage of the story. Following a number of sympathetic pieces from prominent newspapers such as *Nanfang Ribao* and *Guangzhou Ribao,* even more critical opinion pieces appeared on the Internet. One such piece was provocatively titled, "How Many More Union Organizations Will Be 'Raped' by Employers?" and provided an incisive critique not just of management retaliation but also of the union: "If companies can do whatever they want right under the nose of the highest trade union organization in the province, and they haven't paid any attention to workers' legal rights and interests, who would dare hope that the union can represent workers' interests...? Even more frightening, how many other union organizations, union committee members, and union members have in reality been 'raped' by employers?"[61] Another opinion piece argued that the system of management funding of union activities and union chairs' salaries was at the heart of the problem and that "unions should be paid independently."[62] Unfortunately, the huge amount of attention generated by the coverage upset the authorities, and three days after the story broke, all reporting on the case conspicuously disappeared.

Somewhat surprisingly, the furor caused by the media reports caused management to back down, and Liu was quietly allowed to maintain her post. With the media now unable to report on the case, Liu agreed to leave her post. However, over the next year she was engaged in legal battles with management over the amount of compensation she would receive, arguing that the RMB 20,000 offered in April 2009 was insufficient. In December of that year, Liu lost her case, a decision that she did not appeal.[63] And in April 2010, she was finally forced out.

Throughout the incident, the GZFTU's and GDFTU's emphatic neutrality—a "passive repressive" response—was tantamount to siding with management, a fact that was surely not lost on Liu Yongyi or other labor activists following the story. The Guangdong Union Hotel case thus took pole position as one of the most egregious and tragically ironic instances of unchecked managerial retaliation against union activists.

The Institutional Moment in Guangdong?

Thus far, we have analyzed workplaces within the jurisdiction of Chen Weiguang's GZFTU where we should be most likely to find the union playing an important role in bringing about institutionalized decommodification and incorporation of labor: the award-winning Hitachi Elevator joint venture and the GDFTU-owned Guangdong Union Hotel. How should we assess the outcomes of union activity in these enterprises?

It is first important to establish the extent to which labor was decommodified for employees. Hitachi was characterized by a dual labor market in which a portion of workers received relatively good wages, job security, and benefits.

The labor of these regular workers was comparatively decommodified. None of them were laid off when orders dropped in late 2008–9, thus indicating a degree of workplace security. Social insurance payments were made on time, and workers were able to get significant subsidies for medical expenses, both indications of social protection. Wages were good for migrant workers, even if they were far short of what would be required to make a life in the city. And instances in which workers were unhappy with oppressive managerial styles were not resolved.

But if regular workers enjoyed a degree of protection from the market, the temporary interns remained fully subject to the vagaries of managerial autonomy and market fluctuations. These workers were by and large unaware of the union or any other channel for resolving grievances, nor were they allowed to be union members. They did not receive contracts, had wages significantly below those of regular workers, and did not receive benefits. Employees were often kept as interns for much longer than was legally permitted, often for more than a year. And when the economy stumbled during the economic crisis, they were the first ones to lose their jobs. In short, any decommodification that regular workers benefited from was not extended to the interns who made up a large segment of the workforce.

Then we have the question of whether union organizations at either the enterprise or municipal level played a significant role in bringing about the limited decommodification that was secured for regular workers. It is impossible to strictly determine causality in this case, as the union and management both operate with little transparency. I was not allowed to see the collective contract, and my only account of the process of collective bargaining came from union officials themselves. Given workers' complete ignorance of the collective contract, it is impossible to independently verify what the union's role was or to develop a counterfactual as to what might have happened without the union. But there are a number of reasons to believe that the relatively good conditions for regular workers derive more from Hitachi Elevator's capital-intensive nature of production, from the relatively strong market position of its workers, and most important, from the fact that it is partly held by a state-owned enterprise than from the activities of the union *as representative of the workers*. In this sense, the union has not moved in the direction of incorporation.

Although managers in state-owned enterprises in China have continually moved toward an embrace of market principles (Gallagher 2004, 2005; Zhao and Nichols 1996), conditions for workers are in general still better than those in the private sector—at least for those who are lucky enough to work for profitable firms (Chan and Unger 2009). A brief comparison with three other enterprises in Guangzhou—the foreign-owned Ascendant Elevator, foreign owned-Nanhai Honda (both of which will be discussed in greater detail in chapter 5), and the joint venture Guangzhou Honda—is instructive. All four of these enterprises are capital-intensive and employ relatively skilled workers. All four have union organizations. However, workers' conditions (especially wages) are significantly worse at the two privately owned companies, Ascendant and Nanhai Honda. As we will see in the next chapter, such conditions eventually caused workers in these two factories to revolt and led to a highly militant strike action. Despite the strike wave of 2010, which affected mainly Japanese-owned enterprises (mostly in auto but in other industries as well), neither Guangzhou Honda nor Hitachi experienced any labor disturbances. Although conditions for workers in these plants certainly left something to be desired, the ability of regular workers to consistently make more than RMB 2,000 and to have social insurance paid on time was something that workers in the privately held companies could not enjoy. Although such a tiny sample prevents us from drawing any strong conclusions, it is quite likely that conditions for workers improve when the state is a major shareholder in a company, particularly in capital-intensive industries with a skilled workforce—precisely the type of enterprise we have with Hitachi Elevator.

Perhaps the objection may be raised that Hitachi is not a state-owned company but rather a joint venture that is only 30 percent owned by the Chinese partner. Indeed, the state's minority share does indicate that the Japanese investors retain a strong hand in major managerial decisions. However, the managerial hierarchy in the company highly favors the Chinese. First and most important is that the CEO, Pan Shengshen, is Chinese and has had an active political career, holding prominent positions in Guangzhou's municipal legislative body as well as the People's Political Consultative Congress. As the Hitachi union chair put it, "Because he has these positions, the Japanese really trust him."[64] Pan maintains close relations with many prominent political figures in Guangzhou and attended a banquet held by Chen Weiguang in honor of visiting American union leaders. Additionally, all twelve of the high-level managers at Hitachi are Chinese, whereas the Japanese are only deputy managers. In short, while the Japanese maintain a majority share in the company, it is clear that primary operational control is in the hands of the Chinese managers that have close ties to the Party and local government. With these manager/politicians in key positions in the enterprise, the state (broadly conceived) is able to exercise significant control over key decisions, including treatment of workers.

It is because the limited decommodification at Hitachi came about as a result of state action rather than democratic mobilization of the workforce that the "success" is so limited in scope. The continual heavy reliance on interns at Hitachi represents a significant failure and a potential source of instability. Most union officials argue that interns, temporary, and "dispatch" workers are not formal employees of the enterprise and therefore are not a concern of the union. This is a reflection of the narrowly focused service-based orientation of ACFTU-subordinate unions. And in a situation when even regular workers remain highly atomized, ignorant of their collective contract, and disengaged from the union in general, their gains remain tenuous. As the Chinese state always reserves the right to violate its own laws, it would not be surprising to find that the collective contract could be easily ignored by management if deemed necessary. In a slight modification of Feng Chen's (2007) argument that individual rights in China are undermined by a lack of collective rights, we see here that individual material gains can potentially be undermined by lack of collective power. In short, failure to incorporate the workforce implies that material gains are segmented (only certain workers enjoy better treatment) and potentially reversible.

Whereas in Hitachi a degree of decommodification came about for a segment of the workforce as a result of state action, the Guangdong Union Hotel presents us with a very different scenario. Here we saw an activist enterprise union chair who had strong rapport with and support from regular employees. These workers knew Liu Yongyi and were grateful for her leadership within the union. In this sense, the enterprise union was operating *as worker representative* rather than as an expression of state power, and it was able to solve problems through rationalized channels. However, because Liu had begun to consolidate a base of support among the membership, it was likely that the higher levels of the union took a passive repressive position in response to her firing. That is to say, it was precisely at the moment when prolabor leadership from Chen Weiguang (or other high-level union officials in Guangzhou) could have made a difference that such leadership evaporated. Simply by doing nothing (i.e., behaving passively), the leaders unleashed the inherent repressive capacity of capital to hire and fire. Given this structural power asymmetry at the point of production, passivity from union leadership is tantamount to repression.

The Guangdong Union Hotel raises a few additional salient points. The first is that Liu's struggles against management were a clear example of the Polanyian countermovement in action. Her constituency demanded social protection (housing subsidy, social insurance) and workplace security (appropriate overtime wages) to protect them from market fluctuations, the clearest example of which was increased housing costs. Liu mobilized the organizational resources at her disposal to fight for, and eventually win, these protections. Thus we can see that the union structures at the enterprise level maintain the potential to be directed toward decommodifying and incorporating ends. Liu's victories are an indication of the first hints of the institutional moment of the countermovement.

But the fate that befell Liu Yongyi was not a chance occurrence. Indeed, activist enterprise-level union chairs have emerged in a variety of different industries all over the country (A. Chan 2011b) and have on many occasions successfully challenged capital in advancing the interests of membership. But time and time again, these union chairs are summarily fired and almost always in violation of the Trade Union Law (which requires a majority recall vote among a membership congress).[65] The reason that the Guangdong Union Hotel case struck a chord in Chinese society is that it was such a common occurrence but one that many were surprised and angered to see repeated at a union-owned enterprise. The cased revealed the profound vulnerability of these union chairs to unchecked managerial retaliation (F. Chen 2009), even in the enterprises where it is least likely to occur.

This, then, is a very clear indication of how union oligarchy threatened tenuous steps toward institutionalization of the countermovement. To a certain extent, union oligarchy at the enterprise level was diminished as Liu pursued particular goals in response to the wishes of membership. It is important to note that these ends were pursued oligarchically—the rank and file were not actively mobilized. And it was because of this inability to adequately develop the collective power of workers that the victories in the Guangdong Union Hotel were so tenuous. But ultimately it was the oligarchy and heteronomy of the municipal and provincial level unions that allowed for Liu's activism to be effectively crushed. The union was heteronomous in this instance both vis-à-vis the state and in relationship to the market. That is to say, the impetus for the union to tamp down grassroots activism and to generate profit through market mechanisms overrode any capacity it might have had to defend activist chairs within its jurisdiction. And it was oligarchic in the sense that high-level leaders did not use their political and symbolic power to intervene in a situation in which they could have made a difference. Their passive repressive response was eminently political and had important symbolic consequences. Since this case was being closely watched, they knew other potential activists would be aware of the outcome. This unwillingness to support grassroots activism is a strong indication of oligarchy and a continual threat to the construction of an institutional response.

But perhaps it is unfair to blame Chen Weiguang for his failure to act in the Liu Yongyi case. Maybe he wanted to intervene, but because it involved his direct superiors from the provincial federation he was unable to. There is of course no way to know what Chen's personal feelings were on the case. But his feelings on the matter are immaterial, for what I am interested is political *action*. And if in fact he was unable to act out of fears that he would upset his superiors, this reveals the fundamental weakness of the entire Chinese trade union structure, predicated as it is on appropriated representation: officers are beholden not to their constituency but to the political system. Thus we can see strong limitations on what prolabor leaders, even those as prominent as Chen, will be able to achieve in terms of promoting the interests of their membership.

It is also worth noting the mixed results that the GZFTU has had in removing management from trade union leadership (one of Chen's top priorities). The clearest example of this comes from the formation of the prominent Tianhe District Retail Sector Union Federation. As we will see in more detail in chapter 4, the formation of sectoral unions has been at the top of Chen Weiguang's agenda for a number of years, and he has been personally involved in their formation. It then came as quite a surprise that when the formation of the Tianhe district federation was announced in November of 2010, the deputy chair was a man named Wang Honggang, the human resources director for the mega-chain Trust-mart. It is also worth noting that Wang had been, and presumably remained, chair of the enterprise-level union at the Trust-mart store. With a human resources manager as deputy chair of the new federation, management will have a strong voice in the development of the sectoral union as it expands from the Tianhe district to cover the other districts in Guangzhou (as was planned). The selection of Wang as deputy chair was in clear violation of the 2007 measures for implementation, which explicitly ban managers from serving as union chairs or deputy chairs. If three years after the ban was passed management was still able to secure powerful positions in prominent unions being formed under the direct supervision of the GZFTU, it is quite likely that such practices continue unabated in other enterprises. This is a strong indication that Chen Weiguang's attempts at winning greater union autonomy from management continue to be confounded.

Finally, it is important to mention that after Chen's final term in office, he was apparently unable to institutionalize a consistently prolabor political culture. In November 2012 Chen was succeeded by Zhao Xiaosui, a woman with no experience as a worker or in the trade union. Zhao has a professional degree in management and a master's degree in economics, and her longest stint prior to assuming leadership of the GZFTU was as the director and deputy director of the Enterprise Management Office of the Guangzhou Economics Committee.[66] At the time of writing it is difficult to assess her performance, though she was conspicuously absent during the sanitation worker strike wave (discussed in chapter 4) that began the month after her term started. Although it is impossible to predict how someone will behave once in office, there is little in her background that suggests she will continue the prolabor positions of Chen.

This chapter has provided an analysis of the possibilities that prolabor leadership in regional union organizations can play a role in institutionalizing the countermovement. It is evident that traces of the institutional moment are emerging, even within a union structure that at first glance appears to be an exemplar of oligarchic organization. In other words, we can see an attempt to respond to the insurgent moment of the countermovement within existing institutional parameters. However, when we look at two of the enterprises in which relatively decommodified and incorporated labor should be most solidly institutionalized, we see that the gains that have been made are modest, tenuous, and subject to ongoing threats. This is due in large part to the state's categorical ban on the development of worker collective power at the point of production. Thus we can see the consequences of the contradictory nature of labor in China—after Chen Weiguang engaged in widely publicized legislative attempts to reduce retaliation against activist union chairs, even a chair in a union-owned hotel could not be saved from dismissal. While prolabor leadership in Guangzhou has produced some symbolic and policy shifts, as we will see in the following chapters, they have not been able to put the institutional machinery in place to prevent ongoing worker insurgency.

OLIGARCHIC DECOMMODIFICATION?
Sectoral Unions and Crises of Representation

Thus far we have seen cases where ACFTU-subordinate unions have, despite pressure from their membership, not played an active role in the realization of decommodification. While the details of the specific cases vary, the general point is that oligarchy has blocked incorporation and therefore stood in the way of the unions' participation in institutionalizing the countermovement. Worker unrest has failed to produce a realignment of political power in society, and so the countermovement remains stalled at the insurgent moment.

When we turn to the case of Zhejiang, we find very different economic and political dynamics from those in Guangdong. These conditions have given the municipal governments and unions greater capacity than those in Guangdong to organize entire industries in an attempt to rationalize employment relations. I argue that the greater development of sectoral bargaining in Zhejiang is due to the different models of development—specifically the origin of investment, levels of capital mobility, levels of social capital, local economic diversification, and presence of legitimate employer associations. At first glance, it appears that these conditions have allowed unions to play a key institutional role in bringing about decommodification, the clearest indication of which is the conclusion of municipal-level sectoral wage agreements. However, while the Zhejiang and Guangdong cases are quite *dis*similar in terms of the institutional capacity of the state and union to respond to instability in labor relations, the final outcome (i.e., decommodification and incorporation) is quite similar in both places. Although the sectoral agreements reached in Zhejiang seem to imply a degree of decommodification on a formal level, lack of incorporation led to contract nonenforcement and ongoing high levels of commodification. This suggests that attempts by the state and union to find a technocratic solution to labor conflict— what I will call "oligarchic decommodification"—may fail, as illegitimate representative organizations cannot convince their members to abide by agreements reached without their participation or consent.

In this chapter I first seek to explain why the Rui'an Eyeglass Union and Wenling Wool Knitwear Union were able to play a key role in the conclusion of sectoral-level agreements, while unions in Guangzhou have failed in such endeavors. The answer to this question lies in an analysis of the distinct models of economic development and the type of politics that such an economy generates. Finally, I show that under conditions of appropriated representation, even if labor is decommodified at the formal, contractual level, employers and workers alike frequently ignore such constraints on the market in practice. Thus the union's attempts at realizing oligarchic decommodification have failed.

Comparing Zhejiang with Guangdong makes sense for a number of reasons. The two southeastern provinces (see figure 10) are two of the wealthiest in China, have been the most successful with capitalist industrialization, and also have some of the highest levels of worker unrest. Thus, if we are looking for the emergence of a new system (or systems) of labor relations in China, it would be reasonable to assume that it would happen in these regions. And yet we see that the possibilities for establishing new organizational forms are different in each place. Given that unions in both places are subject to similar imperatives from the ACFTU center, this divergence is worthy of investigation. This approach allows us to see how external economic conditions impact union activity, rather than simply focusing on the much-discussed relationship to the Party.

An additional word about my case selection is necessary. A comparison between heterogeneous industries—knitwear and eyeglasses in Zhejiang, sanitation and construction in Guangdong—may seem odd. Indeed, divergent outcomes could be attributed to differences inherent to the industry, such as skill level of the workforce, market position, and capital mobility. It was originally my intention to compare the Zhejiang unions to sectoral unions in manufacturing in Guangdong. But at the time I was doing research there was not a single sectoral union in any manufacturing industry in Guangdong, making such a comparison impossible. As a result, the comparison is between the best examples of sectoral unions in each place. The fact that Guangdong had no sectoral unions in manufacturing is already an indication of the lack of success in this region.

To set the stage, some background in China's paths to development will be necessary.

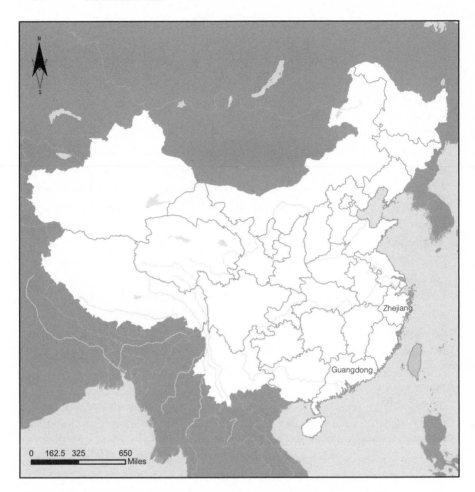

FIGURE 10. Location of Zhejiang and Guangdong provinces in China.
Source: redrawn from *Wikimedia Commons,* http://commons.wikimedia.org/
wiki/File:China_blank_map.svg.

Development and Labor Politics in China

The role of foreign direct investment has been widely discussed in both academic
and mainstream accounts of Chinese economic development over the past three
decades. Although there are some exceptions, the dominant narrative is that
the Chinese government has been able to secure hundreds of billions in foreign
investment, while domestic industry has played a secondary and relatively minor
role in promoting growth. Statements such as the following are representative of
this line of argumentation: "China's export-led manufacturing boom is largely a

creation of foreign direct investment (FDI), which effectively serves as a substitute for domestic entrepreneurship. During the last 20 years, the Chinese economy has taken off, but few local firms have followed" (Huang and Khanna 2003, 75). While some recognize the spatial and sectoral unevenness of FDI (Broadman and Sun 1997), the overall consensus is that foreign investment is good for growth (Chen, Chang, and Zhang 1995) and, despite possible political drawbacks (Eng 1997; Gallagher 2002, 2005), that it is a fundamental part of the story of development in China (Tseng and Zebregs 2003).

I do not wish to debate the validity of these claims. Indeed, total utilized FDI more than doubled from US$40.3 billion in 1999 to $92.4 billion in 2008,[1] making China the largest FDI recipient in the world among developing countries. However, I draw attention to Zhejiang province, an economically vibrant part of the country that has relied relatively little on FDI in its quest for growth. There are significant consequences of this path to development for politics in the province.

The focus of my research is on labor politics, not on determinants of growth. I introduce Zhejiang into the conversation on the Chinese labor movement to highlight the relationship between models of development and the political possibilities for labor. The overwhelming majority of literature on Chinese labor politics has focused either on the state-owned sector (Blecher 2002; Cai 2002; F. Chen 2000, 2003; Hurst 2004, 2009; C. K. Lee 2002) or the FDI-fueled southeast (A. Chan 2001; Chan and Pun 2009; C. K. Lee 1995, 1998; Pun 2005; Thireau and Hua 2003), with Ching Kwan Lee (2007) producing the only significant comparison of the two regions. The dominant narrative about the role of FDI in Chinese development is really a story about the "sunbelt," which is centered on the Pearl River Delta. Footloose transnational capital has been drawn to this region by its well-developed infrastructure, low labor costs, relatively healthy and well-educated workforce, and categorical ban on independent worker organizations. This model of development has produced a certain set of possibilities for labor politics that is too complex to explain at length here. But very briefly, workers in this area have engaged in frequent, cellular forms of protests, which have yet to result in significant decommodification of labor or a realignment of power relations in the determination of the labor process. The local state is committed to attracting and retaining foreign investment, and therefore its ability to push for the interests of labor or to discipline capital is highly curtailed. As has been discussed previously, the inability of trade unions to win recognition from the working class is indicative of this dilemma.

Now when we turn our attention to Zhejiang, we see that the model of development there has produced a somewhat different political environment with more possibilities for the labor movement than one might assume from a reading of the extant literature. While the local state in Zhejiang maintains the alliance with capital that we see in Guangdong, it has a significantly greater *potential* to organize, if not necessarily coerce, employers. This is because a much greater percentage of employers in Zhejiang are locals and are organized into representative associations. As a result, the state has many more political, administrative, and social tools at its disposal. This means that the state has greater capacity to violate the immediate interests of certain capitalists in the service of greater long-term competitiveness for the sector as a whole. Worker insurgency in many sectors has pushed the state to search for a more rationalized approach to accumulation, the clearest example of which is the greater propensity for conclusion of sectoral wage agreements. While such agreements are not necessarily positive from the perspective of labor, they do indicate that there are moments when the interests of the state and at least some segment of capital overlap with those of workers and that under the right conditions, Chinese unions can play an important institutional role in the realization of such contracts. Despite these important political differences, much as was the case in Guangdong, the weakness of trade unions at the grassroots level means that what the union wants to happen and what actually happens are two very different things.

Zhejiang and the Wenzhou Model

Although not nearly as well known internationally as Guangdong, Zhejiang province is in fact one of the most economically vibrant areas in China. Along with the Pearl River Delta, it ought to be considered ground zero for the birthplace of post-Mao Chinese capitalism. The success of the region in promoting economic growth is quite astonishing. Although Zhejiang's output of RMB 313 per capita in 1978 made it only the thirteenth-wealthiest province in China,[2] by 2006 that number had skyrocketed to 31,874. With Jiangsu clocking in at 28,814 and Guangdong at 28,332, Zhejiang could claim to be the most economically successful province in the country by a wide margin.[3] Although Guangdong's official population of 86 million dwarfs the 46 million in Zhejiang,[4] the significance of Zhejiang's vault to economic preeminence among Chinese provinces should not be overlooked.

But in contrast to the typical story about state involvement and reliance on FDI, Zhejiang pursued "capitalism from below" (Nee and Opper 2012). Perhaps the most significant indicator of the extent to which Zhejiang differs from Guangdong is the percentage of output that derives from foreign invested firms.[5] In 2003, a modest 20.1 percent of output in Zhejiang came from foreign firms, and that number crept up to 26.64 percent by 2007.[6] While one-quarter of the economy is clearly significant, it pales in comparison with Guangdong's massive reliance on foreign investment. In the year 2000, 58.28 percent of output in Guangdong came from foreign firms, and it was up to 61.05 percent by 2007.[7]

For the three largest cities in the Pearl River Delta (the focus of my Guangdong study), the numbers are even more astonishing: 64.44 percent in Guangzhou, 67.88 percent in Shenzhen, and 77.85 percent in Dongguan.[8] In Guangdong, foreign investment is not a just a significant part of the economy—it the *foundation* of the economy.

This tremendous divergence is of note in and of itself. But when we dip below the provincial level of aggregation in Zhejiang, we see that the story is a bit more complex. Zhejiang has traditionally been divided into a flat, prosperous, and centrally located Northeast and a mountainous, poor, and remote southwest. However, as Ye and Wei (2005) argue, over the past twenty years regional inequality within Zhejiang has increased between the interior and coastal regions while

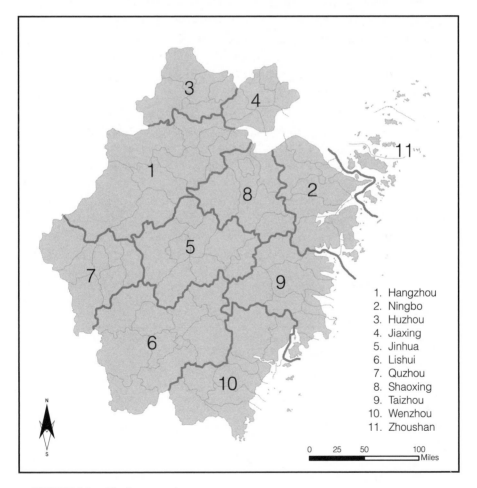

1. Hangzhou
2. Ningbo
3. Huzhou
4. Jiaxing
5. Jinhua
6. Lishui
7. Quzhou
8. Shaoxing
9. Taizhou
10. Wenzhou
11. Zhoushan

FIGURE 11.   Zhejiang province.
Source: redrawn from *Wikimedia Commons,* http://commons.wikimedia.org/wiki/File:Zhejiang_prfc_map.png.

decreasing between the traditional northeast/southwest regions. Because I am interested in the most industrially advanced regions, I will focus for the moment on the Northeast and Southeast regions of Zhejiang. The northeast includes the cluster of municipalities of Hangzhou, Jiaxing, Shaoxing, and Ningbo, while the southeast consists of Wenzhou, Taizhou, and Jinhua (see figure 11). But why is this categorization of regions *within* Zhejiang important? Since the reason I am interested in the province in the first place is that it represents a different model of development from that in the Pearl River Delta, I focus on the regions that best exemplify this model. In this case, the southeast, in particular Wenzhou, is representative of an indigenous, entrepreneurial model of economic development that does not rely on FDI.

This is not to say that the northeast of Zhejiang, centered on the provincial capital of Hangzhou, has been lackluster in its growth. Rather, it is that this region has many advantages that the southeast of the province does not. Hangzhou and its environs have been a major engine of economic growth for many centuries. The Grand Canal, first completed in the seventh century, was built to link Hangzhou with Beijing in the north. Ningbo, just to the east of Hangzhou on the East China Sea, was the premier port city in the region until it was eclipsed by Shanghai in the nineteenth century. Today this region benefits tremendously from its highly developed infrastructure and proximity to both the investors and the markets of Shanghai. These are advantages that municipalities in the southeast have not enjoyed as they have pursued growth.

In particular, the amount of foreign investment in the two regions is remarkably different, as shown in table 3. These data have important implications for a Guangdong-Zhejiang comparison. It is true that aggregated at the provincial level, a much smaller percentage of Zhejiang's output comes from foreign-invested

TABLE 3.   Foreign investment in Zhejiang, 2007

	Value of utilization of foreign capital (US$)	Value of utilization of foreign capital per capita (US$)
Northeast		
Hangzhou	5,580,590,000	830
Ningbo	4,501,070,000	797
Shaoxing	2,365,160,000	542
Jiaxing	3,455,120,000	1,026
Southeast		
Wenzhou	1,049,444,000	137
Jinhua	373,352,000	81
Taizhou	816,810,000	144

Source: *Zhejiang tongji nianjian* (2008) [Zhejiang statistical Yearbook (2008)] (Beijing: Zhongguo tongji chubanshe), 564; *Zhejiang Economic Census Yearbook* (2004) (Beijing: Zhongguo tongji chubanshe), 7–16.

enterprises than is the case for Guangdong. However, the three southeastern municipalities are much more exemplary of the locally driven development that I am interested in and are thus the focus of this discussion.

The Rise of Zhejiang's Local Entrepreneurialism

The distinctive model of development found in southeastern Zhejiang started in the city of Wenzhou. Although the city leadership was condemned for harboring procapitalist tendencies during the Mao era (Forster and Yao 1999, 61), the so-called Wenzhou Model received support from the central government in the 1980s and quickly gained national fame. Though the model was promoted as feasible for imitation nationwide, it is really only in the neighboring municipalities in southeast Zhejiang where such emulation has proven highly successful. Despite the Wenzhou Model's undeniable success in growth, its political feasibility in the formally socialist China of the 1980s was far from guaranteed.

As mentioned previously, Wenzhou was quite isolated from the major hubs of Chinese social life for much of history. In the Mao era, state investment in the region was minuscule, as the city's proximity to Taiwan made it appear vulnerable to military attack. Additionally, Yia-Ling Liu (1992) argues that the relative independence of the Wenzhou Communist Party in the revolutionary era often put local officials at odds with, and willing to violate the directives of, the central leadership. Although these may be only partial explanations, the fact remains that up until 1978, only 1 percent of provincial fixed capital investments went to Wenzhou, despite the fact that the municipality contains 15 percent of the province's population (Forster 1990, 56). While one should take into account the negative effects of the Cultural Revolution on economic growth, in the years 1966–78 Wenzhou measured only a .1 percent average industrial growth rate (Parris 1993, 244). Wenzhou was a place with a rebellious political streak that had been, by and large, excluded from the fruits of the Maoist command economy.

At the end of the Cultural Revolution, things in Wenzhou started to change. With political leadership unable and/or unwilling to stop them, experiments with household-based commodity production began to take off. Whereas in 1980 only 1 percent of industrial output in Wenzhou came from private firms, by 1988 that number had jumped to an astonishing 41 percent (A. Liu 1992, 703). The impact on the labor market was immense: the percentage of the rural labor force employed in agriculture dropped from 89 percent in 1978 to 37 percent by 1985 (Dong 1989, 79). Aside from a "privatization" of the economy and a partial proletarianization of the local populace, incomes jumped remarkably: "Average rural incomes grew from 55 yuan in 1978 to over 447 yuan in 1985, still below the provincial average of 548 yuan but above the national average of 397 yuan" (Parris 1993, 249). Between 1981 and 1985 the municipality's gross industrial output increased by 130 percent (Forster 1990, 57). An area that had been poor, not just by Zhejiangese standards but by national standards, was turning into an economic dynamo, and it was local private enterprise that was fueling the transformation.

But what precisely was the structure of these firms that were quickly gaining renown throughout the country? Calvin Chen (2008), who has done perhaps the only ethnography of enterprise development in southeast Zhejiang (in both Wenzhou and Jinhua), talks about the close-knit, relatively egalitarian organization of production in the early years of the enterprises he studied. In particular, high levels of social capital were crucial in promoting the development of the firm: "These young workers, even their parents if need be, could speak directly with factory officials if they felt dissatisfied. Many did so with ease. These meetings were not simply exchanges between employer and employee; rather, they were discussions between familiar parties who interacted socially outside the workplace." (73) With firms rarely exceeding one hundred employees and more typically employing around thirty-five (Parris 1993, 247), all of whom would be hired from the locality, there was deep social integration between workers and management in Wenzhou firms. This was a double-edged sword: sometimes it meant that workers would accept delayed payments of wages for the good of the enterprise, but other times it meant that managers would work on the assembly line to help quickly fill orders. Chen argues that the socially embedded nature of production allowed "members of the workplace [to] understand and willingly fulfill the duties and responsibilities they [were] assigned." In the view of Burawoy (1982), this might sound like the utilization of dense social ties in the construction of a hegemonic labor regime, but for Chen it allowed for healthy enterprise development. Regardless of one's normative assessment of such a situation, the point is that during the early-mid 1980s, small-scale, socially embedded enterprises that enjoyed a high degree of managerial autonomy (Bramall 1989) quickly became the bedrock of Wenzhou's local economy.

In addition to a reliance on existing local social networks for the recruitment of workers, entrepreneurs also depended greatly on support and protection from local government officials. The first benefit the state provided these entrepreneurs was actually to do *nothing:* it looked the other way as informal and indeed *illegal* capital markets began to develop in the municipality (Tsai 2002). Informal "credit associations," usurious middlemen, and family borrowing all emerged on the scene in the 1980s, clearly violating the legal monopoly of the state banks. Then, in 1986, someone formally opened up a credit union with variable interest rates and was able to overcome opposition from state banks only because of protection offered by local government and Party officials (Parris 1993, 248). Government officials' support of private enterprise also extended to assisting them with the difficult task of registering their businesses. Since originally there was no such thing as a "private enterprise," entrepreneurs had to be very creative with their formal status. The practice of "wearing the red hat" referred to a procedure where village governments (which are below the municipal level) would register private enterprises as "collectives." This allowed the enterprises to appear politically correct and also generated revenue for local government officials.

But this support from the local state became most important in the political struggle that emerged as the Wenzhou Model gained national attention. Though Deng Xiaoping had initiated market reforms in 1978, these centrally mandated experiments spatially quarantined capitalist relations of production into a few special economic zones. Wenzhou presented a much more serious challenge to the still-dominant socialist ideology in the sense that capitalist-style credit, labor, and commodity markets had sprung into existence without any management or affirmation from Beijing. Although Wenzhou had received visits from central authorities as early as 1983, it was not until the 1985 visit of reform-minded Premier Zhao Ziyang that locals felt they had a strong sign of support from central leadership. That being said, there was still heated debate about the emergence of what was undeniably an experiment with capitalist labor relations. Supporters argued that Wenzhou's strength in realizing the development of the forces of production justified the increased wealth disparities and exploitation that inevitably arose. One well-known economist foreshadowed an increasingly uneasy relationship between the Party and Marxism by arguing that exploitation did not exist in private firms in Wenzhou because the firms were still regulated and taxed by a socialist state. Detractors held that the Wenzhou Model was tantamount to the reintroduction of capitalism into China. Three decades later, there is little doubt that they were correct in that assessment. However, the key point is that Wenzhou officials' political protection and support allowed local enterprises to flourish in such a way as to prove their advantages at promoting capital accumulation in poor, remote areas. The material success of Wenzhou entrepreneurs resulted in a victory for promarket Party leaders. The consequences for China's transition to full-blown capitalist labor relations have been profound.

What Became of Wenzhou?

After Wenzhou received a flurry of scholarly attention in the late 1980s and early '90s, the city and its model of development fell out of the spotlight. Perhaps this was because capitalist labor relations were no longer controversial, and the more traditional hubs of Chinese economic and political power put economic reform into high gear. In 1984, fourteen major coastal cities were opened up to foreign investment, and Shanghai's Pudong district was established as an SEZ in 1990 (Ge 1999, 1282). After Deng Xiaoping's "Southern Tour" in 1992, reform continued to accelerate, and the emergence of private enterprises continued throughout the country. Soon national and international attention was focused on the economic juggernauts of the Guangzhou-anchored Pearl River Delta[9] and the Shanghai-anchored Yangzi River Delta. Wenzhou's dependence on private enterprise for economic development was no longer controversial, nor did it seem particularly extraordinary.

On the one hand, the Wenzhou elite had great cause for celebration: their resistance to political pressure and perseverance in "following the capitalist road" had ended victoriously. The entrepreneurs who bucked Maoist orthodoxy ended up looking like heroic trailblazers by the 1990s, and their once-derided political sponsors were seen as visionaries. But it was a bittersweet victory: the flip side of China's full embrace of the market was that Wenzhou-based enterprises suddenly faced much stiffer competition than they had when they first started out. The family-style firms that were innovated in Wenzhou soon spread to neighboring municipalities in southeastern Zhejiang, most notably Jinhua and Taizhou. Foreign-invested factories, equipped with deeper reserves of capital, more advanced technology, more rationalized forms of management, and larger economies of scale began encroaching on their markets. While many Wenzhou enterprises had a first-mover advantage in their respective sectors, they would have to change in order to survive.

The 1990s have been referred to as a time of expansion (C. Chen 2008) and restructuring (Wei, Li, and Wang 2007) for Wenzhou industry. The very small, household-based production that characterized the Wenzhou Model in the early days gave way to increasingly large, differentiated, and rationalized firms in the 1990s. Although many firms reorganized into shareholding enterprises, in most cases single families maintained majority stakes. Companies began setting up branches throughout China and in some cases even relocated their headquarters to Hangzhou and Shanghai in order to secure better access to human and financial capital (Wei, Li, and Wang 2007, 438). The informal kinship networks that were crucial for marketing in the 1980s needed to be updated and rationalized. In order to survive, most firms had to conquer new domestic markets and begin to expand into international ones.

At the same time, internal labor process reforms radically reformulated employment relations. Speaking of the two firms he studied in Wenzhou and neighboring Jinhua, Calvin Chen (2008) has said that "enterprise leaders moved away from the norms of reciprocity, social trust, and collective well-being that had been integral components of the company's previous strategy....The rough sense of egalitarianism that had previously existed was soon replaced by an ever-widening gulf between the skilled and the unskilled, the managers and the managed" (89).

Additionally, Wenzhou locals were less and less interested in the relatively low-paid, exhausting, and frequently dangerous work on the shop floor. As was the case in other coastal cities in China, these firms began recruiting from the waves of migrant workers who arrived in the city. The rationalization and concomitant dissolution of bonds of social solidarity within the factory meant that capital-labor relations became increasingly tense. Open conflict, the type of which was very rare in the household-production enterprises, burst into the open, and strikes, legal disputes, and other conflicts all increased in frequency.

The final section of Chen's 2008 book *Some Assembly Required* focuses on the problem of "reintegration" in such firms: "The core task of reintegration is to simultaneously consolidate improvements in production capabilities made during the expansion stage and restore the tight-knit, trust-filled relationships of the [earlier] era" (126). In both Chen's research and my own investigation, enterprise managers and state actors expressed a strong desire for some sort of reintegration. And this desire unmistakably derives from anxiety over increasing labor conflicts and social instability. In marked contrast to their foreign counterparts in the Pearl River Delta, entrepreneurs in Wenzhou and other areas in southeast Zhejiang began actively seeking the assistance of the Communist Party and other organizations, most notably the trade union, in an attempt to regain stability in production.

Labor Relations in Zhejiang

I was first alerted to the activities of Zhejiang trade unions in casual conversations with officials from the GZFTU. In September 2008, Chairman Chen Weiguang led a delegation from the GZFTU in visiting five cities in eastern China (including Wenzhou) to learn about that region's experiments with industrial (*chanye*) and sectoral (*hangye*) trade unions. Upon returning, members of the delegation were glowing in their praise for Zhejiang unions, with the official internal report saying, "In thirty years, Guangzhou unions have been at the forefront of reform, have developed their own characteristics, and have had enormous success. But we cannot be proud and complacent. This visit has allowed us to see our shortcomings and gaps."[10] In the view of one GZFTU official, there was no question that the success of Zhejiang province in establishing sectoral unions had to do with greater government support for their activities. This was a mutually beneficial arrangement for union and government as "the union there knows how to help the government do things."[11] The official contrasted this with the situation in Guangzhou, where he unequivocally stated, the local government was not nearly as supportive.

TABLE 4. Wage-only collective contracts, 2006

	Total workforce	No. of enterprises covered by WCC	No. of workers covered by WCC	No. of enterprises covered by sectoral WCC	No. of workers covered by sectoral WCC
Zhejiang	31,723,800	84,878	3,689,895	6,311	346,413
Guangdong	52,500,900	41,101	2,075,095	4,062	84,889

Source: *Zhongguo gonghui tongji nianjian* (2007) [China union statistical yearbook (2007)] (Beijing: Zhongguo tongji chubanshe).

This subjective assessment of the superiority of Zhejiangese trade unions in promoting the development of sectoral-level unions and wage negotiation is supported by official statistics (see table 4). We can see that even in absolute terms, the number of workers covered by a wage-only collective contract (WCC) or a sectoral-level WCC was significantly higher in Zhejiang than in Guangdong. But in relative terms, the disparity is even more striking. Whereas in Zhejiang 11.6 percent of workers were covered by WCCs and 1.1 percent by sectoral-level WCCs in 2006, in Guangdong these numbers were only 4 percent and .16 percent, respectively. It is true that a relatively small number of workers have been covered by sectoral-level WCCs in both provinces. However, at over 1 percent, a significant number of Zhejiangese workers are covered by such contracts, while the 84,889 workers in Guangdong under sectoral-level WCCs make up a truly paltry sum.

Sectoral-level collective negotiation requires at least two representative parties—namely, labor and capital. In order to understand what has happened in Zhejiang, it is important to know something about the unique nature of employer associations in the region.

Zhejiangese Employer Associations

Zhejiang, and in particular the southeastern area centered on Wenzhou, is famous throughout China for its entrepreneurial spirit and success at developing the local private economy. Although largely ignored in the English-language literature, a significant amount of research has been conducted by Chinese scholars on the noteworthy development of independent employer associations in the region, with the best examples to be found in Wenzhou (Wang Shizong 2004; Wu Ganying 2004; Yu, Xu, and Jiang 2007). Both these studies and my own research reveal that the emergence of these associations has important consequences for politics in the region and that they are also a strong indicator of the highly classed nature of political participation in China. These relatively democratic organizations allow for member participation in organizing and expressing sectoral interests, which provides a potential bargaining partner for trade unions in their

attempts to engage in sectoral-level wage negotiations. While this is not necessarily positive from the perspective of workers, it does mean that it is easier for
the state to rationalize and organize production within a given sector in a way
that is simply not possible in areas such as the Pearl River Delta (where employer
associations do exist but either are fragmented by national origin or have very
low legitimacy, as in the case of the official associations).

China has two nationally organized employer associations, the China Enterprise Confederation-China Enterprise Directors Association (CEC-CEDA) and
the All China Federation of Industry and Commerce (ACFIC). The CEC-CEDA
was formed in 1979 and has few members and little legitimacy in the eyes of
employers (Ma 2011). This organization was set up in large part to serve as China's
official employer representative to international organizations such as the International Labor Organization and the International Organization of Employers
(62). The ACFIC, on the other hand, was organized shortly after the revolution
and is better established among large firms. In most instances, ACFIC organizations will be dominated by large state-owned enterprises, with government or
SOE officials installed as the chairs. These are typically set up to try to establish
and enforce certain standards within an industry (which will frequently benefit
the SOEs) and therefore are much less beneficial to smaller private employers.
While there have been moments when such organizations behave in a corporatist manner (Pearson 1994) or serve as a bridge between employers and the state
(Unger 1996), they are still subject to significant state control.

In Zhejiang, on the other hand, a type of employer association (*shanghui*)
has emerged, which from a formal level looks a lot more like the representative
organizations one might find in a liberal democracy. Though these organizations still must be formally "attached" (*guakao*) to a parent state organ, their
organizational structure and decision-making procedures are formally autonomous. They do not receive funding from the state but are supported by member
dues. Although there still are some instances in which the government will try
to appoint employer association chairs, the leadership selection process is usu-
ally internally determined. As one indication of this trend, in 2003 77 percent
of employer associations in Wenzhou reported that their chairs were selected
according to their own internal rules (Yu, Huang, and Fang 2004, 37). Such organizations are of course interested in having good relationships with the government and will often invite government officials to hold honorary positions, but
they are more specifically concerned with their membership's interests than are
unions.

As has already been pointed out, industrial development in southeast Zhejiang has been highly dependent on the emergence and success of local, privately
owned enterprises. Although today there is more foreign investment than in the
1980s, it is still a relatively small amount. This fact is reflected in the membership

of employer organizations, which are endowed with very high levels of social capital. In describing the process of setting up the eyeglasses employer association in Rui'an, the organization's director said that since everybody already knew everybody, it was a relatively straightforward procedure.[12] Of the more than one hundred eyeglasses manufacturers in the county-level city, only one of them is a joint venture (with Taiwanese investors), and there are no fully foreign-owned firms. Even more noteworthy, I was told that only two of the Chinese-owned enterprises are owned by people who come from different cities; thus the sector is overwhelmingly dominated by locals.[13] A trade union official in Rui'an commented that members of the employer associations would listen to and obey their chair, since "relationships [among the members] are like brothers."[14] The thick social networks tie together not just employers to other employers but also the business associations to the state. With retired government officials sometimes serving as officers in the employer associations, representatives from each group frequently have long-standing relationships with each other. What this means is that the state and union may have not just administrative but also social resources at their disposal in their interactions with local capital.

There has been debate about the political implications of these organizations and whether they herald the coming of a robust civil society in China (Fewsmith 2005). Given the widely disparate definitions of "civil society," this is not a straightforward question to answer. But in this discussion the relevant political question is, To what extent does the formation of employer associations in Zhejiang present an opportunity for the state to more effectively organize capital? At one time, there was great debate in the West about unequal capacities for labor and capital to expresses class interests through representative organizations (Offe and Wiesenthal 1980; Streeck 1991; Traxler 1993). But since labor is characterized by appropriated representation and political space is highly constrained, the issue of expression of class interests cannot be the question in China. In Zhejiang we see that the organization of capitalist interests is the prerequisite for the state to try, through the auspices of the trade union, to establish sectorwide standards at the municipal level. The formation of representative employer associations in Zhejiang has important implications for labor politics because it provides the union with a bargaining partner. On the other hand, the state in the Pearl River Delta is confronted with a disorganized and highly mobile set of capitalists; under such conditions, it is incredibly difficult to establish wage agreements for an entire sector. This makes it unlikely that conscious human action, rather than the whims of the free market, will determine the substance of the labor process and the price of labor power. In southeast Zhejiang, on the other hand, we have a situation where certain segments of capital decide that a more rationalized approach to production is in their interest, and they are organized into associations that allow for this interest to be expressed. This allows capital in cooperation with the state (again, through the auspices of the union) to establish a more coordinated system of production that could result in decommodification of labor. Let's now turn to the data to see how this process has played out empirically.

Trade Unions and Decommodification in Southeast Zhejiang: The Official Story

Starting in 2004, trade unions in certain industries in southeast Zhejiang began to successfully conclude sector-wide wage agreements that cover nearly all enterprises within a given city. This model has been most successful in relatively labor-intensive industries where there are a large number of small local employers concentrated in a particular district. In all the cases that I am aware of, the final agreement on sector-wide wage standards was possible only through the coordinated efforts of agencies of the state, as well as the trade union and relevant employer association. While the trade union has played a key role in signing such agreements on behalf of workers, the impetus for setting wage standards has come largely from employers and the state after they have become concerned about high turnover and excessive labor conflicts. In order to address this problem, an organizational innovation in the form of sectoral trade unions was necessary. The establishment of sectoral unions mirrored the already-existing employer associations, the primary difference being that employer associations are membership-based while the unions remain an extension of the state.[15] The end result has been the successful conclusion of sector-wide agreements in several places in southeast Zhejiang. In this next section we will turn to two cases—the previously unstudied Rui'an eyeglass union and the much-ballyhooed (within China) Wenling wool union—in order to understand the political dynamics behind that state's attempt at oligarchic decommodification.

Given its prominence in the media and Chinese scholarly literature, the data on the Wenling case come from secondary sources. The general economic and political conditions are very similar between the two cases, but Rui'an has been less celebrated in the media. In this sense it is a better case because the exceptional attention from the state and media likely would have an effect on the operation of the trade union in Wenling. However, I include data from the Wenling case to demonstrate that regional conditions allow for a particular type of trade unionism and because it represents the highest aspirations of the ACFTU. Data on Rui'an come from interviews with workers and managers as well as officers from the Eyeglass Employer Association, Eyeglass Sectoral Union, Rui'an Federation of Trade Unions, and the Rui'an Labor Bureau.

COLLECTIVE BARGAINING IN WENLING

Perhaps the earliest, and certainly the most widely discussed, experiment with sectoral-level collective bargaining took place in the county-level municipality of Wenling, less than an hour away from Rui'an by car. Just as Rui'an is encompassed by the municipality of Wenzhou, Wenling is within the administrative jurisdiction of Taizhou municipality. As was described earlier in the chapter, Taizhou's model of development has been very similar to that of Wenzhou, with a preponderance of local enterprises serving as the foundation of the economy. The establishment and functioning of the Wenling Wool Knitwear Union has been quite similar to that of the Rui'an Eyeglasses Union.

The Wenling wool industry grew very rapidly in the 1990s, and many local entrepreneurs jumped into the market. As of 2004, the industry in Wenling employed twelve thousand workers in 113 enterprises, with a total yearly output of RMB 1 billion.[16] Most of these enterprises are rather small. By the first part of this decade, nearly all the workers in the industry were migrants, and approximately 90 percent of them were female. Although the industry developed quickly, it encountered fierce worker resistance and instability in the labor market. Speaking of the first few years of the 2000s, one labor official said, "At that time, workers were constantly arguing with their bosses about unreasonable wages, and every day there would be employees jumping ship."[17] In 2002, the industry experienced approximately one conflict involving ten or more workers every single day.[18] The highly seasonal nature of the work meant that skilled workers enjoyed strong market position in the May–December high season, during which time they could force employers into bidding wars. As one worker in the wool industry put it, "Jumping ship became the only method workers had to resist and defend their rights."[19] Faced with short lead times and slim profit margins, many employers were concerned about these high rates of turnover and frequent conflicts. Though not framed in precisely such terms, there was a strong incentive to bring about rationalization in the labor market. Both large employers and the state (which, as was the case in Rui'an, was concerned with the development of the sector as a whole) wanted to take action.

The process of setting up a sectoral-level wage agreement was not straightforward at all, despite the fact that conditions in Wenling were much more propitious than in most places. In early 2003, the Wool Textiles Employer Association met with leaders from the Wenling Federation of Trade Unions to discuss the matter. The idea of trying to establish a sectoral-level wage agreement gained support, and the two parties began to move forward with full support from the local government. With such support from state and capital, the establishment of the Wool Knitwear Union was a rather simple administrative procedure. However, it is not surprising that some individual employers were not so enthusiastic about this development. The trade union official who was tasked with investigating wages in the sector (with the end goal of being able to establish commonly agreed-upon piece rates) was originally turned away by employers when he asked to look at their books. In the end, however, the much more powerful local Party committee told these employers that they had to cooperate with the union, and the issue was thus resolved. At the conclusion of the investigation, the union delineated five major categories of work and fifty-nine individual work procedures. However, the piece rates being offered for identical procedures varied greatly between enterprises, with the difference sometimes as high as 1 RMB. The next task of the union was to try to figure out a piece-rate system that all parties involved could agree upon.

Wage negotiations were, of course, complex. In June of the same year, worker representatives were selected by management to participate in an officially sponsored "frank discussion" on establishing uniform piece rates. There were differences of opinion on many items, but after distributing more than five hundred survey questionnaires, holding six negotiation sessions and ten frank discussions, and conducting three wage adjustments, the union and the employer association reached a final agreement.[20] On August 8, the union and the employer association signed the "Wool Knitwear Sectoral Wage (Piece-Rate) Agreement," with the agreement that wages would be renegotiated once every year.

From the government's perspective, the sectoral collective wage agreement was an unqualified success, as it claimed that turnover and conflict in the industry dropped significantly as a result. In the final months of 2003 after the new agreement was implemented, there was a dramatic drop in official complaints coming from the wool industry, with only eleven such incidents involving a total of 120 workers. From 2004 to 2005 there were only three complaints involving 11 workers, and from 2005 to 2006 there was only one complaint involving 3 workers. In 2007 workers in this sector did not file a single official complaint.[21] Additionally, since 2006 there has not been a single labor dispute over wages. With the government claiming that labor strife was way down from its highs earlier in the decade, the Wenling government could make a strong claim that its model of industrial relations was a perfect embodiment of harmonious society.

In fact, it was not long before the Wenling union won national recognition for its activities. As early as 2003, Wenling's accomplishments had been recognized by its national-level parent industrial union.[22] After gaining repute within the trade union, the so-called Wenling Model was officially approved by Premier Wen Jiabao, who proclaimed in a work report that "Wenling's approach can be summarized and popularized."[23] The following month, Zhejiang's Party secretary advised that Premier Wen's advice should be followed and that the popularization of the Wenling Model would start first and foremost in Zhejiang. Constantly on the lookout for practical examples to demonstrate that harmonious society and win-win labor relations were more than just slogans, both the ACFTU and the Party-state more broadly were very impressed that the Wenling union had managed to reduce conflict without affecting productivity.

THE RUI'AN EYEGLASS UNION

Though largely unknown outside the borders of the city, the case of the Rui'an Eyeglass Union is very similar to the Wenling Model. Rui'an is a county-level city of 1.17 million residents that is administratively subordinate to Wenzhou municipality.[24] Its per capita output of RMB 31,525 in 2008[25] was significantly higher than most cities in China, though almost precisely the same as the provincial average for Zhejiang. As one of the more industrialized areas within Wenzhou, it exemplifies the Wenzhou Model of dependence on small, family-owned enterprises. Rui'an is best known for its productive industries, including shoes, textiles, bags, and small consumer goods. The focus of my research is the eyeglass sector that is centered in the small township of Mayu and employs more than twelve thousand workers. For a number of years the city government has been intent on becoming the preeminent eyeglass manufacturing center in the world, and it has begun to actively recruit international eyeglass brands to establish offices in Rui'an.

After the first factory was established in 1978, the eyeglass sector in Rui'an grew quite rapidly for a number of years.[26] Many enterprises that started as household-based units expanded in the 1980s and 1990s, and the total number of eyeglass and eyeglass accessory manufacturers increased as well. Relying on the renowned Wenzhou-style family-based marketing networks, these producers first conquered domestic markets and then expanded internationally, eventually gaining customers throughout the world. By the late 2000s, sales from the Rui'an eyeglass industry totaled more than RMB 10 billion, accounting for half of all nationwide eyeglass sales, and the Eyeglass Employer Association estimated that 60 percent of all eyeglasses worn in China were produced in Rui'an.

But it was the very success of the industry in the 1990s that began to lead to a deterioration of employment stability. More and more entrants to the market increased competition for skilled labor. Armed with relatively strong marketplace bargaining power, skilled workers began pitting employers against each other in an effort to increase their wages. Smaller, younger enterprises did not have the financial or knowledge-based resources to conduct the comprehensive worker-training programs that the larger and more established companies offered. One result of this was that these smaller enterprises began to pilfer skilled workers from other enterprises by offering marginally higher piece rates. In a formal address, the chair of the Eyeglass Employer Association presented this state of affairs as a very serious problem:

> The need for technical personnel and skilled workers has been steadily increasing within the industry, and using high salaries in hiring has been an inevitable decision for enterprises. "Cutting the ground out" from each other is already not a new phenomenon, and this led to lack of order and chaos in enterprise employment. Workers have been jumping ship without order for personal gain and lured by the promise of [higher wages]. This has disturbed order in the industry and destroyed the normal functioning of enterprises. Labor conflicts are obviously up, and there have been instances of using certain articles of the Labor Contract Law to continuously engage in appeals, file lawsuits, and commit blackmail [yaoxie]. According to the social security authorities, labor conflicts have been occurring continuously in the industry, which has led to a worsening of the employment environment, and the positive development of the industry has been restricted.

Though such a situation is not necessarily disadvantageous for skilled workers, large employers were much more concerned. Thus in 2001 a few players in the industry took the first tentative steps toward addressing these problems. Two of the largest eyeglass firms in Rui'an took the initiative in trying to establish sectorwide standards, and they began to appeal to the Eyeglass Employer Association for assistance.

The Rui'an Eyeglass Employer Association had previously been a formal statesponsored organization. Eventually the local government decided to "give them freedom,"[27] which meant greater autonomy for the association but also implied responsibility for raising its own operating expenses. Since that time, the association has operated as an independent civil (minjian) organization, 100 percent dependent on membership dues for its operations. The organization has served as a platform for eyeglass manufacturers in Rui'an, allowing them to communicate common interests to the government and also allowing the government to have an efficient way of communicating with the business owners. Often new laws and regulations that are of relevance to the industry are disseminated through the employer association. As one official from the local labor department said, "These are things the government used to do but they gave this responsibility to the association."[28]

The push for a sector-wide standardization of wages has been one of the most significant tasks taken on by the employer association, and it surely required intense negotiations between firms that might have had conflicting interests. It is not coincidental that the CEO of one of the largest manufacturers in the city, Chen Chengwei, was also the chairman of the Eyeglass Employer Association. Instability in the labor market was most problematic from the point of view of large employers, since smaller enterprises would frequently poach their skilled workers. In coordination with a few other large manufacturers, Chen used his position within the association to begin to push for wage standardization, presumably against protests from smaller employers. Eventually, conversations within the association and with government agencies led them to the idea of collective wage negotiations. As a sympathetic employer argued, "Every year in the busy season, workers would go on strike, and nearby manufacturers would not hesitate to use high salaries to poach skilled workers. If we did not sit down and bargain, it would be difficult for the entire eyeglass industry to continue."[29] The problem now was that the employers needed a bargaining partner.

It was at this point that officials from the Rui'an Federation of Trade Unions (RAFTU) became involved. Following the lead of the Wenling Wool Knitwear Union, the decision was made to establish an eyeglass sectoral union. Leaving absolutely no doubt about where the initiative for such a thing came from, the official document approving the establishment of the Rui'an Eyeglass Union is addressed to the Eyeglass Employer Association.

The next item of business was to initiate collective wage negotiations. The union launched an investigation into wage levels in the various eyeglass enterprises, speaking with managers and workers and conducting a survey. The information was analyzed, and the union put forth a proposal for unified piece rates for 318 specific work operations. After soliciting comments and a holding a few negotiation sessions, in September 2005 a final contract was signed by the respective chairs of the employer association and the sectoral union. The contract was approved by the labor department and thus became legally binding.

As already mentioned, the extent of tensions between different manufacturers is not entirely clear. Officials from the Eyeglass Employer Association have tried to put a positive spin on such intrasector competition. Although appearing reluctant to discuss the issue, the chairman of the association did admit that some small employers refused to participate in the sectoral wage agreement. Since the employer association is not a government agency, it could not "force them to sign."[30] Additionally, he admitted that of the 130 eyeglass manufacturers in Rui'an, about 30 of them were not members of the association. That being said, cooperation between the employer association, trade union, and—perhaps most important—government and Party officials eventually resulted in a binding collective wage agreement.

The actual content of the contract is very limited, as there are only five articles. Article 1 simply states the two-year time period during which the contract is in effect. Article 2 is the meat of the contract and says that workers will be remunerated according to the piece rate established in the "2009 Rui'an City Eyeglasses Employer Association Enterprise Piece Rate Form." Article 3 says that workers must be paid on time but that if an enterprise is having "difficulty," payment of wages can be delayed after consultation with the union. Article 4 states that the contract is legally binding, while article 5 says only that disputes should be handled according to the law.

Since the conclusion of the sectoral wage agreement, union leaders say that they have continued to develop their organizational capacity within the industry. At the time of the establishment of the eyeglass sectoral union, many manufacturers in the city had not yet established enterprise-level trade union organizations. With the help of the employer association, union officials have been making efforts to address this issue, believing that the sectoral union will be more effective with enterprise-level branches in place. Additionally, in June of 2009 the preparatory committee for an eyeglass sector "staff and workers' congress" (*zhidaihui*) was established. Particularly in state-owned enterprises in China, the staff and workers' congress has been, in theory, a mechanism whereby employees can directly participate in the determination of the labor process. Aside from clichéd rhetoric about "democratic participation," it is unclear precisely what function the eyeglass congress will serve. But since Chen Chengwei, former chair of the employer association, was appointed director of the preparatory committee for the staff and workers' congress, it is almost certain that it will remain under the control of employers.

Four years after the conclusion of the collective wage agreement, the unions, government, and employer association leaders were very pleased with the results. The official story is that previous illegal actions on the part of employers, such as holding employees' ID cards or taking deposits, have been eliminated. Turnover was greatly reduced, which stabilized production. Additionally, bosses can no longer unilaterally determine wages but have to engage in the official process of negotiation. Finally, and perhaps most important, the number of labor conflicts has dropped significantly.

In official accounts, both Wenling and Rui'an are great success stories in which labor conflicts have been reduced and production has been rationalized, all through administrative means. The state and higher levels of the trade unions have been impressed with such reports and have gone out of their way to shower praise on these experiments.

Zhejiang: Exemplary Model of Labor Relations?

As was revealed in the descriptive statistics earlier in the chapter, Zhejiang has significantly more workers than Guangdong who are covered by collective wage agreements and an even greater (relative) edge in sectoral-level agreements. This success has not gone unnoticed, as the state has proclaimed for many years the implementation of collective contracts as a primary goal. Indeed, the legal framework for the implementation of collective contracts in China was firmly established with the labor law reforms of 1994 (Clarke, Lee, and Li 2004; Warner 1995), but the union's ability to bargain and enforce such contracts has been highly circumscribed. Thus the apparent success of Zhejiangese trade unions at concluding collective contracts was received with great enthusiasm from both the Party-state and the national leadership of the ACFTU.

On a formal level at least, the Zhejiang government made a strong commitment to promoting collective wage negotiations. In late summer of 2008, the provincial government announced the goal that 70 percent of private enterprises and 100 percent of state-owned and collective enterprises be covered by such agreements by the end of 2010.[31] The state appeared to be taking this task seriously, as all government agencies and Party committees have been exhorted to support this work. To put some muscle behind the demand, the provincial Party committee added success with collective negotiations into its procedure for evaluating the accomplishments of government officials. It is unclear how much weight is given to these accomplishments in comparison with typical criteria such as economic growth, attracting investment, and maintaining social stability, but the fact that they are considered at all is significant. Although some of these plans were likely temporarily derailed by the collapse of the export economy in late 2008 and 2009, it is undeniable that the experiences of places like Rui'an and Wenling convinced the provincial authorities of the viability and desirability of collective negotiation.

Zhejiang's apparent commitment to this project garnered support from the highest levels of the trade union. In addition to the frequent affirmations from Party leadership, the provincial Party committee and provincial government held a conference in Wenling in March of 2008 to learn about the union's experiences with sectoral bargaining. The following month, the ACFTU sponsored a national-level conference on collective negotiation that was held in Zhejiang's capital city of Hangzhou.[32] Entitled "National Union Collective Wage Negotiation Exchange," the conference was attended by the ACFTU's number two in command, Sun Chunlan, as well as the deputy chair of the province's Party committee. The fact that a national-level conference was held outside Beijing is indicative of the extent to which ACFTU leadership was willing to try to elevate the experience of Zhejiang unions. In addition, collective negotiations in Zhejiang have begun to attract the attention of semiofficial scholarship in China (Chen and Huang 2008; Zhu 2008), and even foreign researchers (M. Liu 2009; Pringle 2011).

It is clear that the state and unions were enthusiastic about the perceived success with collective bargaining in Zhejiang. But the question remains, To what extent was the official rhetoric realized in practice? In order to answer these questions, I went beyond the official statements and interviews with union and employer association leaders to talk with factory management and workers in the Rui'an eyeglass industry.

Nonenforcement

During my first brief foray into the field in Rui'an, I interviewed only officials from the labor department, trade union, and employer association. Between conversations with these officials and the documents they provided, the story I pieced together was compelling in its innovativeness. Faced with instability in employment relations, the union, government, and employers came together and through negotiation and compromise, reached an agreement on wage-level standards for the entire sector. It was a true win-win-win for workers, the state, and employers. But upon spending a bit more time in the field, I discovered there was just one problem: the contract was not being enforced.

My first realization that things on the ground were not as I had been led to believe came in a very awkward interaction with a manager from a small factory in Mayu township. I had been brought to this factory by my closest contact in the eyeglass industry, Ms. Du, a human resources manager at Zhilian Eyeglasses who was also the chair of the enterprise's trade union branch. I had first met Ms. Du in a meeting with the chair of the Rui'an Eyeglass Employer Association when I had been given an official, and overwhelmingly positive, account of the development and results of sectoral-level bargaining in Rui'an's eyeglass industry. In previous conversations, she had frequently touted the achievements of both the employer association and the union in bringing about the breakthrough of a sectoral-level wage agreement. However, when she brought me to visit the neighboring Huangwei factory (directly across the street from Zhilian), a different picture began to emerge. With Ms. Du sitting at my side, I began chatting with Huangwei's general manager, Mr. Guo, about the factory's operations. When I inquired about the sectoral-level collective wage agreement, he looked puzzled and asked me what I was talking about. I tried rephrasing the question but to no avail. At this point Ms. Du interrupted and said, "He wants to know how you set your piece rates."[33] Finally Mr. Guo's face lit up in recognition, but his response had absolutely nothing to do with the collective agreement to which his factory was supposedly bound. In fact, he revealed that Huangwei didn't use piece rates at all (as dictated by the collective agreement) but rather used hourly rates. Fearful that I had just embarrassed my most important contact in the industry, I quickly moved to change the topic.

Mr. Guo—ignorant as he was of the wage agreement—was by no means an outlier among those in the Rui'an eyeglass industry. As I interviewed managers from more than ten enterprises over the next several weeks, I discovered that not only were very few employers abiding by the agreement, but hardly any of them had even *heard* of it. Managers from the largest enterprises with up to five hundred workers and those from firms with only eighty employees were equally confused by my inquiries about collective wage negotiations. Even managers from Zhilian Eyeglasses (one of the two large enterprises that promoted the idea of a sectoral collective wage agreement) told me during a factory visit that their wages were higher than those of other neighboring factories, indicating that they were not abiding by any industry standards.

It will come as little surprise that workers were equally unaware of the existence of such an agreement. In my many evenings hanging out with workers at the pool tables in Mayu's industrial zone, I quickly learned that the topics of collective contracts and trade unions would elicit no response. On my first night in Mayu, I innocently asked a few workers from a nearby glasses factory about the collective contract. Not only were they unaware of the existence of a collective contract, but they said that in their factory workers did not sign contracts at all; rather, their employment relationship was based on "trust."[34] Some workers did know what trade unions were, but nobody had any direct experience with them.

The employers in the eyeglass industry were familiar with the concept of trade union, but—in contrast to what I had been told by the Rui'an union officials—very few of the enterprises had established a union branch. Many employers claimed that unions were set up only in the larger enterprises because those businesses operated more "by the books" (*zhenggui*). One manager from a small enterprise with fewer than one hundred employees had this to say about a union branch: "At the moment we don't have one; we can't set it up,"[35] an indication that establishing a union requires resources that smaller enterprises do not have. Somewhat curiously, he then articulated a position widespread among Chinese workers and intellectuals: "In China, I'm not sure if the union has any function."[36] He went on to say that unions in Europe accomplish more things. A manager from one of the largest firms told me in response to an inquiry about a union branch that his company did not have one but that it had set up a Party branch. When asked what the Party did in the factory, he merely laughed and said, "They can help some people."[37] Though the municipal-level union officials had claimed that they used the negotiations over the collective wage agreement as an opportunity to establish more enterprise-level union branches, I did not detect even a suggestion of new organizing initiatives.

As mentioned previously, there are a few enterprises in Rui'an that do not participate in the employer association and therefore are not covered by the wage agreement. However, this was not the case with the firms that I had contact with, as all of them confirmed that they were members of the association. This is not surprising, as I was based in the epicenter of Rui'an's eyeglass industry, Mayu township. Mayu had the highest levels of social capital and was the center of the activities of the employer association. Employers' assessments of the association varied from mild to enthusiastic support. Most noted that the association had helped them to learn about new policies and new market opportunities, but nobody mentioned the group's role in establishing industry standards. All members had to pay dues that were adjusted according to the size of the enterprise. Thus employers' lack of familiarity with the collective wage agreement cannot be attributed to their nonparticipation in the employer association.

The lack of enforcement of sectoral wage standards was further highlighted by employers' frequently expressed angst over one of the main problems that the agreement had originally set out to resolve: high turnover of skilled workers. Senior managers from both small and large enterprises complained about workers jumping ship. One manager from an enterprise with 110 workers described the problem as "very serious" and "very troublesome" but admitted that "there is nothing to be done.... [Workers] have freedom."[38] As one would have expected, large employers were even more agitated about the pilfering of workers. Mr. Wu, a veteran of more than twenty years in the eyeglass industry, had worked for the two largest eyeglass manufacturers in the city, Zhilian and Huakai. Both companies generally have workforces of approximately three hundred, though both have at times reached more than five hundred. Mr. Wu explained in detail that these two enterprises are some of the only factories with extensive worker-training programs. Additionally, they provide workers with a base wage even in the off-season in order to retain talent, something that the small enterprises cannot afford to do. However, during the busy season, small enterprises try to offer marginally higher piece rates to their skilled workers to lure them away. According to Mr. Wu, the first question these enterprises ask potential employees is, "Have you worked for Zhilian or Huakai?"[39] as this is a strong indication of how well trained they are. In general, nobody claimed that the problem of jumping ship had improved in recent years (in the time since the conclusion of the collective wage agreement), with some saying that things hadn't changed and others claiming that the situation had gotten much worse.

Though not directly related to either union activities or the wage agreement, the labor market dynamics in Rui'an exerted a significant influence on employers' capacity to retain skilled labor. Perhaps the single most pervasive complaint from employers was not that the economic crisis had reduced the number of orders they received but rather that they could not hire and retain enough workers. In some cases, manufacturers were unable to accept orders because production was running so far below capacity. On one factory visit, I strolled through a shop floor on which fewer than half of the machines were being used. The manager who was accompanying me motioned to the machines and said, "As a manager when you look at this...it's such a waste."[40]

In sum, it is clear that the sectoral-level wage agreement that was so highly touted by officials from the Rui'an Federation of Trade Unions and the Eyeglass Employer Association was not being enforced. This despite the fact that the enforcement of such an agreement could help resolve the serious problems the industry as a whole faces, namely, high turnover of skilled workers and labor conflicts. Despite a strong possibility of building a cross-class alliance and the exertion of extensive efforts among official representatives, the agreement exists on paper only. And yet when we turn to the experiments with sectoral unions in Guangzhou, we see that the response of the state and union is, *at the formal level,* very different.

Shortcomings of Sectoral-Level Trade Unionism in Guangzhou

As mentioned previously, union officials in Guangzhou held the activities of Zhejiang sectoral unions in high regard and frequently expressed frustration at their own inability to achieve similar success. GZFTU Chairman Chen Wei-guang said that the development of sectoral unions would be one of the primary tasks of the GZFTU in the years going forward. Chen was particularly enamored of sectoral unions because they presented an opportunity to create greater independence between unions and employers.[41] The chair of a sectoral union would not be employed in a particular enterprise (as is the case for most primary units of the trade union), a scenario that could potentially give the chair greater freedom to impose demands on employers. And yet Chairman Chen complained that the work of sectoral unions in Guangzhou was greatly constrained by the fact that they did not have a "partner," by which he meant there was no party with which they could negotiate collective contracts. One of the deputy chairs of the GZFTU was quite explicit about the problem when describing why in Guangzhou the unions were focused only on collective bargaining at the enterprise level: "Our sectoral unions are not mature, and...the employer associations are not mature. They [employer associations] are even less mature! So we don't have an opponent."[42]

During my time in Guangzhou I studied the activities of the two sectoral unions that the GZFTU considered the most successful: the construction and sanitation worker unions. The construction union leadership claimed that its sectoral union was the most developed in the city, having officially established its organizing committee in October 2007. The GZFTU originally set up a union only in the central Liwan district but then expanded to cover the remaining districts in Guangzhou. With two thousand construction sites and around four hundred thousand workers in the city, this was no small task. However, when the leaders were asked what specific activities the union conducted, it was not clear that it was performing any sort of a representative function. The union cadres did say that they provided workers with legal assistance and disseminated information on workers' legal rights. But the activities beyond this remained quite limited. Construction union cadres confirmed that the GZFTU had suggested they look into sectoral bargaining, but they admitted that no progress had been made on this front. Their explanation was that different employers had their own systems for calculating wages and that unifying pay scales would be very difficult. Reverting to free-market ideology as an explanation, one cadre argued that "the market economy is a presupposition, so there isn't any need to intervene here [by negotiating wages]."[43] Even more alarming, the construction union did not even have the capacity to collect dues but instead was fully supported by the GZFTU. Indicating the difficulties Chinese unions have faced in the process of marketization, the chair of the construction union complained, "In the past the construction sector was all state-owned. And we got the dues. But the system reformed, and it is very relaxed [i.e. unregulated] now and we can't collect the dues."[44]

Deregulation also created significant problems for the union's attempts to organize sanitation (*huanwei*) workers[45] in the city. Originally all sanitation workers in Guangzhou were directly employed by the city. However, after China's entry into the World Trade Organization (WTO) in 2001, the government deregulated the industry, and contracts were given to a variety of private companies. By 2008, there were more than six hundred companies involved in sanitation work in Guangzhou, many of them owned by companies from Hong Kong, Taiwan, Malaysia, and Singapore. With privatization came worsening conditions for many workers, and in the spring of 2008 street cleaners in one of the industrial districts of Guangzhou went on strike. Shortly thereafter, the GZFTU decided to establish a sanitation sectoral union, starting where the workers had gone on strike in Baiyun district. However, by December of the same year, little progress had been reported, and Chairman Chen said that the workers needed the "government's strength" to organize the employers into a representative organization.[46] The following October, the chair of the sanitation union still had little claim to success, saying only that the union had continued to expand its presence into more districts of the city. However, in the summer of 2009, several months after I left my field site in Guangzhou, it was reported in the media that the Luogang district union had concluded the city's first sectoral-level collective contract. The contract was reported to cover only six employers, a tiny share of the hundreds of employers operating in the city. Although information remains highly incomplete since I was not able to independently verify the content of the contract, the media report did not mention anything about increases in wages or benefits but emphasized that relevant laws and regulations would be better enforced.[47]

But ongoing strikes among the city's sanitation workers after 2008 indicated that the sectoral unionization effort had not realized its own goals. In January of 2010, approximately three hundred cleaners in Yuexiu district demonstrated at People's Park to demand better wages, housing subsidies, and an end to employer deductions of overtime wages. One worker complained, "Over the past eight years, the cost of goods has gone up continuously, but our wages haven't gone up even once. On average we can make RMB 1,100 per month, but you need 300 just to rent a place; how are you supposed to raise a family?"[48] Similarly, in February 2012 nearly one hundred street cleaners in Baiyun district went on strike over wages that were below the legal minimum.[49] But an even more dramatic confirmation of the union's failure to preempt unrest in the sector came with a massive strike wave in late 2012–early 2013. It began with a strike of more than two hundred workers in Tianhe district on December 24,[50] and eventually hundreds of workers walked off the job throughout the city. In January and February there were strikes in Tianhe, Yuexiu, Panyu, Baiyun, and Liwan districts. As with other strike waves in China, these were copycat rather than coordinated strikes. While the specifics varied somewhat in each case (as the strikers were all employed by different companies), all the workers were dissatisfied with low compensation. Some demanded overtime wages or better benefits such as housing subsidies, while others even demanded an end to the practice of outsourcing. Many of the strikers engaged in public demonstrations, petitions, and sit-ins at government offices, and more than two hundred Liwan workers had a tense confrontation with police.[51] Although each of these strikes targeted a particular private employer, it was amply apparent that there was a structural problem in the industry.

As has been the case with other major strike waves, this upsurge attracted major attention from the state. During the strike in Yuexiu district, the chair of the Yuexiu Sanitation Sectoral Union had somewhat ambiguously suggested that workers should in fact get a raise but that "it requires an orderly process."[52] The *Workers' Daily* ran an article entitled, "Increase Sanitation Worker Compensation."[53] Liu Xiaogang—a deputy chair of the GZFTU during the 2008 strike and subsequent officer in the Guangzhou People's Political Consultative Congress— seemed to support the strikers when he was quoted in the above article as saying that anything less than a 30 percent wage hike would be unreasonable. But in microblogs posted during the strike wave, Liu also evinced the conflicted politics at the heart of the trade union system. A local resident in Guangzhou had posted a picture of a busy sanitation worker who had not participated in the strike, giving her a thumbs-up emoticon and lauding her diligence. Liu commented on the post by saying, "I call on sanitation workers to defend their rights legally, to defend their rights rationally."[54] In a context in which there are no legal strikes, his meaning was clear enough.

It was not just the union that got involved in the response, as the government convened a Guangzhou Sanitation Sector Representative Conference that brought together officials and employers from various districts within the city. Following this, Mayor Chen Jianhua announced that various levels of the government would provide an additional RMB 470 million that year toward increasing sanitation workers' salaries.[55] Not only that, but he suggested that priority should be given to these workers in obtaining local *hukou*. Finally, Chen acknowledged the need for reform of the industry—a realization that the union had already come to in 2008: "In determining the approach to reforming and improving [the industry], we should take a systemic approach to reforming the organization of sanitation. We cannot resolve the problem simply by providing more [funds]."[56]

Two months after the strike wave, the city government unveiled a draft version of the "Advice on Standardizing Employment in the Sanitation Sector." Eventually implemented on May 1 of that year, this was an attempt to achieve through state power what the union had failed to realize five years earlier. The document touched on a broad array of work-related issues, including base salary, social insurance, housing subsidies, high-heat bonuses, vacations, and overtime. It called for a base salary for workers 10 percent higher than minimum wage,[57] and the government estimated that total compensation would increase by 40 percent.[58] Additionally, it established a unified standard for wage composition for the municipality regardless of whether workers were employed directly or by subcontractors. While questions remained about enforceability, this document applied to all districts within Guangzhou.

At the time of writing, it is unclear whether the severity of the 2012–13 strike wave will be enough to push significant and sustainable institutional realignment. It appears that the state is attempting to circumnavigate the trade union system altogether by directly administering wage levels. But similar political constraints that existed during the first centralization attempt in 2008 are still in place, as there is little to suggest that workers have become more incorporated within the polity or that they can exercise coercive power vis-à-vis employers. Thus we have yet another case in which the state is attempting to resolve labor-capital conflict through purely administrative means—a scenario that bodes poorly for enforceability.

It is worth noting that all the sectoral unions in Guangzhou that were in oper-ation or in the planning stages (e.g., restaurant and hotel unions) were in the service sector, a significant contrast with the situation in Zhejiang. In general, one would expect organizing sectoral agreements in manufacturing to be even more difficult than in the service sector, since service work is place-specific. Even given this seeming advantage, neither of the two most prominent sectoral unions in Guangzhou had achieved anything close to the formal success of the sectoral wage agreements that are becoming more and more common in southeast Zhejiang.

At this point it is clear that the formation of sectoral unions is high on the agenda for the ACFTU. However, there has yet to be a critical analysis into the following questions: *Why* have Zhejiang unions been more successful than others (notably those in Guangdong) at reaching sectoral-level wage agreements? What do the particularities about the Zhejiang case imply for sectoral-level bargaining in other regions in China? Why were union and state alike unable to enforce the sectoral agreements that they worked so hard to produce? And finally, has col-lective negotiation significantly decommodified or incorporated labor in any of the industries in which it is prevalent? It is these questions to which we now turn.

Oligarchic Decommodification?

As compared with other regions of China, the volume of worker protest has been particularly pronounced in Zhejiang, Guangdong, and other economically dynamic regions where manufacturing industries employ huge numbers of migrant workers. But in the preceding account, we have seen that the administrative strength of unions vis-à-vis employers varies according to region. Explaining why union and state responses have been different n Zhejiang and Guangdong—despite the fact that they are both within the hierarchically organized ACFTU system—is the purpose of this chapter.

As explained above, both Zhejiang and Guangdong have experienced similar levels of worker insurgency but have had different capacities to address this crisis. Since there have been no systematic studies of labor protest in Zhejiang, it is diffi-cult to know whether the character of this unrest differs significantly. However, as far as government and union officials' *perception* of the unrest is concerned, there is no significant variation between the two regions. Union officials in both places also understand this is a problem that must be resolved and that it is their task to promote the development of "harmonious labor relations." While I would not go so far as to claim that Zhejiang's labor relations are more stable in general, the cases of the sectoral unions are an indication that Zhejiang has had some formal success that has been elusive in Guangdong. In particular, trade unions in Zhejiang have been more successful at setting up sectoral-level unions and concluding sectoral-level wage agreements. While Guangdong unions remained reactive to worker protest, Zhejiang unions managed, in at least a few cases, to establish the formal appearance of a more stable form of labor relations.

My explanation for why sectoral-level wage negotiation has been possible in Zhejiang but not in Guangdong is straightforward: the two regions have different models of development and composition of capital investment. Additional and interrelated factors are the existence of representative employer associations, high levels of social capital, and the geographic density of enterprises in a particular sector that can be found in both Rui'an and Wenling. I have gone to great lengths in this chapter to demonstrate that southeast Zhejiang has been largely dependent on indigenous entrepreneurs in the process of development. While the local state's degree of autonomy is up for debate, the local character of capital allows for it to be highly embedded (Evans 1995). In addition, the high level of social capital among capitalists has provided the union with a representative bargaining partner in the form of local employer associations. Given the high density of a particular industry in a very small geographic region, township-level governments are dependent on the sustainable development of the given industry in order to maintain their tax base, while the highly diversified economy of the Pearl River Delta stands in stark contrast. The combination of these various factors meant that the local state had both an interest and a capacity to work toward an administrative resolution to instability in labor relations.

Thus, because of the character of the Zhejiangese political economy, we appear to have the possibility of oligarchic decommodification as represented by the top-down imposed sectoral-level wage agreements. In these cases, the trade union continues to respond to the demands of the state—even if the state is simply expressing the interests of capital. The state is interested in such a project because of the relative immobility of local capital and because it is in the interests of a relatively large segment of employers. Additionally, such a program is oligarchic in the sense that it does not involve consultation with or participation of workers. Members were never asked whether they thought the sectoral agreements were a good idea, nor was there any attempt to build relatively autonomous working-class power.

Before getting involved in an analysis of outcomes, we can see that as a result of the political economy of Guangdong (as represented by its capital, Guangzhou), there are severe structural impediments to even *attempting* oligarchic decommodification. In line with Atul Kohli's (2004) argument about the difficulty of directing foreign capital toward national goals (382), in Guangdong trade unions are incapable of establishing any standards at the sectoral level. The

sectoral agreement eventually signed in Luogang district covers only six employers out of more than six hundred and appears not to specify wage levels (to say
nothing of other benefits, workplace rules, etc.). Capital in the Pearl River Delta is
cosmopolitan and footloose and is not organized into the types of representative
organizations that exist in Zhejiang. These investors have no social bonds or sense of
obligation to the locality and are willing to threaten capital flight when the state
tries to increase worker protections. While such enterprises do encounter the
same issues with labor conflict that we see in Zhejiang, a prounion strategy is not
something they have pursued, in large part because of the difficulty in organizing
foreign capital. Even if rationalization of employment relations were something
that made sense to some large employers, it would be very difficult for them to
impose sector-wide standards on smaller employers. The inability of the state
and union in Guangdong to discipline transnational capital has negative implications not only for the politics of decommodification but also for future growth
potentials (Chibber 2003).

There are important consequences of this dynamic when one considers the
applicability of the Zhejiang experience to other regions in China. The question of applicability is significant as Wen Jiabao and ACFTU leaders have specifically called for national promotion of the Wenling experience. Union leadership
is particularly keen to highlight these cases because they demonstrate that it is
possible to reduce conflict through administrative processes. But given the relative peculiarity of the model of development of southeast Zhejiang, the ability
of unions in other areas to follow in their steps is questionable. Indeed, when
one union official from Guangzhou was asked about applicability of Zhejiangese union activities to his work, he responded, "If they have some experiences,
I will study it. But I won't accept it just because Hu [Jintao] likes it."[59] Not only
were nearly all the businesses in the Rui'an and Wenling cases locally owned, they
also had the advantage that comes from a high concentration of small enterprises
in a very compact geographical area. This meant that local government had a
strong incentive to focus on the development of one particular industry, as much
of their tax revenue depended on the industry's success. Such conditions do not
hold in cities in the Pearl River Delta, adding yet another obstacle to establishing sectoral-level wage negotiations. The implication is that without the unique
combination of economic and political conditions that exist in southeast Zhejiang, it will be very difficult for trade unions in manufacturing sectors in other
parts of China to emulate the sectoral-level wage agreements found in places like
Rui'an and Wenling.[60]

The question remains, however, as to what extent the Wenling and Rui'an
cases count as successes. Specifically, to what extent was decommodification or
incorporation of labor realized? At this point it is clear that these cases have not

produced meaningful advances in decommodification. There are no greater job protections, no improvement in benefits such as pensions, health insurance, and housing allowances and no wage scales or seniority. The Rui'an contract even specifies that employers have the right to unilaterally violate the contract (and the law): delaying wage payments is deemed permissible granted that the employer is suffering "difficulty" (which is not defined) and that it "consults" the union. The union retains no legal right to reject delayed wage payments. Additionally, there is no mechanism for resolving disputes over interpretation of the contract prior to filing with the labor department. The one possible exception is that there have been reports that wages for many workers in Wenling have increased substantially since the implementation of the sectoral wage agreement (though this may very well be due to a tightening of the labor market rather than union intervention). The area in which some tentative progress could theoretically exist is in determining wage rates. Whereas previously, piece rates in the Rui'an eyeglass and Wenling wool industries were determined according to market principles, the establishment of sectoral wage agreements submitted the determination of the price of labor power to coordinated and conscious human action. True, this "conscious human action" ultimately was very undemocratic and took little account of the interests of workers themselves. But from a formal standpoint, the process of negotiation by which piece rates were determined implies a rejection of free-market logic. Even if the intention was to establish wage restraint (and is therefore not necessarily positive from a normative standpoint), such intervention is nonetheless an attempt to negate the market.

However, when we move beyond an analysis of formal outcomes to interrogate the substantive consequences of divergences in institutional responses between Zhejiang and Guangdong unions, we see that in neither province has labor *actually* been decommodified. The sectoral wage agreement in Rui'an's eyeglass industry is not being enforced and therefore has failed to alter the methods by which the price of labor is determined. The rise and fall of wages in the industry are still determined by the dictates of the free market, and coordinated and conscious human action does not play a role. Despite the efforts of officials from the trade union, government, and employer association, the pricing of labor in Rui'an's eyeglass industry is still determined by the market.

Why did the attempt at oligarchic decommodification fail? The first major factor is, ironically, the very thing that made the institutional breakthrough possible in the first place, namely, reliance on state support. The union was quite happy about the outcomes from Rui'an because it was able to win a contract by relying entirely on the symbolic and administrative power of the state. As one GZFTU staff member noted, this support was crucial since the union did not have other coercive tools at its disposal: "We [the union] lack means to put pressure on the bosses. If we say to the boss, 'sign, sign, sign the contract!' and he refuses there's nothing we can do."[61] What was unique in Wenling and Rui'an was that the interests of a significant segment of capital overlapped with those of the state in bringing about rationalization, and one result of this could have been a degree of decommodification.

Why is it that the thing that made this development possible (i.e., state support) was also a weakness? As has been argued extensively, the state at the local level is strongly beholden to capital and is rarely capable of genuine autonomy. The implication is that in situations when decommodification is *not* in the interest of a significant portion of capitalists within a given sector, that state support for the union will evaporate (and there is a huge amount of evidence to support this claim).With workers continually atomized, the sustainability of sectoral-level wage agreements will be dependent on state support. As the chairman of the Wenling Wool Knitwear Union said to a visiting German delegation, "We can't be like you and just go on strike. We depend on the support of the Party and government."[62]

Thus the primary reason that the contract in Rui'an was not enforced was that there was a crisis of representation in both the union and the employer association—that is, there was a failure to incorporate labor. Just as in Guangdong, the Rui'an eyeglass union's claim to represent and negotiate on behalf of that sector's workers was an act that did not need to be recognized by the members. To refer to eyeglass workers in Rui'an as "members" is even an overstatement, as they did not pay dues, were not aware of the fact that they were members, and were completely unaware of the fact that representatives were acting on their behalf. The union did exert quite a lot of effort in negotiating the contract, but this performance was directed at other government agencies, the employer association, and higher levels of the trade union, *not* toward its supposed membership. Thus we can see how inseparable the political and economic features of the institutional moment are: without incorporation of labor, decommodification can be extremely difficult to secure, even if it has the support of the state and a segment of capital.

While the challenges for the union in gaining recognition are severe, what can explain such a failure of legitimacy in the employer association? Though any answer must remain provisional given the lack of transparency in official maneuverings in the Chinese polity, the explanation can likely be found through an analysis of the power dynamics within the association as well as its relationship to the state. First of all, it would not be surprising to learn that the Rui'an Eyeglass Employer Association lacked the institutional muscle to force all their members to abide by a wage agreement that seriously harmed their bottom line. The attempt to impose sector-wide wage standards clearly plays to the advantage of large employers who have invested significantly in worker-training programs and enjoy economies of scale. Some coercive power would be required to convince smaller employers to abide by such an agreement. But if such coercive power did not exist, than why would the employer association go to such lengths to negotiate an agreement they knew would not be enforced? It would appear that the motivation would come from the promise of some symbolic profits in the eyes of the state. While the conclusion of such an agreement is more clearly beneficial to the trade union (in the sense that it will please their superiors), there are also potential advantages for the employer association. Always mindful of trying to promote scientific development and harmonious society, the employer association may be eager to demonstrate to the state that it is willing to make compromises with the union in order to reduce labor conflicts. Though this has not actually happened in practice, the conclusion of a formal agreement gives the association something concrete it can show to concerned government officials who will likely see the agreement as an accomplishment. Given that few agents of the state have the time or the inclination to independently verify on-the-ground outcomes, the formal appearance of activity is likely sufficient to win accolades. Such a positive review from the state can pay dividends down the line.

Though my fieldwork was focused on the Rui'an eyeglasses union, it is possible that issues with enforcement could develop (or already have developed) in Wenling. Despite the national attention focused on the city's wool knitwear industry, employers and union officials alike expressed deep anxiety about the enforceability of the wage agreement. As one boss in Wenling worried, "We signed a tradewide wage standard, we must respect it; but these worker representatives were all appointed by the government and enterprises, will they be able to represent the aspirations of all the workers? If other workers do not respect the standard and continue to demand a wage increase what can be done?"[63] The chairman of the Wenling Wool Knitwear Employer Association expressed nearly identical concerns: "I can unite everyone to go and control those employers that do not follow the wage agreement. But who can guarantee that workers will follow the agreement and won't go on strike again?"[64] These comments reveal that employers understand the lack of legitimacy the union has with workers. Interestingly, a trade union official from the Taizhou Federation of Trade Unions (the body immediately superior to the Wenling Federation of Trade Unions) expressed the mirror image of this concern: "The sectoral union represents workers in concluding the wage agreement with the enterprise. But what happens if the boss ignores it? There are no specific measures, and no legal protection, we just have to rely on the good will of the employer."[65] So, while employers are concerned that workers will not respect the contract because of the union's lack of legitimacy, union officials fear that employers will violate the agreement because there is no check on their power. Although Pringle (2011) maintained cautious optimism about the Wenling agreement, the possibilities for regression appear strong.

Although it is well known that legal and contractual enforcement in China is particularly weak, I would be remiss if I left the impression that this is an exclusively Chinese problem. Indeed, many states in the global South have consciously pursued weak enforcement of labor laws in the hopes of attracting foreign capital. One consequence of the weakening of "hard law" is that private, nonstate forms of regulation have proliferated over the past two decades, though with uneven effectiveness (Locke, Qin, and Brause 2007; O'Rourke 2003). Outsourcing, informalization, and precariatization (Standing 2011) have presented major obstacles to enforcing labor standards not just in the South but also in workplaces of the global North (Fine and Gordon 2010). The reason that China is particularly notable, however, is that continual weak enforcement comes in a context of major legislative initiatives as well as a nationwide unionization and collective negotiation campaign. While Cooney, Biddulph, and Zhu (2013) show that the new laws have had some effect in improving enforcement, "they fall short of the far-reaching reform that may be needed to raise compliance levels very significantly and deal more effectively with widespread workplace conflict" (142). Thus what is striking about China is that ongoing lawlessness appeared at a time in which labor law and collective negotiation appeared to be undergoing a revitalization—thus making it quite distinct from most other countries (where the latter is not occurring).

What, then, are the consequences for theory? At first glance, it appeared as if the countermovement was able to overcome appropriated representation because a degree of decommodification could be oligarchically administered by state and trade union. The sectoral-level collective wage agreements reached in both Wenling and Rui'an indicate some capacity to determine wages through nonmarket mechanisms, even if such control is exercised in a nondemocratic manner. After my first trip to Rui'an, it seemed as if, given the unique characteristics of southeast Zhejiang's political economy, oligarchic decommodification could be a reality.

However, on deeper investigation, it is clear that neither decommodification nor incorporation of labor has been realized in the Rui'an eyeglass industry. Trade unions in Rui'an are similar to their counterparts in other parts of the country, either unwilling or unable to involve membership in contractual negotiations or any other features of political life that impact employment relations. Workers remain unaware of the actions that are taking place in their name, and so they have no allegiance to (or cognizance of) contracts to which they theoretically are party. Unions have not incorporated workers, and this has undermined their attempts at decommodification. As we have seen previously, labor is strong enough to win formal victories but not strong enough to enforce those victories, and a crisis of representation within the employer association only added to the difficulties. Thus, even in the region with the most propitious external conditions, oligarchic decommodification could not be realized.

Why, then, if the outcome with regard to the institutional moment is essentially the same as in Guangdong, is this research significant? First of all, one of my overarching concerns relates to the relationship between the insurgent and institutional moments of the countermovement, or in general terms, assessing the outcomes of disorganized worker movements. Even if labor remains similarly commodified and unincorporated in both regions, the institutional response of the union is quite different in Zhejiang than it is in Guangdong. Different models of development have generated different possibilities for labor politics, the result of which is that unions in Zhejiang have the capacity to negotiate collective wage agreements at the sectoral level, something that has not happened in Guangdong (as made clear by recurrent strikes among sanitation workers). In Zhejiang we can see, in embryonic form, the emergence of the institutional moment of the countermovement. On a strictly formal level, labor *was* decommodified in these cases, and in this sense we have a strong divergence from what has happened in Guangdong. It is of course significant that on a *substantive* level the outcomes are the same, a fact that speaks volumes about the structural deficiencies of trade unions in China and reveals the importance of incorporation. And yet in both Rui'an and Wenling we see that even a highly oligarchic union is groping about for an institutional response to the chaos engendered by a free labor market. Additionally, the structures and modes of negotiation that were established by the sectoral agreements in Zhejiang hold the potential for increased decommodification and rationalization, while Guangdong unions are mired in trying to resolve labor conflicts after the fact. That Zhejiangese unions developed the form of an institutional response is incredibly noteworthy.

This divergence in the organizational responses of Zhejiang and Guangdong unions is important because it indicates that scholars should pay more attention to external determinants of union activity. The overwhelming majority of literature on ACFTU unions has focused on how its activities are tightly constrained by Party control—a claim I do not dispute. But unions both in Guangdong and in Zhejiang have been attempting to establish sectoral unions capable of engaging in collective bargaining, something that has been encouraged by central leadership. While Rui'an and Wenling do not represent strong successes, it is evident that the peculiar regional model of economic development allowed them to make advances that were impossible in Guangdong.

Finally, an analysis of trade union activity in southeast Zhejiang is significant because of the high esteem afforded to local unions by higher levels of the trade union and the government. The attention showered on Wenling in particular is an indication that the state has high hopes for oligarchic decommodification-style labor politics. Though their concerns and responses vary, different levels of the state are all concerned about worker unrest and are currently searching for various methods of dealing with the problem. However, the key precondition is that workers themselves do not attain any organized and autonomous power. The consequence is that the state and the union are left with only administrative responses to social problems. The enactment of the Labor Contract Law in 2008 as well as the sectoral agreements in Zhejiang should be seen as just such responses. However, the failure of the Rui'an wage agreement bodes poorly for this approach: the state's goals of keeping the working class deeply cellularized while restoring order to employment relations may end up contradicting each other.

WORKER INSURGENCY AND THE EVOLVING POLITICAL ECONOMY OF THE PEARL RIVER DELTA

In previous chapters we have seen how union responses to worker resistance have encountered severe challenges in realizing decommodification or the realignment in power relations at the point of production necessary to politically incorporate migrant workers.[1] Each case has revealed the state and union's deep-seated fear of social instability—a fear so profound that they would rather have laws go unenforced than devolve organizational capacity to workers. Even when higher levels of the state are interested in promoting decommodification in the service of rationalizing production, these efforts have been confounded by the nonenforcement of laws and contracts within the enterprise. This has been made evident in cases where sympathetic elites first provide a degree of support to workers but then backtrack from fear that workers will begin to formulate more expansive demands. In Zhejiang we have seen instances where intermediate bodies of the union exert great effort in establishing the form but not the substance of top-down, rationalized, and decommodifying collective contracts. However, the strong alliance between state and capital at the local level has left mangers with incredibly high levels of autonomy, the results of which have been continual nonenforcement of laws and contracts, poor working conditions, and high levels of resistance among migrant workers. Paradoxically, the one way out of this conundrum—the emergence of an organized countervailing force at the point of production—is categorically opposed by all levels of the state and union. This paradox is what I have termed insurgency trap.

But by the spring of 2010 it became clear that not all incidents of worker insurgency are treated equally. In this chapter I compare two strikes that in many ways are similar—the little-known Ascendant Elevator strike and the famous Nanhai Honda strike—but that produced very different outcomes. In the Ascendant case we see insurgent workers resisting commodification, encountering inaction and passive repression from the union, and ultimately failing to win any victories. We see that union oligarchy has caused the countermovement to stall at the insurgent moment. In the Honda case, on the other hand, the strikers were able to "boomerang" (Keck and Sikkink 1998) around repressive local authorities to win the support of the provincial and central state, which then opened up the space for better organization and greater militancy. As a strike wave engulfed the entire foreign-owned auto industry in China, the capacity for the local state and union organizations to maintain low-cost and highly repressed labor—already challenged by the myriad daily labor conflicts around the country—began to waver. Significantly, the position of the higher levels of the state had evolved between late 2007 and 2010, affecting both the process and the outcome of the strikes. The Honda strike dissolved the ideological image of a unified state edifice, as the central and provincial government showed relative tolerance toward the workers while the local state resorted to coercion in a failed attempt to bring the deadlock to a close. The 2010 strike wave marked an important turning point in Chinese labor politics and in the trajectory of the nation's political economy more broadly.

My main argument in this chapter is as follows. The transition from the insurgent to the institutional moment of countermovements can—particularly in nondemocratic states—be accomplished only with the accumulation of countless, often relatively anonymous instances of class struggle. As we can see in China, it is not until the unstable equilibrium has been severely upended that the capitalist state, or at least significant segments of it, will be ready for compromise. For years, a strong alliance between capital and the lowest levels of the Chinese state meant that strikes were dealt with either through police repression or through an ad hoc system of mediation by union and government officials that was focused almost exclusively on resuming production, regardless of the outcome for workers. But by 2010, the Chinese central government and Guangdong provincial authorities not only were ready to seek a new model of accumulation in the Pearl River Delta but were willing to (indirectly) ally with insurgent workers in attempting to realize this goal. Just such an alliance, conditional and ephemeral as it may have been, emerged in the course of the Nanhai Honda strike, which in turn allowed the strikers to win economic concessions and begin to develop political goals. In large part because of this small political opening, the character of protest in the 2010 strike wave displayed some unusual (if not unprecedented) tendencies, most significantly that demands were offensive rather than defensive in nature. By comparing the strikes at Ascendant and Nanhai Honda, we can see that the position of the provincial and central authorities shifted in the interven-ing two and a half years, even if the lowest level of the state remained committed to low-cost labor. However, even if Honda employees won economic gains that eluded the Ascendant strikers, we see that all levels of the state and union remain vigilant about the development of autonomous bases of worker power. Although economic gains were made in the 2010 strike wave, worker disillusionment with unions from the enterprise level on up persists, and the state's exit from insur-gency trap remains murky.

The Countermovement in China

To briefly review, I originally posited that countermovements as conceived of by Polanyi are too mechanistic and that he fails to account for the complex rela-tionship between anticommodification social struggles and the consequences for state action. Subsequent theorists have tended to conceive of the countermove-ment primarily either as resistance pure and simple (Chin and Mittelman 1997) or as represented by state policy. By pointing to expanded social spending in China since the beginning of the twenty-first century, Wang Shaoguang (2008) falls into the latter category. With little discussion as to *why* such spending has increased, how and whether it has been distributed, or what the implications are for decommodification, Wang has implied that the double movement has already been realized in China. But in this work we see a conflation of social rejection of commodification and actual decommodification. Because in China there is hardly any space in which workers can develop autonomous power to counter the hegemony of market and state (Burawoy 2003), worker rejection of com-modification is confined to cellular activism (Lee 2007), which has yet to cohere into the type of political force that can articulate specific political demands.[2] In Wang's view, we are led to believe that simply because there were some negative consequences of marketization, the state decided to initiate the double move-ment. Society, or in this case cellular resistance, and the deeply entrenched inter-ests of state and capital are eliminated from the formula—that is, the political aspect of the countermovement is obliterated in the analysis. Thus we are left with no explanation for why the state (and which levels of the state) might or might not initiate reform, aside from the fact that it is *necessary*.

In the existing literature, it is clear that the new Chinese working class has been engaged in frequent acts of resistance against the incursion of the mar-ket (C. K-C. Chan 2010; Chan and Pun 2009; C. K. Lee 2007; Pun, Chan, and Chan 2009; Pun and Lu 2010). I have shown that higher levels of the state are sometimes supportive of anticommodification struggles, particularly when they threaten rationalized accumulation, and that they are keen to integrate workers into regularized and legal modes of contention. And yet, even when proworker legislation is adopted at the national or regional level, actual implementation is frequently confounded by vaguely worded laws (Cooney 2006) and the alliance between the local state and capital. Commodification on a national scale produces new interests and new power arrangements in society. When certain segments of society (and possibly the state) revolt against further commodification, they must struggle to realize these goals; decommodification severely impacts the interests of capital and various levels of the state and so is not easily won. As a result, it is incredibly important to analyze specific cases of worker insurgency and the response of state and union to see the dialectic between resistance and institutionalization in action. Additionally, while national-level policies on increasing social spending are worth noting (particularly because they indicate that a segment of the state is interested in class compromise), they cannot be accepted at face value as large swaths of migrant workers have been excluded from the potential benefits (Frazier 2010).

Because of this, I have argued that in the early stages of capitalist development, countermovements against the market must be broken down into two constituent moments: the insurgent moment, when workers and others negatively affected by marketization rebel and engage in nonregularized forms of contention; and the institutional moment, when decommodification of labor comes to be institutionalized at the social level and the working class is politically incorporated by the state. The central argument up until now has been that persistent oligarchy within the ACFTU—workers' only legal representative—has caused the countermovement in China to stall at the insurgent moment (i.e., fall into an insurgency trap). Until we descend to the shop floor to see how and why workers organize strikes and what the concrete responses of union officials are when such an event happens, we cannot fully understand the relationship between the insurgent and the institutional moments of the countermovement.

Particularly in a country as vast as China, it is important to understand how insurgent workers interact with various levels of the Chinese state. Kevin O'Brien and Lianjiang Li (1996, 2006) developed the influential concept of "rightful resistance" to describe how protesters use the language and concepts of the state in attempting to circumvent local officials in attracting attention from higher-ups. Ching Kwan Lee (2007) has discovered the political economy undergirding similar forms of resistance among workers, in what she terms "decentralized legal authoritarianism." This allows us to see that the ideological image of a benevolent central authority counterposed to corrupt and rapacious local officials is produced through a specific economic and political arrangement—one that not coincidentally allows for a more stable form of domination. And Yongshun Cai

(2010) has argued that one of the key determinants in protesters' ability to get their grievances addressed is whether they cause enough of a disturbance that higher-level officials (especially the central government) cannot maintain the illusion of ignorance. I concur with these scholars that the lowest levels of the state often appear to be, and in fact are, aligned with powerful interests against workers and that higher levels (especially the central government but sometimes the provincial or even municipal authorities) are more likely to be sympathetic. But as we will see in this chapter, there is an ongoing dialogue between the central authorities and insurgent workers. During the first thirty years of China's transition to capitalism, increasing iterative flashes of worker insurgency have not merely dissipated into the ether. Rather, in a complex and highly mediated process, residual particles of insurgency have settled on the political field, eventually remaking the landscape and changing the attitudes of the state toward wildcat strikes. Gaining the attention of the central government through social and economic disruption not only is helpful in resolving a particular case (as argued by Cai) but has ongoing consequences for contours of resistance. This dynamic is clearly illustrated in the following empirical account.

The Ascendant and Honda cases make for a good comparison. Both are capital-intensive wholly foreign-owned operations, with Ascendant located in Guangzhou and Nanhai Honda less than twenty-five miles away in the adjoining municipality of Foshan. Production in both factories requires skilled labor, and most workers are graduates of technical schools. Workers enjoy somewhat better working conditions than in most labor-intensive industries in the Pearl River Delta and other export-oriented regions. And Honda and Ascendant alike employ the labor-force dualism so prevalent in capital-intensive industries in China (L. Zhang 2008), in which a large number of employees are hired with fewer job protections, lower wages, and worse benefits than the regular workers receive (Yu Jing 2009). And yet we will see that different organizational capacity and labor market dynamics, as well as different overall political conditions, forced the union to adopt varying responses to the respective strikes. Additionally, we will see that various levels of the union had very different responses to each strike.

Commodification, Resistance and More Commodification

I first heard about the Ascendant Elevator factory from the GZFTU chair Chen Weiguang during an official visit he made to the United States in the spring of 2008. As is the case with most trade union leaders from China, Chen was aware that many foreign labor activists take a rather dim view of the ACFTU and its subordinate unions. Thus he was eager to demonstrate the efficacy, and perhaps potential advantages, of the Chinese model of trade unionism. In pursuit of such an end, he brought up the case of the Ascendant Elevator factory several times during his U.S. trip. Nearly a year and a half later, in October 2009, another GZFTU delegation came to the United States, this time headed by deputy chair Zheng Yiyao. Zheng repeated the story of Ascendant Elevator to a group of labor scholars and activists at UCLA,[3] indicating that it was still considered a prime example of union efficacy.

The story as Chen and Zheng related it went like this. Ascendant Elevator is an American-owned company that has a production site in the Baiyun district of Guangzhou. In the late fall of 2007 the company announced to workers that it would be switching from an hourly-rate system to a piece-rate system in order to increase productivity. It announced how much workers were going to be paid per piece and demanded that all employees sign a letter of intent that indicated their acceptance of this change in factory rules. Workers were quite upset with this because, according to their calculations, their salaries would be dramatically reduced by the change. They tried to get assistance from their enterprise-level union chair, but he was ultimately unresponsive.[4] Feeling that they had no choice, the workers went on strike to demand that the hourly-rate system remain in place. After the strike occurred, the GZFTU got involved to mediate. Union leadership met with workers and managers and eventually reached a resolution. Although the piece-rate system was to be implemented, the union successfully negotiated an increase in the rates. Several months after the strike, productivity was up, workers' wages were up, and everyone was satisfied. It was a win-win outcome, and it revealed that Chinese unions were capable of defending workers' interests without being antagonistic toward management.

Chen told this story because he thought it was a good demonstration of the fact that Chinese unions are quite capable of promoting worker interests. In reality, not only was the union completely incapable of realizing any decommodification, but its negotiated resolution was unable to prevent further outbreaks of worker insurgency. The actual events of this case reveal the immense challenge Chinese unions will face if they are to significantly decommodify labor without challenging the interests of state or capital.

First of all, it is not at all insignificant that the Ascendant Elevator story was widely covered by the Guangzhou press. The GZFTU did not get involved until *after* the story began gaining a lot of public attention. An unfortunate but common phenomenon is that trade unions (and other government agencies) refuse to address mounting social conflicts until they pose a real threat to their image. Time and time again, the union hopes that conflicts can be glossed over and that they will just go away. Workers understand this logic of the state, as is reflected in the clichéd phrase "create a big disturbance, get a big resolution, create a small disturbance, get a small resolution, create no disturbance, get no resolution." Ascendant Elevator employees had tried to resolve their grievance by approaching their enterprise-level trade union chair, and some workers reported trying to get assistance from the labor bureau. But it was not until they went on strike and received widespread coverage in the media that the municipal-level union decided to intervene. This consistently reactive stance of the union is in line with general practice.

While Chen's account was more or less accurate in describing the events up to the final resolution, it is still important to fill in some additional details. Tensions in the factory began building up in mid-December when the company first announced the switch to a piece-rate system. Workers were quite angry about the announced switch, since according to their calculations, their salary would be decreased by 60 percent, and they would be forced to do more overtime. On December 18, 128 of the workers went on strike, completely shutting down operations at the plant. Two days later, the company sent a "gentle reminder" saying that anyone who refused to sign a letter of intent accepting the piece-rate system by the following day (December 21) would have his or her contract terminated at the end of the month.

Unbeknownst to the workers, the enterprise-level trade union chair, Cheng Weiji, had already discussed the new piece-rate system with management and claimed to have represented the interests of the workers. In order to further grasp the farcical nature of Cheng's discussion with management, it is worth quoting at length a section of a newspaper article that appeared on December 21:

> Yesterday around 1 p.m. this reporter was finally able to see the chairman of Ascendant Elevator Company, Mr. Cheng Weiji. It was surprising to find that every one of his statements came under fierce attack from the 128 workers at the scene of the incident.
>
> Cheng Weiji said, "Today we convened a staff and workers' congress. Workers were present."
>
> "This didn't happen," said the workers.
>
> Cheng Weiji said, "The union contacted the representatives that you all selected to discuss the piece-rate issue."
>
> "No, who are you saying participated?" the workers said.
>
> Cheng Weiji said, "The night before last, the union held a meeting to discuss this issue. We informed all of the workers that there is going to be a negotiation conference today at 1:30."
>
> "We didn't receive any notification," the workers said.

Cheng Weiji said, "Just because you didn't receive the notification does not mean that it wasn't sent. We sent it out by e-mail."

"We don't even have computers, how can we receive something by e-mail?" responded the workers.

In an interview with this reporter, Cheng Weiji said that the union had discussed the matter of the piece-rate system with Ascendant Elevator Company two times, and that they convened a union representative congress. The union representatives transmitted the spirit of the congress to the employees. This reporter inquired what the union was prepared to do if the company terminated the contract of employees, some of whom have been at the company for ten or more years, if they refused to sign an agreement on accepting the piece-rate system. Cheng Weiji said that he is not an administrator, so it wouldn't be appropriate for him to give a response.[5]

Clearly, the enterprise-level union was not up to the task of resolving the impasse, as its representation was formalistic at best. At this point the GZFTU and the Electrical and Machine Industrial Union dispatched officers to Ascendant Elevator Company to do an investigation. As a symbolic indication of the gravity of the event, the ACFTU sent someone from Beijing to attend the investigation. The goal was to determine whether the company had gone through the appropriate legal procedures for implementing the new system, whether workers' legal rights were being protected, and whether the enterprise-level union chair had fulfilled his appropriate duties. At the same time, the union began its own evaluation of the proposed changes, with the intent of coming up with an alternative piece-rate system. Chairman Chen, legal experts, and other trade union leaders planned to personally visit the company the following week to engage in negotiations.

The labor bureau also jumped into the fray. Though initially giving cautious warning to the company that its approach could violate labor laws, the bureau quickly did an about-face. The chief of the Baiyun District Labor and Social Security Bureau, Xie Xijian, was quoted in the newspaper as saying, "The enterprise has sovereignty over the determination of labor contracts. As long as it is above the minimum wages for the province and the city, the labor bureau cannot intervene."[6] Since the bureau understood that a reduction of wages to levels below that of the legally mandated minimum was not under discussion, this comment was equivalent to removing the government from adjudication of the issue. Management's confidence in the support of the government was evident when it said that if it was unable to come to a resolution, it would "encourage" workers to file for arbitration. The procapital position of the state was not lost on workers, as is evidenced by this comment from a temp worker about the strategy of workers in a second strike that took place in

August 2008: "Some people said we should go report it to the labor bureau, but others opposed this. Those in opposition said that when there was a conflict last time, some people went to the labor bureau, but it didn't have any effect. The labor department doesn't help workers, it protects bosses. So if you go it will be useless!"[7]

After garnering much attention in the print media and on various blogs (where the overwhelming majority of people supported the striking workers), a gag order was imposed and the story disappeared from public discourse. It is of course significant that this gag order was issued before the resolution of the conflict, since the likelihood that the union or other government agencies would have their image tarnished was thus greatly reduced. However, the Ascendant Elevator incident did appear in the papers one more time at the end of the following January. Chen Weiguang, displaying some of the characteristics that had given him a good reputation among foreign trade unionists, publicly criticized the inaction of the enterprise-level union in Ascendant Elevator: "On the surface, the Ascendant incident is a conflict between labor and capital, but in the background it magnifies the crisis of our enterprise-level trade unions, something which is worth our contemplating."[8] Chen went on to make a more general critique, saying that "some enterprise-level union chairs are taking the wrong position and are completely servile toward capital. They have completely forgotten their primary responsibility as a worker representative."[9] The fact that Chen's leadership and insistence that unions more effectively represent workers were unable to affect managerial authoritarianism reveals a fundamental weakness of the trade union.

What was the actual outcome of the Ascendant Elevator incident? In interviews with workers conducted more than a year after the strike, there was universal displeasure with the results. Most of these workers participated in the strike but said that in the end they had no choice but to sign the letter of intent. Otherwise, they said, they would lose their jobs. Contrary to the promises of management and the reassurances of the union, wages for workers declined significantly after the implementation of the piece-rate system. One worker claimed that 90 percent of workers' salaries had declined since the strike. He said that before the strike temporary workers like him earned between RMB 2,000 and 2,500 but that their wages had since been reduced to 1,300–1,600. Another temp worker said that he had made only 1,100 the previous month. The original salaries for regular workers had been between 4,000 and 4,500 but had since been reduced to 3,000–3,500. Though I could not verify these numbers with official documents, all interviewees confirmed that their wages had been significantly reduced.

This leads to a secondary point that was not addressed in any of the media coverage: Ascendant Elevator Company's employment of temporary workers.

The implementation of labor-force dualism has become increasingly common in many enterprises throughout China,[10] both as a method to break employee solidarity and in order to maintain greater flexibility in human resources management. This was the case in the Ascendant factory, where a very significant number of employees were hired as temp workers through a hiring agency. The long-term maintenance of this sort of labor regime is in violation of the legal requirement of equal pay for equal work. Indeed, interviewees from Ascendant Elevator pointed out that as temp workers they did exactly the same work as regular workers but were compensated at a much lower level. This system was not addressed at all in the negotiations at the end of 2007. The failure to address this issue is significant because temp workers went on strike briefly in August of 2008, protesting low wages and unequal treatment. I was unable to get more detailed data on this event, but two workers mentioned it in interviews.

Finally, there is little evidence that the union did anything to secure increased recognition from workers. Many interviewees, despite participating in the strike, were unaware that the factory had a union:

> INTERVIEWER: Before the strike, what actions did the Ascendant
>   Company union chair take?
> RESPONDENT: I didn't know our company had a union!
> INTERVIEWER: Well then, how about the higher-level trade union?
> RESPONDENT: Higher-level trade union? Is that the labor bureau?

In response to the same question about the behavior of the union chair, a different respondent said, "My friend said that the union chair and the boss 'wear the same pants,' he just speaks for the boss!" This respondent said that the union chair eventually told them that management's actions were legal and that they would either have to obey the new rules or leave the company.

But perhaps the most succinct summary of the outcome of the Ascendant Elevator case came from a temp worker who was asked whether there was a win-win resolution: "Where is there win-win? It was an absolute and thorough defeat for the workers. An absolute defeat!"[11]

The Honda Conflagration

On May 17, 2010, more than two years after the Ascendant Elevator strike, hundreds of workers at Nanhai Honda walked off the job to demand higher wages.[12] Over the next three weeks, all of Honda's production facilities in China would be shut down, and a strike wave would have cascaded throughout the auto industry, plunging the union into perhaps its deepest political crisis of the reform era. Although the original organizers in Nanhai did not have the intention of sparking a string of worker revolts, that is precisely what they accomplished. As we will see in a moment, the changing dynamics of worker insurgency produced a response from the union that revealed simultaneous continuity and evolution.

The Honda case presents both similarities and differences with Ascendant. It is similar in that the enterprise unions were completely unable to either effectively represent their membership or even to stave off insurgency. Although on the surface the initial reasons for going on strike were different, underlying both incidents was the general process of commodification of labor. But the outcomes of the two strikes were quite different. Although Honda workers did not win everything they asked for, it would be impossible to describe the outcome as an absolute defeat. The organizational capacity of workers was much greater at Honda, and they made specifically political demands. These changes in the dynamics of resistance as well as changes in the overall political economy resulted in a different response from both the union and the state than what we have seen previously.

Nanhai Honda

Honda's production chain in China consists of a somewhat convoluted system of ownership. The most significant company is Guangzhou Honda, a 50–50 joint venture with the state-owned Guangzhou Automobile Group Corporation, where a majority of units are produced. Additional assembly plants include Honda Automobile (China), which produces for foreign markets, and the joint-venture Dongfeng Honda located in Wuhan. These plants are served by a variety of parts manufacturers, including the wholly Japanese-owned Nanhai Honda. Starting production in March of 2007 with an initial investment of USD $98 million,[13] the company was Honda's fourth integrated automatic transmission production plant in the world.[14] Aside from producing transmissions, the plant also makes drive shafts and connecting rods for engines.[15] In part because Honda believed that work stoppages were highly unlikely in authoritarian China, the Nanhai plant was established as the sole supplier of several key parts for the entire China operation. As stated in the press release accompanying the company's establishment, "The start-up of production at [Nanhai] enables Honda to secure an adequate supply of powertrain components to support expansion of Honda's automobile production in China, and also to further increase local content of powertrain components, which will help cost-reduction efforts and strengthen Honda's competitiveness in the market." By sourcing from within

China rather than from Japan or Southeast Asia, Honda could reduce costs by saving on transportation and labor.

In part because of the key position that auto manufacturing plays in the economy, the government put a high premium on maintaining good labor relations in this sector. As a result, all the Honda assembly and parts manufacturing plants in Guangdong established unions. The union at Guangzhou Honda had been awarded several official accolades for its good work and frequently hosted visiting delegations of foreign trade unionists. But there were strict limits on how much even this model union would do for its workers. During a lunch meeting in December 2008 between the chair of Guangzhou Honda and visiting union leaders from the United States, talk turned to international cooperation between auto unions. The union chair said that he had visited Japan previously to hold exchanges with other auto union representatives and that he felt they had much in common. Alluding to the difficulties American auto manufactures were facing at the time, he joked that he had told his Japanese counterpart, "We have a strong union, like you. But we don't want to be too strong; just look at all the problems they have in the United States!"[16] In fact, it turned out that the very weakness of the union at the Nanhai supplier plant would make it impossible for workers to have their demands heard without going on strike; not just the Nanhai plant but Honda's entire China operations would be shut down as a result.

Although workers at Nanhai had long been unhappy with the wages and had discussed going on strike, hardly any of the workers knew that Tan Guocheng was going to initiate the strike when he did.[17] One week before the strike, Tan met with fifteen people from the assembly department were he worked; previously they had only "had random talks on the shuttle bus to work."[18] One worker from this department said that the idea had been discussed but that nobody wanted to lead it. In separate interviews, workers from other departments confirmed that they had heard nothing of the strike until it had begun. But according to Tan, more than twenty people, most of them from Hunan, had been in on the plan by the time it was put into action.[19]

On the morning of May 17, just as production began at the usual time of 7:50, Tan hit the emergency stop button, and both production lines in the assembly department were shut down. Tan and co-organizer Xiao shouted out at each assembly line, "Our wages are so low, let's stop working!"[20] For most of the plant's nearly two thousand workers, this was to be the first they heard of the strike. Even one worker who was from the assembly department and had heard discussion about the possibility of the strike was caught unaware: "I didn't know the strike was going to happen....I wasn't there at the time [because I went to the bathroom]. When I was finished in the bathroom I came out and there weren't any people. I stood there looking, 'huh, how come they aren't at work?'"[21]

As workers from the assembly department fanned out throughout the facility, they shouted to their coworkers to stop work and join them in fighting for higher wages. They initially received a somewhat cool reception in the other departments and eventually began a sit-in in front of the factory with only about fifty workers. But given the critical position of the assembly department in the production process, the other departments were forced to shut down in a matter of hours. By that afternoon, management had set up suggestion boxes and pleaded with the workers to resume production, promising them that they would consider their demand for higher wages and provide a full response in four days. Perhaps because of their relatively small numbers, the strikers took management at their word, and production resumed that very day.

On the twentieth, management, government officials, union officials, and worker representatives engaged in negotiations. The workers' demand at this point was simply to raise all wages by RMB 800. In the meantime, the strikers returned to work, though production was greatly reduced during these few days. On the twenty-first, negotiations broke down, and the strike continued. Over the weekend, organizers continued their outreach, and the number of strikers in front of the factory grew to over three hundred. Then, on the twenty-second, management announced that Tan and Xiao, the two original strike leaders, were having their contracts terminated. But this attempt at repression completely backfired, as the following day the strike only grew in strength. Now concerned for their livelihoods, workers covered their faces with surgical masks but continued to hold the line.

Throughout this process, the enterprise union alternated between passivity and hostility. Workers complained that during the bargaining session the union representative did not say anything at all but merely observed the proceedings. When the strike initially began on May 17, a team of investigators from the district labor department and trade union were dispatched to the factory. Leaving no doubt which side of the struggle they were on, the officials announced, "According to relevant regulations, we did not find that the factory is in violation of any laws."[22] One worker who was selected as a representative was quite disappointed with the behavior of the enterprise union chair, Wu Youhe, in the first round of negotiations:

> [The enterprise union chair] invited a lawyer [to the first round of negotiations]. The lawyer said that our strike was illegal. He [the union chair] didn't have any views of his own and couldn't make any decisions. He always asked the general manager what to do. At bottom he is a chairman and isn't controlled by the company; he has this power. But for him, everything had to go through the general manager, and he would help the general manager refute the things we said.[23]

On the twenty-fourth, worker representatives were convinced to come back to the table in a negotiation session chaired by the enterprise union head. Still trying to serve as an intermediary, the union chair attempted to persuade the workers to accept management's offer of a RMB 55 increase in food subsidies—a far cry from the RMB 800 they were demanding. This ineffectiveness was not lost on the workers, with one striker commenting, "The union said it stood for our interests. They said we employees could give them any demands and they would pass them on to management, and they would resolve things for us. But they didn't do this in the slightest."[24]

The strikers refused management's offer on the twenty-fourth, and the situation escalated. On the twenty-fifth things became much more tense when all of Honda's assembly plants in China were completely shut down because of lack of parts. Originally counting on a well-disciplined workforce, Honda had only one supplier for transmissions in the country, and all four assembly plants in China were therefore highly dependent on Nanhai. The combined daily losses of the five plants were estimated to be RMB 240 million.[25] Management further yielded by producing a second offer for wage increases on the twenty-sixth. This proposal called for increasing regular workers' salaries by RMB 200 a month, along with 155 in living expense subsidies, and a wage increase of 477 for interns who had been at the plant for more than three months.[26] But workers rejected this offer as well, and the strike continued. At this point, workers formalized their demands, and in addition to the primary demand of increasing wages for all employees by RMB 800, they also demanded that the fired workers be rehired, that there be no retribution against strikers, and that the enterprise union be "reorganized" (chongzheng). According to some strikers, the demand for union reorganization emerged after they saw that the union had failed to actively represent them in the previous negotiation sessions.

With the losses mounting, management became desperate and did its best to try to break the resolve and unity of the strikers. The most direct attack was on the twenty-eighth, when managers attempted to force workers to sign a pledge saying that they would "not lead, organize, or participate in slowdowns, work stoppages, or strikes anymore."[27] But this tactic completely backfired as almost nobody agreed to sign it, with one worker saying, "as soon as I saw it [the agreement] I threw it away. We won't sign."[28] One group of female workers said that "nobody moved a hand." When asked if they were afraid of refusing management's demand, one worker insisted, "Nobody was afraid! Who would be afraid? If they want to fire us, then they'll have to fire all of us!"[29]

The strike was entering a decisive stage. Likely already the longest strike ever waged by migrant workers in the reform era, the situation had become a political crisis for the local state. Despite the mounting economic and political costs, the events of May 31 took everyone by surprise.

The Union as Strikebreaker

When workers arrived at the factory on the morning of May 31, they were informed that each department would be holding meetings to further discuss strike resolution.[30] As the workers were waiting in various rooms of the main administration building, a large contingent of vans and buses pulled up in front. The vehicles were filled with dozens of men, all of whom were wearing yellow hats and badges reading, "Shishan Township Federation of Trade Unions," which is the union organization immediately superordinate to the enterprise union branch. Shortly thereafter, the assembly department, crucial to reviving production, met with the general manager of the plant, during which time he made a new offer for a wage increase. Although still dissatisfied with management's new offer, the workers were persuaded to return to their assembly lines. Indications began to emerge that the strikers' unity was crumbling as some departments began to start up their assembly lines. People from the union dispersed to each of the departments and encouraged workers to immediately resume production.

When some workers from the assembly department moved to return to the area in front of the factory where they had been demonstrating over the previous nearly two weeks, a confrontation with the union group emerged. As confirmed from multiple independent sources, the union people began filming the workers and demanded that they return to the factory and end the strike. A tense situation quickly escalated and soon devolved into a physical confrontation during which several workers were struck by people from the union. This infuriated the workers, and a strike that had appeared to be losing steam was quickly reinvigorated. Workers from other departments who had resumed production rushed to the scene as soon as they received news of the violence, and a large crowd quickly gathered. Another physical confrontation occurred, and this time the union side was even more violent than before, with several workers suffering light wounds. Among those hit were some women workers. The aggressors quickly retreated to their vehicles and refused to come out.

At this point, the government decided things had gone too far, and it took steps to settle the conflict. Riot police were deployed, though they never engaged the workers. The authorities additionally cordoned off the road into the factory, and nobody was allowed entrance. Whichever government agencies had supported the peaceful strike were not interested in more violent confrontations or the possibility that the strikers might leave the production grounds.

It is certain that most of the strikebreakers were not actually union officers. The first thing mentioned by many workers was that it seemed preposterous that the township-level federation, with only a few paid members on staff, could recruit so many officers from other union branches. One worker involved in the scuffle said that some of the strikebreakers (all of whom were male) had earrings and tattoos, items that union officials would be very unlikely to sport. But if most of the thugs were not actually union officers, it is nevertheless undeniable that the district union federation had a hand in organizing the strikebreakers, a point made obvious in a letter it wrote to workers (see below). A foreman from the assembly department was blunt in his assessment: "Of course it was the union's idea. Who else would have such a stupid idea? Only Chinese unions would think of this."[31] It is, however, unclear to what extent the union federation was acting at the behest of management or whether it was taking independent action.

When workers received an open letter from the Shishan Township and Nanhai District Federations of Trade Unions the following day, the local union leaders provided a tepid apology and did not denounce the violence that had occurred the previous day, nor did they attempt to deny that they had organized the strikebreakers. The letter is worth quoting at some length:

> Yesterday the trade union participated in mediation talks between the workers and management of Honda. Because a portion of Honda employees have refused to return to work, factory production has been severely curtailed. In the process of discussions with forty or so employees, at one point there occurred some misunderstandings and verbal imprudence from both sides. Due to the impulsive emotional state of some of the employees, a physical conflict ensued between some employees and representatives from the union. This incident has left a negative impression on employees. A portion of these employees, after receiving word of the incident, seem to have misinterpreted the actions of the union as siding with management. Yesterday's incident came entirely as a shock to us. If people feel that some of the methods used in yesterday's incident were a bit difficult to accept, we apologize.
>
> The behavior of the above mentioned group of forty or so workers has already damaged the interests of the majority of employees. In addition, such behavior harms factory production. The fact that the union has stood up and admonished these workers is entirely in the interests of the majority of employees. This is the responsibility of the union!
>
> It would be unwise for workers to behave in ways that go against the interests of themselves and others because of impulsive emotions. Some employees are worried that representatives who are willing to stand up

and enter into talks with management would later receive the reprisals of management. This is a misunderstanding.[32]

The letter went on to admonish workers for refusing to accept the offer that management had made. In a final attempt at damage control, it closed by saying, "Please trust the union. Trust each level of Party officials and government. We will definitely uphold justice."[33]

Unsurprisingly, the letter from the Shishan and Nanhai union federations was unsatisfactory to the strikers. As one worker activist put it, "Their apology letter wasn't an apology letter at all, so we were pretty enraged."[34] An open letter from worker representatives that appeared two days after the union's apology letter was defiant: "The union should protect the collective rights and interests of workers and lead the workers in the strike. But up until now, they have been looking for excuses for the union people's violence against striking workers, and we seriously condemn this."[35] Additionally, the letter went on to express "extreme rage" at the union's claim that it was the union's hard work that had caused management to increase its offer of wage increases, arguing rather that these were "won by the blood and sweat of striking workers facing extreme pressure."[36] Relations between the strikers and the township-level union could not have been worse, and they certainly heightened the tension of the unfolding drama.

Resolution

Whereas the tactics of the township-level union failed to break the deadlock, higher levels of the union and Party were much more sympathetic to the strikers. I heard from GZFTU leadership that Guangdong Party secretary Wang Yang supported the strike and the workers' wage demands and even that there was support in the central government. The Central Propaganda Department did not issue a reporting ban until May 29, nearly two weeks into the confrontation, at which point the strike wave had spread to other factories.[37] But this was an indication that the central government was willing to allow more pressure to build on management, as it is rare for coverage of strikes to go on for so long. The GDFTU deputy chair, Kong Xianghong, took an active role in the negotiations and supported the wage demands. Particularly after the confrontation between the Shishan union and the workers, the provincial-level authorities were eager to resolve the conflict quickly.

In order to find an orderly resolution, the various government agencies that had become involved in the strike demanded that the workers select representatives. Although a hastily arranged set of negotiators had been selected for the first round of talks, strikers had become reluctant to produce representatives, particularly after the two people who initiated the strike were fired. This unwillingness to negotiate was unacceptable to the state, and it brought in the Guangzhou Automotive CEO and National People's Congress delegate Zeng Qinghong to speak with the workers. Through gentle and paternalistic persuasion, late on June 1 Zeng convinced the strikers to select representatives and to begin a conditional resumption of production. In their open letter, the worker representatives had said that if management did not meet their demands within three days, the strike would be resumed. Furthermore, the letter had stated that "bargaining representatives will not accept anything less than the above-listed demands without the authorization of a general meeting of employees."[38] Finally, negotiations began on the third.

On June 4, the worker representatives were joined by Chang Kai, a well-known labor scholar from Beijing, who served as their legal counsel. Negotiations went late into the night, and eventually an agreement was struck. Regular workers were to receive wage increases of approximately RMB 500, bringing their monthly wages above RMB 2,000. The underpaid interns who worked alongside regular workers saw their wages increase by more than 70 percent, to more than RMB 600. Such large wage increases in response to strikes were unprecedented in China.

Strike Wave

Before discussing the political fallout from the Nanhai strike, it is important to note that the ongoing coverage of the struggle had sparked widespread resistance among industrial workers around the country. The central government had given the OK for media coverage to continue, as it fit in with their inclination to raise wages for skilled workers. Additionally, the fact that Honda is a Japanese-owned factory was important, as it appeared possible to divert anger about worker mistreatment in nationalistic rather than class-based directions.[39] And yet the central government certainly got more than it was bargaining for as strikes ripped through the auto industry, even spilling over into other sectors. Though many strikes targeted Japanese-owned factories, this was certainly not true in all cases. With workers experiencing generalized dissatisfaction, a small relaxing of media controls was all it took to ignite an outbreak of intensified insurgency. It is important to keep this uptick in class struggle in mind to understand the context in which both the Nanhai and subsequent strikes were resolved.

In each strike, the primary demand was for large wage increases. Though the insistence on union reorganization was not highlighted as much in these other struggles, it was included as a demand by many strikers. Perhaps most noteworthy among the copycat strikes was that initiated on June 21 at Denso in the Nansha district of Guangzhou. Employing 1,100 workers, the Japanese-owned

Denso is a major auto parts supplier, in particular for the Toyota assembly plant located in Guangdong. On several occasions, workers in the plant had brought up issues related to pay and living conditions with the enterprise union, but nothing changed. Indeed, a shop-floor union representative admitted that the "small group" (*xiaozu*) meetings that were supposed to happen once a month had been held only one time and that there had never been an employee congress (a meeting for all enterprise employees).[40] Just as had been the case at Nanhai, stagnating wages and the inability or unwillingness of the union or management to take worker grievances seriously were the impetus for the strike. Although they were clearly following the lead of the Nanhai workers, one Denso employee said, "We wanted to go on strike for a long time."[41]

The most significant thing about the Denso strike was its militant and tightly organized nature. During the weekend before the twenty-first, a group of up to two hundred workers gathered in secret to discuss plans. At this meeting, the "three nos" strategy was decided upon by workers. It required that for three days there would be no work, no representatives, and no demands. Workers knew that within three days lack of parts would cause a shutdown in the neighboring Toyota assembly plant. Additionally they had strong reason to believe that representatives would face retaliation or co-optation. By waiting three days before issuing any demands, they would be bargaining from a position of great power, as they anticipated that losses would be mounting not just for Denso but for the entire Toyota supply chain.

Their calculation was correct. They started the strike on the morning of the twenty-first, and workers blocked trucks from leaving the plant. By that afternoon, six of the other parts plants in the "auto city" industrial zone where Denso was located were also shut down. The following day, the nearby Toyota assembly plant closed for lack of parts.[42] And on the third day, workers elected twenty-seven representatives and went into negotiations. Their central demand was simply a wage increase of RMB 800. The negotiations were attended by worker representatives, the CEO of Denso (who had flown in from Japan), and officials from various levels of the union, as well as Zeng Qinghong, who had played a key role in resolving the Nanhai strike. After the negotiations, management and Zeng pleaded with the workers to return to work and promised them a resolution by the twenty-fifth. Worker solidarity broke down somewhat at this point as many began to return to work, although output on the twenty-fourth was far below usual levels. And on the morning of the twenty-fifth it was announced that they would be granted an RMB 800 wage increase.

The evolving political position of the union was evident in the Denso strike, which took place within the jurisdiction of Chen Weiguang's GZFTU. When the workers first went on strike, they rejected the intervention of the higher levels of the trade union, likely with the Nanhai incident fresh in their minds. Chairman Chen was aware of this problem, saying, "When the Denso strike exploded, the enterprise union lost the trust [of workers]."[43] In response he said, "The union represents only the interests of workers, and will no longer play the role of a mediator [as had been requested by the local government]."[44] Additionally, and quite significantly, the local public security bureau told the union it wanted to speak with worker representatives, but the union refused to comply.

Workers struck in another nearby Honda supplier, again severely disrupting production. At the Guli Lock Factory in Zhongshan, they marched in public and blocked roads. As early as May 28, Hyundai Automobile workers walked off the job. And an absolutely massive strike wave engulfed a development zone in the northern city of Dalian. From the end of May through August, seventy thousand workers in a variety of sectors went on strike, affecting seventy-three enterprises in the zone. As reported by union officials, workers won an average wage increase of 34.5 percent.[45] This was the third time the Dalian development zone had experienced a strike wave since 1994. Some Japanese companies that had *not* experienced strikes decided to give their workers a preemptive raise, with National increasing wages by RMB 500 and Panasonic by 200–300.[46]

It is not clear how many workers went on strike in the summer of 2010, but it is certain that the dozens of reported cases are merely a small portion. Around the country, workers were granted unprecedented wage increases. In the fallout from the strike wave, union officials and media commentators declared the end of low-wage labor in China.

Response to the 2010 Strike Wave

In the wake of Nanhai and other strikes, the public position of many union officials, particularly in Guangdong, began to change. Chen Weiguang, always somewhat more daring than his other union colleagues, publicly stated that the strikes had been a force for encouraging trade union reform and that they were allowing labor negotiation systems to become more mature.[47] He additionally expressed concern that unions had continued to be passive and that they were "tailing" workers, publicly stating that unions could not "hide forever."[48] But he believed that the strike waves also presented the union federation with the opportunity to engage in reform: "Recent events at Nanhai Honda and Foxconn have presented the union with a serious problem: what should the position of the union be?...[After the strike wave] we believe that the conditions for Guangzhou to establish a new form of union are mature....The GZFTU is going to grab this opportunity and engage in bottom-up reform to gradually construct this new form of union."[49]

In October, the GZFTU issued "Advice on Strengthening Union Work and Developing the Organizational Function of the Union," which emphasized that in the course of resolving labor conflicts, "the union must be clear on its role, that it cannot be a mediator but rather only represent the side of workers."[50]

At the provincial level, Kong Xianghong was quite explicit in his criticism of the lower levels of the union, as indicated by the following statement: "The union must not be antagonistic to striking workers, but the local unions were precisely standing in an antagonistic position. So the workers said that they want to disband the union, that the union is a running dog and a traitor."[51] While hardly a radical position, Kong's solution to the problem indicated a remarkable divergence from earlier positions held by most union officials: "I think that controllable strikes are a right which should be enjoyed in order to govern a stable and harmonious society. What is harmony? Harmony is admitting conflicts and integrating the conflicts into a systematized path for resolution. Many of us Party cadres are lacking precisely the correct recognition of this problem."[52] Even the GDFTU chair Deng Weilong, not known for his prolabor politics, admitted that very few enterprise-level union chairs in Guangdong were democratically elected. Deng went on to say that one consequence of this was that "in the eyes of many workers, unions are an organization subordinate to the boss....When labor conflicts become acute, unions represent the interests of the boss."[53] The position of ACFTU leaders was considerably more conservative, as they mostly repeated old exhortations to increase unionization in private enterprises. However, they did issue a new specific call for increasing the wages of production workers.

In some ways, the central Party leadership was ahead of the ACFTU in its position. Zeng Qinghong—the former Politburo standing committee member and vice president of China, not the Guangzhou Automotive CEO—wrote a long statement on the value and necessity of expanding and strengthening collective bargaining. While he stopped short of calling for the legalization of strikes, his argument implied that it was something worth considering:

> In other countries, the strike is only the last resort and frequently is used as a threat; domestically, employees strike first and then negotiate. That is to say, they use strikes and other extreme measures to win the right to negotiate. First, the production line stops, and then they consider how to resolve the problem. This sort of preemptive coercive approach expends a large volume of social resources, giving workers a high cost to protect their rights, employers a high operating cost, and the government high costs in protecting stability. This constitutes an unfortunate lose-lose situation.[54]

Zeng was referring in quite precise terms to the costs that worker insurgency exacts on accumulation; a situation that, as he argued, requires an institutional response in the form of substantive collective bargaining. Staking out a more reform-oriented position, the other Zeng Qinghong (writing in his capacity as a National People's Congress delegate) said in a published article that in the process of resolving the Honda strikes he "deeply felt the necessity of legislating rights for economic strikes."[55] Although the Party did not immediately embrace his call for national-level legislation, the topic was no longer taboo.

Even representatives of capital began to question the sustainability of deeply authoritarian management systems. Li Chunbo, an auto industry analyst at the investment bank Citic Securities, argued that in light of the strike wave, "the government should intervene and help enterprises establish an internal system. For example, they should allow employees to have interest representatives, and allow labor and capital to have a platform for communication. There may be fears that people will use this platform to argue, but it can also be an emotional outlet and used for resolving problems. This may allow for a reduction in extreme actions."[56] The unambiguous implication of such a statement is that it was precisely the *lack* of meaningful interest representation that led to the strikes in the first place.

The moment, it seemed, was ripe for an institutional realignment. Linking the government's desire for economic "rebalancing" with union reform, Chen Weiguang said, "We believe that the conditions are mature for establishing a new form of union in Guangzhou. China's economic development is in a period of transformation, and union development should also put forth demands for transformation. Now the conditions for transformation are becoming more mature each day."[57] The Guangdong provincial government reissued a proposed set of laws entitled Regulations of Democratic Enterprise Management, which had been considered in 2008 but put aside when the economic crisis deepened that fall. The regulations included an article that allowed for collective bargaining if one-fifth of enterprise employees demanded it. Once such a decision was made, employees could democratically elect their negotiating team, albeit under the supervision of the enterprise or regional trade union. Once the request for collective bargaining was submitted to the employer, bargaining had to begin within fifteen days. In addition to these seemingly prolabor provisions, the law also explicitly forbade workers from engaging in strikes or slowdowns while negotiations were taking place. However, as the government was seeking public opinion on the draft regulations, it encountered stiff resistance from representatives of capital, most notably the Hong Kong General Chamber of Commerce. Before the regulations could be passed into law, they were once again shelved, although union officials claimed this was done out of concern for disrupting the Asian Games being held in Guangzhou in November rather than because of pressure from employers.

Even if voices calling for reform were gaining ground, it is important to note important limitations. Though Chen Weiguang argued that strikes could be legalized, he consistently affirmed his opposition to "political" strikes. Additionally, he frequently said that he could accept the "reasonable" demands of workers—suggesting therefore that there was a category of "unreasonable" demands. "Reasonable" was meant to imply that these demands could not go beyond immediate workplace issues and that the authorities retained the paternalistic authority to determine what constituted reasonableness even among strictly economic demands. Additionally, trade unionists by and large maintained the obsession with "stability maintenance" that characterized all government agencies during this period. In September of 2010, a conference was held in the Luogang district of Guangzhou, which in part was focused on how unions could effectively respond to strikes. After the conference, the district union published a book summarizing the experiences of various enterprise unions, in which it argued that "when handling spontaneous mass incidents, enterprise-level unions definitely must objectively analyze and recognize the cause and substance of the mass incident. When the conflict is just sprouting they must quickly communicate with the relevant government departments, and quickly devise a strategy to contain the incident from expanding and intensifying."[58] Even if collective bargaining was coming to be embraced by more unionists, it seemed likely that most enterprise unions would continue to be reactive to strikes.

One Year Later—Assessing the Outcomes

But while major political changes were beginning at the provincial and even the national level, what happened at Nanhai Honda in the months following the strike? Of particular importance is whether the promised wage increase actually materialized, whether union elections took place and collective bargaining mechanisms were established, and what workers' perceptions were of subsequent changes. Although there are continual reasons for pessimism, some important changes did in fact take place at Nanhai.

The announced wage increases of approximately RMB 500 for regular workers and RMB 600 for interns did materialize, thereby distinguishing this case from many others. But few workers were satisfied with the settlement, feeling that their wages were still too low (and indeed they remained lower than those of workers in the joint venture Guangzhou Honda). And with the possible exception of union reorganization (see below), the other hundred-plus demands put forth by workers had seemingly been brushed aside, something that was quite clear in this comment from one worker: "Actually, I'm not satisfied with the results of the strike. We also demanded an hour for our lunch break, and they didn't agree to this. And we women wanted a day of rest for when we're menstruating, but they didn't agree to this. Menstruating is so uncomfortable for girls, and they wouldn't agree to even one day."[59] It is thus apparent that even if management was willing to accede to some wage demands, other workplace issues continued to be ignored.

Even during the strike, some worker activists had been aware of the pressing need to build collective power, with some claiming that this was even more important than wage increases. While such a politicized point of view was not generalized among the workers, it was certainly an important current, particularly among the leaders. Although there were no open calls for an independent union during the course of the strike, it is important to recognize that this was something that had been under discussion among the organizers:

> WORKER A: I think the union issue is more important than raising wages now. Actually, at the time we considered a huge issue, whether to establish China's first union. A democratic union.
> WORKER B: If it really happened, we'd be quite proud.
> WORKER A: Really proud. When we wrote that open letter, we discussed establishing the first one in China.... There isn't anyone who really does things for us, and other unions of course are the same, or even worse. So we wanted to take the union...because at the end of the day, the union is the representative of workers.[60]

That workers did not end up calling for an independent union is of course due to their recognition that this would certainly be met with harsh repression. A less contentious framing was to call for union "reorganization," which implied holding new elections for enterprise-level officers while remaining within the structure of the ACFTU.

What, then, was the outcome with regard to the demand for union reorganization? Such an important problem was not to be resolved by the consistently procapital township union federation but rather by the provincial authorities. Kong Xianghong, who had been involved in strike resolution negotiations, took up responsibility for responding to the Nanhai strikers' demand for new union elections. Kong was personally torn between simply appointing a new enterprise chair from above and allowing the workers to hold a democratic election, as they had demanded. Indicating consultation with the central government, Kong announced shortly after returning from Beijing that a democratic election would in fact be held in Nanhai, though it was announced only in the

Hong Kong media.[61] In an unprecedented move, union leaders said that they would allow students and researchers from Sun Yat-sen University to observe the election proceedings. However, there was some subsequent backtracking. Rather than allow workers to immediately hold a general election to replace the discredited enterprise chair Wu Youhe, they permitted elections only for team (*ban*) representatives—the lowest level of the enterprise hierarchy. In each of the approximately thirty-person teams, there was a relatively democratic election, although interns were not allowed to run. Subsequent research revealed that the elections at the branch level (the unit just above the team) were subject to serious managerial manipulation (Chan and Hui 2012), and mostly white-collar employees won the elections (Liang 2012).

From the perspective of most workers, there was no significant change in the union following the strike. More than a month after the strike concluded, one worker expressed continual dissatisfaction with the enterprise union:

> If you're an employee it's impossible for you to be heard by the higher-ups. It doesn't matter who you talk to, it won't work because you can't get in a word with the office [management]. The union doesn't come down to the shop floor at all; they just collect the dues and whatever, or organize one outing a year. To be honest, I don't know even a couple people from the union. It was just that when we first came, there was a woman and she said she was from the union. So they just collect the dues each month and that's it.[62]

When a different worker who had been at the plant since 2008 was asked whether he would participate in elections for union representatives, he said, "No, I won't, because the union is just those government people, it's just for the managers."[63] Even more alarming, one of the workers who was elected as a union representative (at the team level) was completely dismissive about the possibility of union reorganization: "Anyway, they have this idea, but...the union is useless. Go ahead and change [the union officers], but I'm indifferent to whether they change or not. If they change or not, there isn't any use....I think they can't help me with anything....So if this company has a union or not, it makes no difference." This representative even said that the union was unnecessary for collective bargaining and that having a union "is just another expense."[64] But the difficult position of the workers vis-à-vis the union was revealed by one worker's frustration when asked if he still trusted the provincial union federation: "We have to trust them; even if we don't trust them we have to trust them. Who else is there to trust now? Nobody."[65]

Though workers remained suspicious and/or indifferent toward the union, by late winter 2011, it was clear that power relations at Nanhai Honda had shifted in the wake of the strike. Starting in February, the enterprise union, working with the direct supervision of Kong Xianghong from the provincial union federation, entered into collective wage negotiations with management. The democratically elected team-level representatives were able to take part, and their initial wage demand was for a monthly wage increase of RMB 800. In three rounds of negotiations that appeared not terribly dissimilar from similar processes in liberal democracies, offers and counteroffers were exchanged. Because of both the intervention of the provincial union federation and an awareness of the possibility that workers could mobilize independently, management bargained in good faith. In the end, the union got management to increase its initial offer quite significantly, and workers won a monthly increase of RMB 611.[66] It appeared that a meaningful system of collective bargaining—one in which real bargaining takes place—was beginning to take shape.

This seeming breakthrough must of course be qualified with many significant provisos. The first is that wages at Nanhai were very low when compared with those in the joint-venture assembly plants. Strikers had specifically cited the much higher wages at Guangzhou Honda as a reason for their actions, and poststrike their wages remained lower than those at the joint venture. Second, the structural power of workers at Nanhai is much more significant than that of workers in either the service industry or other manufacturing sectors. Perhaps only workers in transportation or energy exercise a comparable capacity to inflict damage on the economy by withholding their labor. A third and directly related point is that the wage increases coming from the strike resolution and from the winter 2011 round of collective bargaining were presided over by the provincial authorities. In less critical industries and in less economically developed regions of the country, the likelihood that workers would have backing from provincial authorities is slim. And finally, it is worth emphasizing again that nonwage issues were completely unaddressed in the subsequent round of collective bargaining. After the second wage raise, Kong Xianghong proclaimed that "collective wage negotiations at Nanhai Honda will become a classic case of Chinese unions for MBAs."[67] Perhaps so, but their replicability is dubious.

Insurgency and Institutionalization

What does the comparison between Ascendant and Nanhai Honda tell us about the relationship between insurgency, decommodification and incorporation, and development? Why did strikes in similar factories in neighboring cities produce dramatically different results?

To review briefly, the strike at Ascendant was, in the view of one of the participants, an "absolute and thorough" failure. Worker sentiment aside, the implementation of a piece-rate system fits my definition of commodification of labor. Management argued that this system needed to be implemented because fierce competition in the industry required an increase in productivity. Piece rates are a key strategy of capital to shift risk onto individualized workers and dissolve potential bases of solidarity and thus they increase the submission of needs satisfaction to the logic of the market. Additionally, the dramatic decrease in wages that was experienced by workers across the board meant that they had fewer financial resources at their disposal to satisfy their needs. This meant that they were increasingly compelled to sell their labor power at whatever price management offered. Increased financial reserves that come with a higher salary decrease the urgency of this situation. And finally, the manner in which the union, capital, and the state combined forces to reject any worker participation in the determination of the labor process reinforced a lack of labor-process control, a key measure of worker incorporation at the firm level. Though it would be difficult to argue that labor-process control suffered as a result of the strike (since there was none to start with), the complete rejection of workers' ability to have meaningful participation or representation was reinforced by this incident. In short, though workers rejected and rebelled against increased commodification, state, union, and capital allied in repressing this mini-countermovement. The commodity character of labor was not only maintained but *enhanced*. Unsurprisingly, a second attempted strike took place less than a year later. Through this process, workers came away with little reason to believe that the union at any level would effectively represent them in the future.

In Nanhai and other workplaces that were affected in the 2010 strike wave, the results were quite different. Workers at Nanhai won a huge wage increase (in percentage terms) in June of 2010 and gained an even larger wage hike (in absolute terms) without striking in the winter of 2011. This increase in wages enhanced the workplace security for the employees, albeit to a limited extent. Of course, two worker activists were fired without protests from the union, indicating continuing managerial authoritarianism. There was no agreement to promote temp workers into regular workers, a situation that implied ongoing precariousness for a huge portion of the workforce, as well as compromised social protection (since temporary workers do not receive social insurance). Demands related to workplace issues continue to be ignored by union and management alike, indicating that there have not been improvements in labor-process control. Thus, from an economic standpoint, workers in Nanhai were able to make gains in workplace security while other issues were left unresolved. Ascendant workers, on the other hand, experienced increased commodification.

When we look at indicators of the political incorporation of workers into the union, we see some important differences as well. At Ascendant, GZFTU and ACFTU officials intervened to try to broker a resolution to the strike. But there was no attempt made to reorganize the union or to build a sustainable organization capable of bargaining with capital. As soon as union higher-ups moved on, management reneged on the deal, and workers were subject to the very enhanced commodification that they had originally resisted. In this case, the union was acting merely to ameliorate the immediate crisis of suspended production; as soon as that issue was resolved, they returned to passive repression, which allowed managerial authority to continue unabated. Workers continue to hold the union in contempt and are unlikely to be able to resolve future grievances through the enterprise-level union organization.

Nanhai represents a somewhat different outcome in this regard. It is true that regular workers continue to think that the union is useless and that even some elected representatives are highly doubtful of its capacity to bring about important change. That being said, a number of team-level representatives were elected and subsequently were allowed to partake in collective wage negotiations. These negotiations produced a very significant wage increase for the workers. Although it is unclear what has happened with the Nanhai enterprise union since the provincial union federation withdrew from direct supervision, a precedent for continual rationalized modes of contention was nonetheless established. Depending on the specifics of how collective bargaining takes place (e.g., are rank and file involved in formulating demands, mobilized during contract fights, kept in regular contact with leadership, and able to democratically ratify contracts?), there is a possibility of increasing worker identification with the union. In the aftermath of the strike, it did not appear that workers had any greater interactions with the union or hopes that it could improve things for them in the future. Even when the provincial unions preside over substantial wage increases, such actions may be insufficient to result in the political outcome of worker incorporation. This suggests that union oligarchy may be a greater obstacle to political incorporation than it is to decommodification.

When trying to explain the different outcomes in these two incidents of worker insurgency, one could refer to the differences between elevator and auto parts manufacturing. Certainly, elevator production is less crucial to the economy than auto production, and the construction industry does not depend on just-in-time manufacturing (as is the case in the auto sector). That being said, with real estate speculation coming to be a key element in national development in China (Hsing 2009), elevators are hardly *un*important. Because of the structure of the supply chain, the stoppage at Nanhai had immediate effects for a number of other plants, something that was not true at Ascendant. And

Ascendant workers started with wages that were closer to those at Guangzhou Honda and therefore considerably higher than those of the Nanhai workers.

Without discounting the differences between auto parts and elevator manufacturing, I argue that these differences cannot account for the divergent outcomes between our two cases. Rather, between late 2007 and early 2010, two interrelated currents—one political and one economic—led the provincial and central authorities to change their approach in responding to worker insurgency. On the political level, 2008 and 2009 saw unprecedented levels of labor conflict (with the Pearl River Delta as the epicenter), in which labor arbitration courts were completely overloaded and worker insurgency frequently spilled out into the streets. As unions did little to help workers thrown out of work by the economic convulsions, conflicts between representatives and their membership were intensified by the crisis (Friedman 2012). Economically, the onset of crisis increased the central government's determination to shift away from a model of development so wedded to exports. And in Guangdong, the provincial authorities gained confidence that they occupied a less subordinate position vis-à-vis transnational capital than had previously been the case.[68] When Ascendant workers went on strike in late 2007, the impetus of provincial and central authorities was merely to avoid instability and to get workers back on the line, regardless of the outcome; but by spring of 2010, they were interested in resolving the strike *and* improving the consumption capacity of workers—even if they were still a long ways away from realizing the Fordist ideal of being able to purchase the cars they were producing. As a result, once the Nanhai strike started, the higher-level authorities decided to open up more space for insurgent workers to overcome the repressive tendencies of the local state, a tendency that was made apparent when the township union federation physically attacked the strikers. And the provincial union's continual attention to the plant is an indication that it would like to build up institutional capacity at the enterprise level that will be resilient enough to overcome the opposition of capital and the local government. Whether it will be able to do this while keeping the genie of autonomous worker power in the bottle remains unclear.

Although this book does not focus on the specific dynamics of migrant worker resistance, the topic is worth briefly addressing here. Two relatively unique features appeared in the Nanhai strike and other strikes in the summer of 2010. The most significant difference with most previous outbursts of insurgency (including those during the major factory closures in 2008–9) was that workers were on the offensive and that they won economic gains. And second, the issue of union reorganization became more central, an indication of the germination of political consciousness. But there were many ways in which older patterns of resistance continued, both of which are somewhat counterintuitive. The first is that worker protest remained highly cellular. Despite the fact that there was a major strike wave in which workers were clearly inspired by what was occurring in other factories, there was no coordination between strikers from different factories. The other is that workers' sense of fidelity to the law remained quite strong. In the course of an interview, one Nanhai striker revealed the contradictory consciousness that was prevalent among insurgent workers. On the one hand, he recognized the efficacy of legally ambiguous strikes: "That's right, [the company's internal complaint system] was not at all effective. Stopping work is effective; as soon as we stop work we see the Japanese people, as soon as we stop working the Japanese will immediately ask what the problem is." And yet just a few minutes later the same worker said, "I hope [the union] will teach us about labor laws, so in the future we'll be better able to defend our rights according to normal procedures."[69] None of the workers from Nanhai expressed discontent with the laws themselves, a remarkable confirmation of the persistence of highly legalistic modes of thought, if not always action, among workers.

A comparison between Nanhai Honda and Ascendant allows us to see the insurgent-institutional dialectic unfolding during the key years of 2007–11. Up to and during the economic crisis of 2008–9, oligarchy had blocked a substantive institutional response from the union. However, with the 2010 Nanhai strike the higher-level authorities allowed the strike to continue in order to overcome the strong state-capital alliance at the local level and to raise workers' wages. A combination of continual insurgency as well as a degree of elite support produced gains that serve as an indication of the institutional moment of the countermovement. And yet, even if material conditions improved, continual worker disillusionment and the involvement of the provincial union are indications of persistent oligarchy, a phenomenon that should cause us to consider how sustainable and exportable the compromise at Nanhai really is. Indeed, as one striker at Nanhai implied, it is not just economic but also political issues that underlie generalized worker discontent: "Of course we don't take the same position as those in power....A lot of people have the same difficulties as us, and have the same thoughts. Actually, the reason our Honda factory ended up like this [causing a strike wave], is because this is already a social problem; it's not just as simple as raising wages."[70]

The state and union at all levels maintain a steadfast dedication to the isolation of political from economic struggles; whether such a separation will continue to be feasible in practice is unclear.

CHINESE LABOR POLITICS AND THE GLOBAL ECONOMY

This book has provided an analysis of the dynamics of labor politics in China during capitalist industrialization.[1] I began with an empirical observation: during the decade after the Chinese central government began making symbolic and material moves toward class compromise in 2002, migrant worker insurgency grew rapidly. Although there are a number of factors behind this, the overarching reason is that while the country experienced an economic boom of historic proportions, migrants' relative socioeconomic position stagnated or declined. For China scholars intimately familiar with the internal tensions and conflicts within the state apparatus, this phenomenon may not have come as such a surprise. Indeed, the past three decades of reform have resulted in the emergence of a well-documented alliance between the local state and capital, a scenario that has resulted in the nonenforcement of many potentially prolabor laws and collective agreements. But if this is the case, how can we explain a situation in which labor is strong enough to force concessions from the central state but not strong enough to significantly benefit from (i.e., enforce) these concessions?

Throughout I have used the term "insurgency trap" to refer to the situation of growing worker resistance despite moves in the upper reaches of the state toward class compromise. Efforts by the central and sometimes provincial and municipal governments to improve conditions for workers have been systematically undermined by the specific political economy of China, in which the interests of the lowest levels of the state are tightly aligned with the short-term interests of capital. This sort of alliance and ensuing lawlessness are not unusual phenomena in the early stages of capitalist industrialization. During twentieth-century (second-wave) marketization, the one reliable way to break this alliance and ensure compliance was to open up space for the development of a potentially coercive countervailing force at the point of production—that is, independent worker organizations. These relatively legitimate unions channel worker unrest into legalized and rationalized modes of contention, most notably collective bargaining. But given postsocialist politics in China, independent and potentially politicized unions remain anathema to higher levels of the state, since they fear it would threaten their monopoly on power. The consequence is that the task of realizing class compromise (what I have termed the institutional moment of the countermovement) is left up to an ACFTU that was born under conditions of semicolonialism and operates according to the logic of the state. Thus far, this organization—which has always viewed national interests as more or less synonymous with working-class interests—has proved unable to realize its self-proclaimed goal of rationalizing labor relations. In short, the state has created the conditions that produced insurgency through marketization and decentralization but has also deprived itself of the one tool likely to reduce insurgency—hence the *trap*.

The delineation of insurgency trap additionally allowed me to distinguish between the insurgent and institutional moments of the countermovement. The insurgent moment consists of the sort of decentered, fractured, and ephemeral resistance to marketization that Chinese migrant workers have been engaging in for years. This resistance is spontaneous (at least from the perspective of state and capital) and seemingly apolitical in that it focuses on immediate and economic demands. But a countermovement is not complete until new class relations are institutionalized in durable organizations capable of ensuring compliance with mutually agreed-upon arrangements. During the twentieth century, this was realized in many countries through expanded social spending, granting collective bargaining and strike rights to unions, and establishing the infrastructure for a rationalized employment relations system. I have argued that the institutional moment consists of *decommodification* in the economic sphere and *incorporation* in the political. However, the movement from the insurgent to the institutional moment that we would expect based on Polanyian theory and historical precedent has been stymied in China by the fact that the ACFTU maintains a monopoly that is backed up by the coercive power of the state.

I have theorized these postsocialist labor politics as appropriated representation. This refers to a situation in which the state unilaterally grants exclusive rights of political representation of an entire class to a particular organization in the absence of substantive or formalistic delegation by membership. During China's transition to capitalism, a new class of migrant workers has emerged outside the auspices of the state. Specifying the relationship between unions and migrant workers helps us to understand why it is that labor is strong enough to win con-cessions from the state (at various levels) but is not strong enough to enforce these advances. On the one hand, dispersed worker insurgency has become a power-ful political force at the aggregate level, since it represents a strong threat to the stability of the system. This has strengthened the hand of unions in pushing for prolabor legislation, widespread increases in the minimum wage, and sectoral-level collective bargaining agreements, instances of which have been discussed in the preceding chapters. Especially given the declining fortunes of workers in the developed world, these gains seem exceptional and are certainly an indica-tion of the strength of labor. On the other hand, we find that at the particular level—on the shop floor—unions remain quite weak. The specter of generalized insurgency is a concern for the higher levels of the state but not nearly so much for a particular employer or local official. Finally, we can see that in instances in which workers build strength on the shop floor, there emerges the possibility of drawing on the general power of labor (winning support from higher levels of the union and state) in bolstering unions within the enterprise.

It is important to clearly distinguish the particular and potentially general-izable features in this story. Most important, I contend that the insurgent and institutional moments are observable in countermovements in various national and historical settings. This conceptual distinction should be useful in assessing the relationship between social rejection of marketization and institutionalized forms of politics. On the other hand, insurgency trap refers to the specific empir-ical situation in contemporary China that grows out of the combination of state socialist representative institutions and rapid capitalist development. Depending on the dynamics of the countermovement, especially with regard to the question of politics, insurgency trap is only one of a variety of possible scenarios. However, given that twentieth-century representative institutions in many countries have been unable to respond effectively to neoliberal capitalism, it is conceivable that insurgency trap–like politics could emerge in other settings. And although I have focused exclusively on labor politics in the process of capitalist industrialization, the theoretical framework developed here could be deployed in studying other forms of antimarket resistance.

There are many features of labor politics in China that will not come as a surprise; for example, unions on the shop floor are weak, workers are suspicious of union leadership, and unions work with state and capital to repress resistance. But in addition to the central theoretical concepts described above, there are several empirical advances that are worth reviewing.

First, we have seen how factors other than control by the Party constrain and/or enable union activity. These include both internal organizational and external economic factors. The historical context of the formation of the ACFTU led the union both to its alliance with (and subordination to) the Party and to the development of a particular organizational logic. This practical orientation was established at the founding of the ACFTU in the 1920s and has persisted to the present, despite instances in which individual leaders sought reform. This basic principle has been to promote the interrelated goals of ethnonational autonomy and an expansion in productive capacity (which are of course shared by the Party). Such an organizational logic developed because capitalist development in China originally took place in the context of semicolonial subjugation, a marked difference from the political situation for labor in Western countries. Thus the union has always seen the interests of the working class as a particular subset of the general interests of the nation, a formula that persists to this day. With this perspective, we can see the continuity between the ACFTU's radical past and its bureaucratized present. While the approach to advancing ethnonational autonomy and an expansion in productive capacity has changed (mass mobilization in the 1920s, the iron rice bowl in the Mao era, and marketization since the late 1970s), the basic organizational ends of action have not. Thus we can see that ACFTU practice derives not just from the external constraint of subordination to the Party but also from a particular internal logic that results in a very different orientation vis-à-vis capital and the nation from the one we find in liberal democracies. While I do not dispute the major constraints that Party control places on union activity, this research suggests that even if the ACFTU were to become formally independent, there would not be a fundamental change in its political outlook.

External economic conditions can be as crucial in determining union activity as the political constraints that have received much more attention in the literature. Through an analysis of cases that vary across space (Zhejiang vs. Guangdong) and time (Ascendant vs. Honda strikes), we see that different models of development and the dynamics of the global economy have a profound impact on the possibilities for organizational change and collective bargaining. Based on an analysis of two regional political economies in China, I have highlighted how a variety of markedly different systems of labor relations may emerge within a single country.

I have presented new material on ACFTU unions that reveals previously understudied trends and have documented the emergence of sectoral unions in China, an organizational form that will be an increasingly central feature of Chinese trade unionism and industrial relations in the future. By linking developments in sectoral-level collective bargaining to regional political economy, I have shown that the success of such efforts will be geographically uneven. It seems that a European-style region-based approach to collective bargaining will be more likely in Zhejiang than in Guangdong, while the latter appears headed toward a more American-style firm-based approach.[2] Perhaps most important, the glowing terms in which trade union officials around the country refer to the perceived success of Zhejiang sectoral unions reveals a fundamental feature of the organizational logic of contemporary ACFTU unions. While new forms of organization and bargaining are proliferating around the country, the old problem of weak enterprise unions emerges as an issue here as well. In any event, sectoral-level unionization and bargaining are sure to remain high on the agenda of Chinese unionists, and these organizational forms are likely to shape the contours of worker resistance in the future.

The organizational innovation of sectoral unions is a response to worker resistance in general, but this book also documents union responses to a number of specific incidents of strikes. I concur with existing literature that unions are nearly without exception reactive to strikes and other forms of bottom-up activism, even in the least likely cases (such as the Guangdong Hotel). However, the comparison in chapter 5 reveals that changing dynamics in political economy imply that, at least in certain industries and in certain regions, unions may begin to leverage autonomous worker resistance in pushing for increased wages and benefits.

A more fundamental argument is that contestation over representation is and will continue to be a defining characteristic of worker movements in China. Representation in all political contexts "connects and cuts, attaches and separates" (Hardt & Negri 2004, 241) as representatives are by virtue of their position related to *and* distinct from their constituents. But conditions of appropriated representation lock representers and represented together in an uncomfortable relationship in which the "attachment" is unilateral and the "separation" profound. While emphasizing that there is no normative assessment involved in the term, I argue that the ACFTU *does* represent the working class if only because the authoritarian state demands it, a scenario that has important practical consequences. Thus, worker insurgency results in organizational responses from the union, the best examples of which are the experiments with sectoral unions. At the same time, shifts in union activity shape the dynamics of worker resistance. This was eminently apparent in the case of the Honda strikes, where workers initially started with simple wage demands but in responding to union repression and inactivity quickly came to insist on union reorganization. Subsequently, elections of limited scope took place that allowed some members of the rank and file to participate in two rounds of collective bargaining. Finally, one of the consequences of the Honda strikes has been a rhetorical shift in which it is now permissible to openly discuss legalization of strikes. If enacted, such legislation will certainly yet again alter the dynamics of worker resistance. The dialogue between insurgency and institutionalization within the representative relationship is apparent enough.

And yet, we have also seen that unions respond positively to worker strikes only in exceptional situations. The tension between workers and unions, between represented and representer, has already become and will continue to be a key site of class struggle. Ching Kwan Lee's argument that legal reforms are both shaped by and end up shaping worker struggles increasingly applies to organizational reforms within the union. Again, this is quite different from twentieth-century experiences of labor politics during industrialization, during which time unions and the working class developed relatively in tandem.[3] Given conditions of appropriated representation and the much greater repressive capacity of the state, migrant workers in China are forced to fight traditional battles against employers but also must confront and transform their own unions to a much greater degree than was true previously. Whether or not dispersed worker insurgency will create enough political pressure to force changes in the union sufficient to reduce unrest is unclear; however, struggles over representation—*political* struggles—have emerged and are likely to increase.

With this background in mind, let us now consider (1) the ways in which China's labor politics and geography of class conflict are exceptional when compared with those of other countries in East Asia and the postsocialist world; and (2) the implications of Chinese labor politics for the global political economy.

China's Labor Politics in Comparative Perspective

As Chinese government and union officials are always quick to remind outsiders, China is special—even exceptional (Alden and Large 2011; Rozman 2012). When coming from the state, this is either a totally banal statement or a self-essentializing ideological intervention meant to defuse external criticism. But even if every country in the world is obviously different from every other country, it is worth considering the particular ways in which China is different, and specifically how its labor politics are likely to play out differently than those in other countries that have undergone capitalist industrialization in the relatively recent past. In particular, the experiences of Taiwan and South Korea are worth noting as both are relative newcomers to capitalist industrialization, pursued export-led development, had some variety of a developmental state, and most important, had monopolistic state-controlled union federations (at least up until democratization in the late 1980s). Despite these similarities, workers in China are more unruly, the official union is more tightly controlled, and the state's repressive tendencies and capacity are greater than was the case in South Korea or Taiwan. Additionally, Vietnam is an obvious case for comparison given its postsocialist legacy, export-oriented development, and high levels of worker unrest.

The similarities in union organization between martial law–era Taiwan (which lasted until 1987) and the PRC are striking. The "semi-Leninist" (Cheng 1989) China Federation of Labor (CFL) was "patronized, financed and staffed by the KMT and, as a result, labor unions became mere extensions of state rule" (Ho 2006). These unions penetrated deeply into workers' everyday lives to assert political control (Ho 2010) and to encourage production and defuse conflict (Chang and Bain 2006,101; Li and Zhao 2008). For a variety of reasons (including but not limited to conservative unions), Taiwan experienced great stability in employment relations until martial law ended in 1987 (Huang 2010, 193), and the country had no real labor movement prior to the mid-late 1980s (Li Jianchang 1991; Xiao 1989). As Taiwanese workers had often understood their grievances through an ethnic rather than class-based lens (i.e., that KMT rule and Chinese chauvinism, rather than exploitative practices by capital, were the issue), they came to have a strong affinity for the pro-independence Democratic Progressive Party (DPP). When the DPP was allowed to begin contesting local elections in the mid-1980s, the independent labor movement was largely channeled into electoral politics, and worker militancy failed to develop (Y. Lee 2011).

Although the relationship between the official Federation of Korean Trade Unions (FKTU) and the regime was never as strong as the CFL-KMT bond (Kong 2005,168), some similar political dynamics held with unions in South Korea. After the coup in 1961, the labor movement was "reorganized" into the renamed FKTU with the aim of enhancing control by the military regime and depoliticizing labor (No 2007). Labor laws enhanced the monopoly of the union federation by restricting most union activities to the enterprise level and by forcing new unions to register through the FKTU (Yi 2005). But in contrast to government-controlled unions in Taiwan and China, unions in South Korea were more likely to be dominated by management—in part because the largest enterprises were not SOEs but rather the private *chaebol* (conglomerates).

Despite the infamous repressive practices of the South Korean Central Intelligence Agency (widely expanded in 1971), South Korean workers were not nearly so deferential as their counterparts elsewhere in twentieth-century East Asia (Kwon and O'donnell 1999, 275; Koo 2001). By the late 1970s, independent (and extralegal) unions were appearing around the country, and the labor movement had constructed strong linkages to other social-movement sectors. As a result, the South Korean state faced a much greater challenge from the working class than was the case in Taiwan. Despite employing a mix of repression and accommodation, neither Park Chung-hee (in office until his assassination in 1979) nor his successor, Chun Doo-hwan, successfully stamped out autonomous and often highly militant worker unrest. Even though the "democratic unions" (*min-ju no-jo*) were not granted official recognition, by the 1980s, "a variety of quasi-labor organizations began to weave themselves around and through the official structures of unionism" (Ogle 1990, 108).

Without a doubt, the processes of democratization that were initiated in Taiwan and South Korea in the late 1980s dramatically changed labor politics in each place. Independent union federations gained official recognition, and political controls were loosened. Each country experienced a major uptick in worker resistance in 1987 (with much greater scope and militancy in South Korea), but labor as a political actor has remained relatively weak in both places. Given that transition to liberal democracy is quite unlikely in today's China, it is not worth investigating these dynamics closely.

On the other hand, when we turn to the case of contemporary Vietnam, it becomes apparent that not all Leninist party-states are created equal. Indeed, there is scholarly consensus that the Vietnamese state takes a much more relaxed attitude toward worker organizing than does China and is much more likely to intervene on behalf of striking workers (A. Chan 2011a). This is not to say that the state is willing to permit independent unionism, as the Vietnam General Confederation of Labor (VGCL) maintains a monopoly on worker representation. Given the administrative complexity and broad array of conditions that must be met in order to strike legally (Tran and Coleman 2010), strikes in Vietnam are essentially without exception wildcat. Insurgent workers in Vietnam have shown increasing sophistication and audacity in organizing strikes over the past fifteen years, as indicated by massive and recurrent strike waves in the country's export processing zones (A. Chan 2011a; A. N. Tran 2007a). And foreign managers complain bitterly that the local state tends to side with workers when such disputes arise. As Simon Clarke (2006) has noted, "A remarkable feature of strikes in Vietnam is that there have been no reports of police action against strikers or strike leaders, either during or after a strike, even when the strikers block the public highway" (355). Additionally, more aggressive and consistently prolabor media have a major impact on the development of labor conflicts (A. N. Tran 2007b). Despite this relative permissiveness toward worker insurgency, the workers regard the VGCL as illegitimate, and a system of rationalized labor relations seems as far off as it does in China (Clarke, Lee, and Chi 2007; Pringle and Clarke 2011). The possibility for insurgency trap–style labor politics in Vietnam appears strong.

Martial law–era Taiwan and South Korea under the military dictatorships were hardly friendly to labor, nor is Vietnam under Communist Party rule, but the Chinese state is much more committed to nipping any independent organization in the bud. Whereas in South Korea, "authoritarian suppression of the workers had been interrupted periodically by intervals of relative leniency" (Chu 1998, 193), the Chinese state has been quite consistent in ensuring that durable worker organizations cannot persist.[4] In Taiwan, the KMT was similarly vigilant about worker organizations, but by the 1980s it was allowing for political opposition to emerge through free elections at the local level. And in Vietnam, underground labor leaders have played an important role in organizing strikes that are much more likely to be met with tolerance by the state. Even if the state still refuses to grant recognition to independent unions, the repressive apparatus is much less likely to be deployed than is the case in China. Whether it is a question of intention or mere capacity, Chinese workers have much less independent political space than their counterparts in neighboring countries. While this may seem like a major advantage for capital, it also means that the Chinese state has fewer means of co-optation.

Finally, it is important to note the distinct geography of labor-capital conflict in South Korea and Taiwan (Vietnam is a somewhat different issue given its stage of development). Just as the working class in each country was enjoying new freedoms of association and swelling union membership, a new threat emerged, one more tenacious and inexorable than state repression: outsourcing. It would be an overstatement to say that capital was self-consciously fleeing freedom of association, as it was likely rising labor costs that were the primary push factor. And yet both countries began rapidly losing manufacturing jobs, especially in labor-intensive industries, beginning in the 1990s. As can be seen clearly in figure 12, the portion of the workforce employed in manufacturing peaked in Taiwan in 1987 and in South Korea in 1989, after which both suffered significant declines. This is a particularly important problem for unions, as manufacturing has traditionally been the greatest source of labor's power. Unsurprisingly, this process resulted in a concomitant decline in union membership. Union density peaked at 18.75 percent in 1989 in South Korea and 53.21 percent[5] in 1994 in Taiwan (Kuruvilla, Das, Kwon, and Kwon 2002, 432) and has declined since. While the fixed costs associated with certain industries—notably heavy industry in South Korea—place restrictions on capital mobility, even some of these seemingly stable enterprises have come under attack. This was made quite clear when 2009's militant but ultimately unsuccessful occupation at the Ssangyong Motor Company failed to prevent mass layoffs. It is clear enough that nationally based labor movements were unable to adjust to the major structural shifts taking place in the global economy, chief among which was the increased openness of China to foreign investment. This opening provided East Asian capital with abundant exploitable resources and a welcoming political environment.

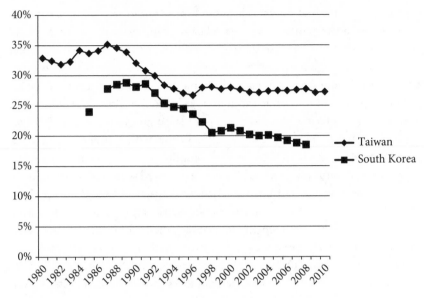

FIGURE 12. Percentage of workforce in manufacturing.
Source: Taiwan Statistical Data Book, Council of Economic Planning and Development, Republic of China, 2002, 2009, 2011; KLI Labor Statistics 2012 (Seoul: Korean Labor Institute).

In other words, in the 1990s and 2000s capital exercised its ability to relocate sites of accumulation and their attendant crises to areas with more favorable political, economic, and social conditions—the "spatial fix" (Harvey 1982; Herod 2001; Silver 2003). Relocation of production is the most effective weapon in capital's arsenal for crushing politicized and/or well-compensated working classes. Though we must of course recognize the varying mobility of different forms of capital, it is clear that increased labor costs and militancy (the former is particularly true in Taiwan, while both appeared in South Korea) were primary drivers of deindustrialization in the Asian Tigers during the 1990s and 2000s. The crucial point here is that when capital relocates abroad, the barriers put in place by the nation-state are generally insurmountable for labor. As Harvey (1982) has noted, "The unrestrained mobility of capital is therefore more appropriate to accumulation than the unrestrained mobility of labour—which may account for the twentieth century trend to restrict the mobility of labour power relative to that of capital" (412). Enhanced asymmetry in spatial mobility between labor and capital is a primary feature of neoliberal capitalism, and this advantage was exploited fully as manufacturers fled the Asian Tigers—frequently ending up in China and increasingly in Vietnam.

But the social geography of capitalism is quite different in China than in small countries like Taiwan, South Korea, or Vietnam. As is well known, the coastal areas of China were the first parts of the country to be opened up to outside investment (Broadman and Sun 1997), and most of this capital came from places in East Asia such as Hong Kong, Taiwan, and South Korea (Gallagher 2005; Hsing 1998). Investment was lured by low production costs, a lawless regulatory environment, highly repressed labor, and relatively good infrastructure. But after a generation of unimaginably favorable conditions, a number of push factors have emerged—especially worker militancy, labor shortages, increased costs of labor and land, and greater efforts at legal regulation.[6] As a result, industrial capital has been looking to either diversify or completely relocate from established manufacturing hubs in coastal China. While some of this capital is fleeing overseas to places in Southeast Asia or elsewhere, much of it is relocating to China's interior. The 2011 percentage growth rates of the interior provinces of Hunan, Henan, Chongqing, and Sichuan were respectively 14, 11.6, 16.5, and 14.7, far outpacing those of traditional powerhouses like Guangdong (10%), Zhejiang (9%), Jiangsu (9.2%), and Shanghai (8%).[7] And indeed, there are the same pull factors in China's interior that once lured capital from abroad to the country's coastal regions: low cost and abundant labor (or at least the perception thereof), cheap land, access to new consumer markets, and local governments much more interested in attracting investors than in strictly implementing laws or collective bargaining agreements.

The salient point is that there is an important difference when capital relocation takes place between countries rather than within. South Korean and Taiwanese workers could not possibly "follow" capital to China, especially if they wanted to bring their unions with them. But insurgent migrant workers can move about within China—and in a totally literal sense, they will be more at home in the interior than they have been in coastal regions. Part of the reason that worker insurgency has remained so fragmented and ephemeral is that migrants remain tied to the countryside and are unable to establish durable communities in coastal cities, in large part because of the *hukou* system (F. Wang 2005, 2010) but also because of social discrimination (Zhan 2011). Migrants will have an easier time getting urban *hukou* in the interior and will be much closer to their rural hometowns. This raises the possibility—though it remains speculative at this point—that these workers will cease to be migrants and will have greater ability to embed themselves in a stable community. It then becomes possible to imagine how workplace struggles could be linked up to community-based (reproductive) struggles over public education, social services, and usage of public space. In addition to these greater social resources that could be brought to bear in labor struggles, former migrants will bring their experience with labor conflict from the coast back home with them. Finally, if the state begins to grant enhanced labor protections such as collective bargaining or strike rights in regions with ongoing labor unrest, it will be hard to prevent workers in other areas from demanding the same treatment. In this sense, China is quite distinct from South Korea, Taiwan, and Vietnam (and other small countries) in that capital can employ the spatial fix within rather than across national borders. Important social and political consequences follow from this.

While Russia and other postsocialist countries in Eastern Europe may seem like an obvious point of comparison, they differ from China remarkably in certain key characteristics. There is clear evidence that many of the Leninist union organizations in the former Soviet Union have remained weak and have therefore continually sought alliances with the state and/or management (Crowley and Ost 2001; Crowley 2004; Pringle and Clarke 2011), and in this sense there appear to be strong parallels with the situation in China. However, as noted in chapter 1, there are two fundamental differences that confound this line of comparison. First, former state socialist countries in Eastern Europe are today much more pluralistic than China, even in relatively closed environments such as Russia. Second and more fundamental is that China is undergoing the shift from an agricultural to an industrial society, and it is economically ascendant. Additionally, Eastern European countries have not pursued export-led development, and so their relationship to the global economy is fundamentally different. Such conditions imply that authoritarian East Asian states in their period of industrial takeoff make for a much stronger comparison.

It is now clear how political and geographic space in China produces a distinct form of labor politics during the process of capitalist industrialization. It is true in a general sense that "where capital goes, conflict goes" (Silver 2003, 41), but such a general formulation must be specified in order to account for particular social and political conditions. This research has been an attempt to analyze instantiations of the general antagonism between labor and capital within the peculiar but immensely important particularity that is contemporary China. Now let us consider how Chinese labor politics might develop in the future and what the consequences will be for global capitalism.

Chinese Labor Politics and the Future of Global Capitalism

As early as 1999 Giovanni Arrighi and Beverly Silver (1999) argued that the core of the capitalist world system was shifting away from United States and toward East Asia—China in particular (286–89). With the United States accumulating a massive current account deficit (due in large part to trade with China) and descending into expensive military quagmires overseas, the passage of the "Belle Époque" of American hegemony became increasingly evident in the first decade of the twenty-first century (Silver and Arrighi 2003). But if a China-centered global economy is becoming more of a reality every year, the consequences of such a massive shift are not immediately evident:

> How drastic and painful the transformation is going to be—and, indeed, whether it will eventually result in a commonwealth rather than in the mutual destruction of the world's civilizations—ultimately depends on two conditions. It depends, first, on how intelligently the main centers of Western civilization can adjust to a less exalted status, and, second, on whether the main centers of the reemerging China-centered civilization can collectively rise up to the task of providing system-level solutions to the system-level problems left behind by U.S. hegemony. (Arrighi and Silver, 1999, 286)

There is of course debate about what precisely will result from China's rise. Arrighi, while adding several conditions and provisos, maintains a great deal of optimism about the possibilities that an emergent China holds for the stability and fairness of the world economy (Arrighi 2007). Minqi Li is far less sanguine, as is evident in the title of his book, *The Rise of China and the Demise of the Capitalist World Economy* (2009). In addition to concerns about ecological catastrophe (M. Li 2007), he fears both internal social chaos and the possibility of downward wage convergence (M. Li 2005, 436). Both Li and Ho-fung Hung (2008) express concern that high levels of investment and reliance on foreign consumer markets leave China vulnerable to severe economic shocks.

This then brings us back to Arrighi and Silver's second condition for avoiding severe upheaval in the world system: the necessity for a "system-level solution" from the "China-centered civilization." The systemic problem to be addressed is precisely the issue of underconsumption in China that Hung identified even before the intensification of the financial crisis in 2008—and a key feature of the much-discussed "rebalancing" (Blanchard and Giavazzi 2006; Lardy 2007). It is here that the specifics of labor politics become of central importance. The introduction of some form of class compromise will be necessary to reduce China's high savings rates and to develop a new class of domestic consumers. Ongoing economic troubles in the world's developed countries only enhance this imperative. But making such a transition is of course a *political* problem, one that will likely require the incorporation of the working class. In my terms, the institutional moment represents a potential solution to one of the central system-level problems.

A New Class Compromise?

The problem as defined above of course echoes the situation found during an earlier systemic crisis—the Great Depression. Keynesianism and the construction of the welfare state were primary means for addressing this crisis, steps that allowed for the brief flowering of American hegemony.[8] In the West, social democratic and other nonrevolutionary leftist parties allied with unions in demanding a greater share of profits from capital, which in the postwar era led to three decades of relatively high growth and a reduction in inequality. But contemporary China is of course very different from Euro-American countries of the mid-twentieth century, as is the global context. This book has addressed the question, Under what conditions has the Chinese state attempted to realize the sort of class compromise and decommodification (that we would expect from Polanyian theory) through the means of a highly oligarchic trade union structure? And there are many reasons to believe that such a program will continue to encounter severe obstacles.

The first reason, which has been an empirical focus of this book, is the crisis of representation within the ACFTU. We have seen that a particular organizational logic has rendered unions in the workplace—the space where formal laws either have material effects or dissipate into the ether—frequently incapable of enforcing their own agreements. Model trade unions in Guangzhou and sectoral unions in Zhejiang bearing the blessing of the premier have by and large failed to incorporate or decommodify labor (even if the formal mechanisms seem to be in place, as in Zhejiang). In enterprises rocked by militant and autonomously organized strikes during the spring and summer of 2010, we see that workers are able to make material gains, but it is unclear to what extent union organizations will be forced to engage in substantive reform. Certainly, postsocialist labor politics continue to present a challenge to institutionalizing class compromise.

A second and related challenge to the realization of class compromise in China is the lack of a developed radical political agenda. Particularly in many of the European cases, the threat of social revolution appeared quite real in the early twentieth century. The potential for the elimination of private property was of course quite unsettling for capitalists (and their allies in the state), and so labor unions and parties were able to exact relatively high concessions in exchange for abandoning a revolutionary agenda. It is important to recall that class compromise, as traditionally conceived, implies concessions by *both* labor and capital. Labor agrees to "trade-off the abolition of private property of the means of production" (Przeworski 1980, 56) in order to secure lower rates of exploitation by capital and expanded social protections from the state. Additionally, labor consents to efficiency-producing arrangements in production so as to maintain the profitability of the firm. However, worker activism in China is not a traditional social movement but an *insurgency;* thus few if any formal political demands (e.g., abolishment of private property) are articulated. While particular instances of worker insurgency can result in heavy losses for capital, there is no credible threat to capital at the class level. Without a unified effort from various levels of the state, something that has yet to emerge, it is difficult to imagine how capital could collectively agree to some sort of compromise.

Related to this last point is a third difficulty, namely, the problem of the strong alliance between the local state and capital and the resulting nonenforcement of relevant labor laws. This is of crucial importance because in order for a class compromise to work, the "state must enforce the compliance of both classes with the terms of each compromise and protect those segments of each class that enter into a compromise from non-cooperative behavior of their fellow class members" (Przeworski, 1985, 202). Even in instances when relatively decommodifying legislation or collective bargaining agreements are enacted, implementation remains a severe problem. The mutual lack of trust resulting from such a situation was amply apparent with the sectoral unions in Zhejiang. Even when management follows the letter of the law, the spirit of the law is often violated. This has been most evident in the large increase of precarious "dispatch" labor since the enactment of the 2008 Labor Contract Law, something that local governments have in many cases actively encouraged. Given the significant individual incentives for violating potentially decommodifying legislation, it will be difficult to enforce a substantive compromise at the class level until the state can act as a credible broker.

Finally, there is the extent to which China is deeply integrated into the global economy. International trade and investment are not new phenomena and were certainly quite prevalent in the period of British hegemony in the nineteenth and early twentieth centuries. But given China's heavy reliance on exports and foreign investment, not to mention WTO agreements, the imposition of institutionalized decommodification at the national level in today's world would be tenuous at best. As argued by Peter Evans (2000, 2005), it is likely that a contemporary countermovement against the market must be as globalized as capital. Although globalization certainly presents possibilities for greater transnational labor solidarity, thus far the relationship between the ACFTU and foreign unions has hardly developed beyond rhetorical overtures (David-Friedman 2009; Luce and Bonacich 2009; Umney 2011). Given the nationalist orientation of the ACFTU, it is almost impossible to imagine a situation that would cause Chinese unions to attempt to forge deep connections with foreign actors to challenge global capital. Although insurgent workers occupy a key position in a variety of global supply chains, their resistance has not scaled up to the regional level, to say nothing of the national or transnational level. At present, the globalized nature of the contemporary economy presents challenges to institutionalizing the countermovement at the national level, a potentially major stumbling block, given strong nationalist currents in China.

If a class compromise of the type that industrialized nations pursued in the twentieth century seems unlikely in contemporary China, that does not mean that certain segments of the state won't continue to try. The central government and certain lower levels of the state (particularly in highly industrialized areas with lots of labor conflict) seem to have become conscious of the "reverse J" problem described by Eric Olin Wright (2000). That is to say, the interests of capital are, in certain regions and sectors, being negatively affected by the *lack* of associational power for Chinese workers. An increase in organized worker power could have the effect of coordinating collective action on the part of capital, thereby leading to rationalization and efficiency gains. In other words, "[capital] must find ways to have its own needs put forward by its enemies" (Tronti 1971).[9]

The failure to secure substantive compromise in China has meant that worker insurgency continues and the system-level problem persists. It is likely that labor conflict will not continue to grow at the same fantastic pace of the first decade of the twenty-first century—if only because it is already so high. But it appears that insurgency will not decline significantly in the short to mid term, and it is therefore likely that the state and union will continue to experiment with institutional responses. Since only the formal outlines of compromise have begun to emerge, what might we reasonably expect from the ongoing dialectic between the insurgent and institutional moments of the countermovement?

Future Developments

I have postulated that marketization in China has resulted in the development of an insurgency trap. Divergent interests between the central and local state, combined with the center's categorical ban on independent labor organization, have produced a situation in which worker insurgency has remained at very high levels. While the state may be trapped at present, the situation is not static. How might things develop in the future, and what are the implications for global capitalism?

The first possibility is the realization of *benevolent technocracy,* currently the highest aspiration of the central state. Here the state reduces unrest through decommodifying legislation and top-down imposed collective contracts while continuing to politically exclude the working class. Under such a system, laws and regulations are determined by elite experts and faithfully carried out by a professionalized and highly rationalized bureaucracy. The state is then able to act as a neutral broker between labor and capital, making material concessions to the former while ensuring property rights for the latter. Labor unrest falls while productivity rises, and authoritarian politics are able to persist. As I have indicated throughout, this scenario is unlikely to emerge, as unions are presently unable to ensure basic legal compliance in China's workplaces. Whereas politicization resulted in social instability during the Cultural Revolution, today depoliticization ensures ongoing insurgency. Nonetheless, it is likely that over the short to mid term the central state will continue legislative efforts to improve workers' economic conditions while using coercion to ensure an atomized and depoliticized working class.

The next possible scenario is *stalemate,* or the persistence of insurgency trap. The state maintains its ban on independent unions, workplaces remain in a legal vacuum dependent on highly commodified labor, and worker insurgency remains high but stabilizes. This insurgency remains highly cellular and therefore does not threaten basic social order. As a result, workers do not exact a high enough cost on the state and capital to force reforms, and the basic setup remains unaltered. High levels of economic and social polarization persist, and China fails to develop significant domestic consumer markets. Over time, such a stalemate could sap the strength of economic growth if capital is not forced into actively pursuing gains in efficiency. Elites strive to maintain existing political arrangements in order to preserve their privilege, thereby preventing the sort of realignments necessary to reestablish rapid accumulation on a more sound sociopolitical foundation. Given persistent economic malaise in Europe, the United States, and Japan and few signs of sustainable capitalist dynamism in other developing countries, this increases the likelihood of ongoing stagnation, social resistance, and repression at the global level.

The third option is *reform.* In this scenario, insurgency strengthens the segments of the state that are committed to compromise, and they then promote the development of associational power for the working class. The existing union structure is deeply reformed, and/or new and independent unions are legalized. Such organizations would have to be much more democratic than the ACFTU and would have the potential to confront state and capital over issues of economic, and potentially political, concern to their members. These relatively autonomous unions then play a key role in forcing compromise from their own constituency (something the ACFTU has not been capable of) while simultaneously wielding potentially coercive power vis-à-vis employers in the form of a credible strike threat. This may push the state to force employers to participate in interest-aggregating business associations, thereby increasing the possibility of regional or national-level collective bargaining. Additionally, it is possible to imagine such unions pushing for greater citizenship rights for migrant workers and an expansion of formal democracy,[10] although this scenario would *not* result in social revolution.[11]

Currently the state is unwilling to make the political compromises necessary for substantial reform. The central government remains deeply anxious about social instability, and local governments are in most instances too concerned with short-term accumulation.[12] But if worker insurgency exacts a high enough economic and political toll over the mid to long term, this may change and the central government could need the help of relatively independent but potentially co-optable trade unions. Additionally, local governments may come to see that expanded associational power for workers could help with the long-term development and stability of particular industries, as has already been the case in some places. They will need unions with higher legitimacy among workers (i.e., incorporation of labor) to enforce rationalizing and efficiency-producing reforms. Additionally, inability to expand domestic consumption may come to seriously hamper China's economic development. In short, reform implies a Keynesian-style solution to the problem and may hold the greatest promise for the long-term stability of capitalist development in China.[13] Such a compromise will likely be necessary to address the system-level problem identified above.

A final scenario is that of *expanded radicalism* that results in revolutionary outcomes. Here the state at various levels digs in its heels and continues to repress any attempts at substantive union reform, while worker insurgency continues to expand in scope, intensity, militancy, and organization. Strikes and various forms of direct action are directed against capital but increasingly against the state as well as labor struggles become explicitly political. In other words, the cell walls separating sparks of insurgency are eventually worn down, and horizontally organized tissues of resistance begin to take form.[14] Worker organization develops outside the legal auspices of the state and therefore in opposition to it.[15] From this perspective, insurgency trap is not a limit on proletarian politics but a facilitating factor in that the state has deprived itself of the institutional machinery to co-opt worker radicalism. I do not wish to make any wildly speculative remarks on what sorts of politics might characterize such a movement. But one could imagine a variety of forms of working-class radicalism that would seriously destabilize current power arrangements, potentially leading to social breakdown or liberatory outcomes. Given China's centrality in a variety of transnational supply chains, the impact on global capitalism would be immediate and profound.

Might China be on the precipice of a long period of stagnation and social decay? Or will we look back at this moment a generation from now as the beginning of a movement toward a somewhat more equitable and embedded form of capitalism? Could labor politics become sufficiently radicalized that the working class could break free of the domination of both state and capital?

Regardless of one's political orientation, there is now general consensus that the model of growth predicated on wage repression in China and an expansion of debt-financed spending in the North is outmoded. The central government hopes that domestic consumption, urbanization, and development in the interior of the country will fuel another generation of high-speed growth. But fundamental social and political reforms will be needed in order for these aspirations to be realized, and such changes will require overcoming powerful interests that have benefited immensely from current arrangements. The central state remains terrified of the singularity of proletarian politics, and yet unarticulated insurgency is already exacting high economic and political costs. The dynamics of insurgency trap and the politics of labor representation will be decisive for the future of China—and for the future of global capitalism.

Notes

CHAPTER 1

1. June 16, 2011. "Chaozhou guxiang shijian: Laodong baohu piruan, dagongzhe kao tongxianghui 'chutou'" [Chaozhou Guxiang incident: Poor labor protection, migrant workers depend on hometown association to 'come forward'], *Dongfang Zaobao,* June 16, 2011.

2. Ibid.

3. See the white paper "China's Employment Situation and Policies" from the State Council's information office, www.chinadaily.com.cn/english/doc/2004–04/26/content_326356.htm.

4. The Labor Contract Law has had contradictory effects with regard to decommodification. On the one hand, its formal parameters seek to restrict conditions under which employees can be dismissed—a clear move toward decommodification. But practically speaking, it has triggered a massive increase in "dispatch" labor, a highly precarious form of subcontracting.

5. I'm referring here to the Tonggang steel incident and the Liu Hanhuang case.

6. Chris Buckley, "China Domestic Security Spending Rises to $111 Billion," Reuters, March 5, 2012.

7. A separate but related question is, Why in this period has inequality also continued to grow rapidly? Although I do not aim to explain inequality here, the inability to enforce prolabor legislation is certainly a major factor.

8. While there are some areas of overlap with Minxin Pei's (2006) "trapped transition," I should be clear that an insurgency trap is actually quite different. Pei argues that China has failed to transition to a fully marketized and liberal-democratic society and that this "trap" may inhibit future growth potentials. He believes that this stalled transition is due to the particular, contingent decision making of high-level leaders. An insurgency trap, by contrast, develops because of the structure of the state, model of accumulation, and in particular, modes of class domination. Pei argues that the stalled transition will have negative effects for Chinese society as a whole, while I draw attention to the classed nature of domination and unequal gains from growth.

9. "Quanwei baogao cheng 'laowu paiqian' da 6000 wan ren quanzong jianyi xiugai 'laodong hetongfa'" [Authoritative report claims 'labor dispatch' has reached 60 million people, ACFTU suggests revisions to Labor Contract Law], *Jingji Guancha bao,* February 25, 2011, http://www.eeo.com.cn/eeo/jjgcb/2011/02/28/194384.shtml.

10. Lee is not the only one to have written about "rule of law" and labor politics in China, but she has produced the most important analysis in terms of the consequences for collective action. For other works on labor law see J. Chan 2009; F. Chen 2004, 2009; Cooney, Biddulph, Li, and Zhu 2007; Cooney, Biddulph, and Zhu 2013; Keith 1991, 1994; Wang, Appelbaum, Degiuli, and Lichtenstein 2009.

11. Caraway (2009) argues that individual labor rights are a strong suit of East Asian countries and that protection of such rights in the region is somewhat stronger than the world average (156).

12. Xinhua, http://news.xinhuanet.com/english/indepth/2013–03/27/c_132266201. htm.

13. This is not to discount major worker struggles under state socialism. Today's labor unrest is much more similar to worker unrest in other capitalist countries than it is to earlier examples under socialism.

14. *The World Factbook,* https://www.cia.gov/library/publications/the-world-factbook/ rankorder/2078rank.html.

15. The World Bank, http://data.worldbank.org/indicator/BX.KLT.DINV.CD.WD.

16. Block (2003) argues for a much more contingent conceptualization of the countermovement, while Silver and Arrighi (2003) see more or less predetermined pendular swings between commodification and decommodification. But perhaps such views are not totally contradictory, as I view the countermovement as a general tendency (identifiable only from a historical and system-level analysis), the specifics of which are highly varied and contingent. Additionally I do not see any necessary endpoint toward which countermovements inexorably proceed.

17. For an analysis of the passage of the National Labor Relations Act in the United States that does *not* fit this description but rather delves into the nuanced relationship between worker insurgency and decommodification, see Goldfield 1989, 1257–82.

18. Miguel Abensour (2011 [1997]) has also proposed an insurgency/institutionalization dyad. But for Abensour, insurgent democracy is institutionalized *against* rather than *by* or *within* the state. Though from a normative position I am more inclined toward his formulation, it seems unlikely at present that Chinese worker insurgency will produce the sort of institutionalization he has in mind: "a political relationship…a vital, intense, non-hierarchical political bond distinct from order, [a setup that would] preserve the people's ability to act and to prevent the bonds among citizens from degenerating once again into a restrictive, vertical, hierarchical, top-down order" (xxiv–xxv).

19. As Burstein and Linton (2002) argue, social movement organizations, "define public problems, propose solutions, aggregate citizens' policy preferences, mobilize voters, make demands of elected officials, communicate information about government action to their supporters and the larger public, and make relatively coherent legislative action possible" (381–82). This suggests that "relatively coherent legislative action" is more difficult where these organizations don't exist, such as in contemporary China.

20. C. K. Lee (2007) has referred to these conditions as "decentralized legal authoritarianism."

21. Lee follows Beverly Silver (2003) in making a distinction between "Polanyi-type" and "Marx-type" worker unrest. The former refers to resistance to the incursion of the market by a previously protected working class, while the latter describes worker unrest in the process of class formation. Lee therefore characterizes the migrant worker insurgency that I am describing here as Marx-type rather than Polanyi-type unrest. Why, then, am I relying on Polanyi rather than Marx? While I understand the utility of distinguishing between the resistance that attends the unmaking and the making of a working class, respectively, I do not see the utility in restricting the Polanyian framework to defensive struggles. After all, Polanyi discussed at length the development of social unrest in the West during the late nineteenth and early twentieth century, at which point these working classes were certainly not being unmade. As I've already mentioned, the New Deal was his key example of a successful countermovement. But the more fundamental reason for engaging Polanyi more directly than Marx is that Marx (famously) undertheorized the capitalist state. The central government in contemporary China more closely resembles the Polanyian model than it does a rigid "executive committee of the bourgeoisie." Even if Polanyi's theory of politics is weak (and indeed can be enhanced by reference to Marxist

theory, broadly conceived), the idea that segments of the state might promote decommodification has been validated historically and appears to be the case in contemporary China.

22. That is, increased rhetorical support from the state for worker grievances.

23. I do not mean to suggest that migrant workers have become constituted as a class in the fullest sense of the term. If class formation is a multilayered process, migrant workers certainly do not engage in collective action as a class (Katznelson 1986) and thus cannot really be considered a "class in reality" (Bourdieu 1985, 725).

24. States demanded the submission of the immediate needs of the working class to national interests, particularly in state socialist (see chapter 2) and fascist regimes. See Sarti 1971, 1974.

25. Or to the township level in nonurban areas.

26. For instance, in Dalian, where a massive strike wave involving seventy thousand workers swept through a development zone. "Dalian tinggong chao 7 wan ren canyu boji 73 jia qiye, yi gongzi zhang 34.5% gaozhong" [Dalian strike wave of 70 thousand workers affects 73 enterprises, results in 34.5% wage increases], *Caixin,* September 20, 2010.

CHAPTER 2

1. For example, the ACFTU letter to all national unions, which begins with the phrase *juguo tongchou* (the entire country has a common enemy) (*Shenggang da bagong ziliao* 1980, 151).

2. The Northern Expedition was a KMT military campaign to defeat warlords that controlled large swaths of China.

3. Li Lisan, "Guanyu fazhan shengchan laozi liangli zhengce de ji dian shuoming" [A few explanations on the policy of developing production and benefits for both labor and capital], *Renmin ribao,* May 1, 1949.

4. Ibid.

5. Ibid.

6. Ibid.

7. Ibid.

8. *Workers' Daily,* January 1, 1951 (quoted in Sheehan 1998, 29).

9. The four basic principles were established by Deng Xiaoping in the wake of the 1978 Democracy Wall movement. The principles are to (1) uphold socialism, (2) uphold the people's democratic dictatorship, (3) uphold the leadership of the Communist Party, and (4) uphold Marxism-Leninism-Mao Zedong Thought.

10. "Collective Bargaining a Goal for Chinese Unions," *China Daily,* July 29, 2010.

11. Xinhuanet, http://news.xinhuanet.com/politics/2012–07/18/c_112467783.htm. Both the accuracy and the meaning of this number must be interrogated closely. While no quantitative data exist, an incredibly large number of these people would not identify themselves as members of a union and do not pay union dues. A somewhat smaller percentage would not have any idea what a union is.

12. There is greater variation in the selection of union chairs at the enterprise level, which is discussed below.

13. In 2002, the Daqing oilfields were rocked by huge protests by workers angered over the theft of their pensions. While it is unclear what precisely Wang's role may have been in this crisis, as a high-level executive and Party committee member, he was certainly involved in some manner.

14. Biographical information comes from China Vitae, http://www.chinavitae.com/index.php.

15. PRC Trade Union Law, http://www.china.com.cn/chinese/LP/75992.htm.

16. Some readers may notice that there are two industrial unions responsible for financial workers. Because I did not undertake a study of these unions, I cannot explain this redundancy; this is how the industrial unions are listed in official ACFTU literature.

17. "Guangzhou san nian nei jiejue qiye fuzeren jianren gonghui zhuxi wenti" [Guangzhou will resolve the problem of enterprise managers' having joint positions as union chairs within three years], *Guangzhou Ribao,* July 24, 2009. Of course, the real number is likely much higher, but this is what was reported publicly.

CHAPTER 3

1. Guangzhou International, http://www.gz.gov.cn/publicfiles//business/htmlfiles/gzgov/s2768/list.html.

2. *Zhongguo laodong tongji nianjian* (Beijing: Zhongguo tongji chubanshe, 2010).

3. Additionally, some literature suggests that some combination of bottom-up and top-down mobilization can be most effective (Milkman 2006).

4. Weber (1946) uses the term "cultivated man" in a "completely value-neutral sense; it is understood to mean solely that the goal of education consists in the quality of a man's bearing in life which was *considered* 'cultivated,' rather than in a specialized training for expertness" (243) This has resonance for those who study Chinese unions, as leaders are generally chosen not for their "expertness" in labor issues but rather their "cultivation" within the Party.

5. See Chibber 2012 for an extended discussion on the question of the universality of working-class interests.

6. I have kept the city ambiguous to protect the identity of the informant, who openly criticized her superior.

7. Field notes, May 2009.

8. Field notes, April 2009.

9. Field notes, December 2007.

10. Ibid.

11. I initially asked union officials in interviews to provide me with a definition of socialism, but respondents fumbled for words, which resulted in a highly embarrassing situation. I decided to drop the question since it provided me with more of a "gotcha" moment rather than illuminating important phenomena and raised the risk of alienating potentially important contacts.

12. Field notes, November 2009.

13. I use quotes here because the terms "Western" and "foreign" are often consciously conflated by union and government officials in China. This conflation derives from the essentialist claim that "Asian" culture is fundamentally different from "Western" culture, particularly in that it is less amenable to democracy and confrontation.

14. Field notes, October 2008.

15. Field notes, November 2009.

16. Field notes, December 2007.

17. "Gonghui zhuxi bu zuowei wo zhichi gongren gao ta" [I support workers suing union chairs in dereliction of duty], *Guangzhou Ribao,* November 16, 2006.

18. Field notes, December 2007.

19. Field notes, August 2008.

20. Field notes, May 2008.

21. Field notes, August 2008.

22. It is quite unusual for union officials to come to university classes and nearly unthinkable that they would accept spontaneously generated questions from students.

23. Field notes, December 2008.

24. Field notes, October 2008.

25. One need look no further than the number of strikes, protests, and riots in China—which certainly outpaces those in any Western country—to verify that Chinese people are engaged in frequent acts of confrontation and dissent.

26. Interview with GZFTU officer, October 18, 2008.

27. Interview with GZFTU officer, October 2008.

28. Interview with Gao Haitao, December 2008.

29. To fully disclose my own involvement in this process, I originally tracked Gao down through one of the reporters that had written an article about the Nanchang Walmart. When I met him in December 2008, he had recently left his position as union chair and was trying to figure out how to stay involved in labor activism. I then introduced Gao to the foreign labor scholar mentioned, who then made the suggestion to Chen. In this sense I am guilty of "contaminating" the study, but this fact in no way diminishes the remarkableness of Chen's hiring an activist who was thought of as a troublemaker by other union federations.

30. Interview with GZFTU officer, October 2008.

31. Ibid.

32. Interview with GZFTU director of international affairs, October 2008.

33. Field notes, December 2009.

34. "Guangzhou zuidi gongzi biaozhun jinnian bu tiaozheng" [Guangzhou's minimum wage will not be adjusted this year], *Nanfang Ribao*, February 18, 2009.

35. "Guangzhou san nian nei jiejue qiye fuzeren jianren gonghui zhuxi wenti" [Guangzhou will resolve the problem of enterprise managers' having joint positions as union chairs within three years], *Guangzhou Ribao*, July 24, 2009.

36. Such measures for implementation are common in the Chinese legal system and allow local governments to adapt national laws to particular conditions.

37. "Guangzhou tuijin gonghui gaige he jianshe, qiye lingdao bu ren gonghui zhuxi" [Guangzhou promotes union reform and construction, enterprise leaders can't serve as union chair], *Guangzhou Ribao*, July 24, 2009.

38. "Guangzhou tuichu xin guiding: Qiye lingdao bude jianren gonghui zhuxi" [Guangzhou unveils new regulation: Enterprise leaders cannot hold joint appointments as union chair], *Xinxi Shibao*, July 24, 2009.

39. Guangzhou International, http://www.gz.gov.cn/business/htmlfiles/gzgov/s6981/201006/523293.html.

40. "Gongzi jiti xieshang mei nian zhishao yici zhigong xiang zhangxin qiye bu licai jiang fakuan" [Collective wage negotiations at least once a year, if employees want to raise wages and the enterprise ignores it, they will be fined], *Dushi Kuai Bao*, March 18, 2010.

41. Qiye gonghui gongzuo tiaoli (shixing) [Enterprise Union Work Regulations (trial)], http://www.acftu.org/template/10004/file.jsp?cid=561&aid=42680.

42. O'Brien and Li's (1999) argument about "selective policy implementation" was developed to describe rural politics but has analytical value for urban labor politics as well.

43. Interview with Shanghai union official, July 2009.

44. Interview with GZFTU officials, October 2008.

45. Interview with Guangzhou union chair, April 2009.

46. Website of Hitachi Elevator, http://www.hitachi-helc.com/about/index.html.

47. Interview with union chair at Hitachi Elevator (China), April 2009.

48. This document was provided to me by Hitachi workers.

49. Guangzhou Statistical Information Network, http://www.gzstats.gov.cn/tjsj/zy.htm.

50. Interview with Hitachi intern, April 2009.

51. Interview with Hitachi regular worker, April 2009.

52. Ibid.

53. Information in this paragraph is derived from media sources.

54. "Gonghui zhuxi bang yuangong weiquan jing zao jiegu" [Union chair helps employees protect their rights, is fired], *Nanfang Ribao,* April 23, 2009.

55. Ibid.

56. Ibid.

57. Ibid.

58. "Guangdong gonghui dasha gonghui bang yuangong weiquan dezui lingdao bei cai" [Guangdong Union Hotel union chair helps employees protect rights, offends leaders and is fired], *Yangcheng Wanbao,* April 22, 2009.

59. "'Gonghui zhuxi zao jiegu' xu, dasha zongjingli cheng zhong le quantao" ['Union chair fired' continued, hotel manager claims he was set up], *Nanfang Ribao,* April 23, 2009.

60. "Guangdong gonghui dasha gonghui zhuxi bei chao" [Guangdong Union Hotel chair is fired], *Guangzhou Ribao,* April 23, 2009.

61. "Hai you duoshao gonghui zuzhi bei qiye 'qiangjian'?" [How many more union organizations are "raped" by employers?], *Xibu Wang,* April 24, 2009, http://news.cnwest.com/content/2009–04/23/content_1993667.htm.

62. "Gonghui zhuxi zao jiegu qianyin houguo, gongzi fafang duli cai you diqi" [The cause and effects of union chairs being fired, salary should be paid independently in order to have courage], *Longhu Wang,* April 23, 2009, http://news.longhoo.net/gb/longhoo/news/guonei/userobject1ai963305.html.

63. China Labor Bulletin, http://www.clb.org.hk/schi/node/1301260.

64. Interview with Hitachi union chair, April 2009.

65. To be more specific, there are three steps in recalling a current union chair: (1) more than one-third of members must request a recall; (2) a congress of members or member representatives must be convened, with at least two-thirds in attendance; and (3) more than half of the congress participants must vote in favor of the recall.

66. Guangzhou International, http://www.gz.gov.cn/publicfiles/business/htmlfiles/gzrdzxs.

CHAPTER 4

1. PRC Ministry of Finance, cited at http://www.uschina.org/statistics/fdi_cumulative.html.

2. Zhejiang Provincial Government, http://www.zhejiang.gov.cn/gb/node2/node1619/node1622/userobject13ai697.html.

3. *Gonghui tongji nianjian 2007* (Beijing: Zhongguo tongji chubanshe, 2007).

4. PRC Ministry of Commerce, http://provincedata.mofcom.gov.cn/people/list.asp?ptypeid=16.

5. This of course includes firms from Hong Kong, Taiwan, and Macau.

6. *Zhejiang tongji nianjian 2008* (Beijing: Zhongguo tongji chubanshe, 2008).

7. *Guangdong tongji nianjian 2008* (Beijing: Zhongguo tongji chubanshe).

8. Ibid.

9. Of course Guangzhou's role in "anchoring" the Pearl River Delta is less absolute than that of Shanghai's in the Yangzi River Delta. In the Pearl River Delta Shenzhen was the first SEZ, and Hong Kong has provided the lion's share of the investment. Such "competitors" do not exist in the same way in the Yangzi River Delta, where the supremacy of Shanghai is unquestioned.

10. This report was provided to me by an officer of the GZFTU.

11. Interview with GZFTU official, October 2008.

12. Interview with director of Rui'an employers' association, July 2009.

13. Interview with local entrepreneur, December 2009.

14. Field notes, July 2009.

15. This confirms Unger's (1996) hypothesis that elites are more likely to have more autonomy in forming sectoral associations.

16. "Wenling xieshang hangye gongzi wending laodong guanxi" [Wenling sectoral bargaining stabilizes labor relations], *Gongren ribao*, December 31, 2003.

17. "Wenling gongzi xieshang jieya laozi maodun" [Wenling wage negotiations relieve pressure from labor-capital conflicts], *Minzhu yu fazhi shibao*, September 22, 2008.

18. Ibid.

19. Ibid.

20. "Zhashi tuijin gongzi jiti xieshang: Zhejiang wenling hangye gongzi jiti xieshang jishi" [Solidly promote collective wage negotiation: An account of Zhejiang's Wenling sectoral collective negotiations], *Gongren ribao*, April 14, 2008.

21. "Zhejiang jiceng minzhu de zhidu chuangxin" [Breakthroughs in Zhejiang's grassroots democratic system], *Xuexi shibao*, March 31, 2009.

22. "Yan Jiamin: Nuli kuoda hangyexing jiti xieshang fugaimian" [Yan Jiamin: work hard to increase the coverage of sectoral collective negotiations], *Gongren ribao*, August 4, 2009.

23. "Wenling zhigong gongzi yu qiye xiaoyi tongbu zengzhang" [Wenling's employee salaries and enterprise productivity increase together], *Taizhou ribao*, April 16, 2008.

24. "2008 nian rui'an shi guomin jingji he shehui fazhan tongji gongbao" [2008 report on Rui'an's economic and social development], http://www.ratj.gov.cn/tjgb/2008.htm.

25. Ibid.

26. The data in this section section are derived primarily from official union documents.

27. Interview with government official, July 2009.

28. Interview with local labor department official, July 2009.

29. "Zhejiang goujian hexie laozi guanxi chutan" [First explorations in Zhejiang's construction of harmonious labor relations], *Ban yue tan*, February 5, 2008.

30. Interview with chairman of Eyeglass Employer Association, July 2009.

31. "Zhejiang to Promote Collective Wage Negotiation," September 8, 2008, http://www.chinacsr.com/en/2008/09/08/3043-zhejiang-to-promote-collective-wage-negotiation.

32. "Quanguo gonghui gongzi jiti xieshang gongzuo jingyan jiaoliu hui zai hang zhaokai" [National union collective wage negotiation exchange conference commences in Hangzhou], *Zhejiang ribao*, April 11, 2008.

33. Interview with human resources manager at Zhilian Eyeglasses, December 2009.

34. Field notes, December 2009.

35. Interview with manager in small eyeglass factory, January 2010.

36. Ibid.

37. Interview with manager in large eyeglass company, December 2009.

38. Interview with manager in small eyeglass enterprise, January 2010.

39. Field notes, December 2009.

40. Ibid.

41. Field notes, December 2008.

42. Field notes, October 2009.

43. Interview with leader in Guangzhou construction worker union, April 2009.

44. Ibid.

45. The category of "sanitation worker" is broader in China than in the American context, as it includes not just garbage collectors but other workers involved in cleaning activities such as street sweepers and janitors.

46. Field notes, December 2008.

47. "Huanwei gongren qian jiti hetong hushen "[Sanitation workers sign collective contract for protection], *Yangcheng Wanbao*, July 21, 2009.

48. "Guangzhou yue 300 ming huanweigong bu man daiyu 'bagong.'" [Approximately 300 cleaners in Guangzhou dissatisfied with treatment, 'strike'], *Yangcheng Wanbao*, January 19, 2010.

49. "Guangzhou baiyun qu huanwei gongren bu man gongzi daiyu bagong" [Cleaners in Guangzhou's Baiyun district strike over dissatisfaction with wages], *Nanfang Ribao*, February 23, 2012.

50. "Nianzhongjiang 10 yuan, guangzhou tianhe huanwei gong bu man tinggong" [Year-end bonus of 10 yuan, cleaners in Guangzhou's Tianhe are dissatisfied, stop work], *Gongda Zaixian*, December 26, 2012.

51. "Guangzhou liwan 200 duo ming huanweigong bagong wei jingche yaoqiu zhangxin" [More than 200 cleaners strike and surround police car, demand wage increase], *Jinyang Wang*, January 11, 2013.

52. "Guangzhou shu bai ming huanweigong tinggong yaoqiu gongzi zhang zhi 3000 yuan" [One Hundred sanitation workers in Guangzhou strike to demand a wage hike to 3,000 yuan], *Nanfang Dushi Bao*, January 21, 2013.

53. "Tigao huanwei gongren daiyu" [Increase sanitation worker compensation], *Gongren Ribao*, January 21, 2013.

54. Liu Xiaogang's Microblog, http://www.weibo.com/1943359432/zfuzSpih1.

55. "Chen jianhua: Jifen ruhu yao xiang huanwei gongren qingxie" [Chen Jianhua: Obtaining residence permits should be tilted toward sanitation workers], *Xin Kuai Bao*, April 26, 2013.

56. "Guangzhou shizhang chen jianhua chengnuo: Jinnian qi tigao huanweigong shouru" [Guangzhou mayor Chen Jianhua promises to raise sanitation worker wages starting this year], *Yangcheng Wanbao*, February 4, 2013.

57. "Guifan huanwei hangye yonggong, jiaqiang gaijin xiaofang gongzuo" [Standardize sanitation sector employment, strengthen and improve fire prevention work], *Guangzhou Ribao*, April 23, 2013.

58. Sanitation News, http://www.hwxx.com.cn/index.php?m=content&c=index&a=show&catid=34&id=2173.

59. Field notes, December 2008.

60. It is, however, more likely that sectoral unions will have more success in the place-specific service industry. As just one example, a food and beverage union in Wuhan bargained a collective contract covering 450,000 workers in early 2011. See "Wuhan 45 wan canyin congyezhe tanpan shixian zuidi gongzi shangfu 30%." [450,000 food and beverage workers in Wuhan collectively bargain a 30% increase in base wage], *Guangzhou Ribao*, May 3, 2011.

61. Field notes, December 2008.

62. "Wenling gongzi xieshang jieya laozi maodun" [Wenling wage negotiations relieve pressure from labor-capital conflicts], *Minzhu yu fazhi shibao*, September 22, 2008.

63. "How Bosses and Workers Can Become 'One Big Happy Family': A Report on an Inquiry into the Introduction of Collective Wage Consultation in Wenling City, Zhejiang," *Chinese Labor and Social Security News*, January 25, 2008 (translated by China Labor News Translations).

64. "Wenling hangye gongzi jiti xieshang zhisu—yige laowu guanxi xin jumian de kaichuang" [The Wenling sectoral collective wage negotiation System—The start of a new phase in labor relations], *Guancha yu sikao*, May 1, 2008.

65. "Wenling gongzi xieshang jieya laozi maodun" [Wenling wage negotiations relieve pressure from labor-capital conflicts], *Minzhu yu fazhi shibao*, September 22, 2008.

CHAPTER 5

1. Much of this chapter appeared previously as Friedman 2013.

2. My perspective is quite different from that of Teresa Wright (2010), who contends that various social groups in China "accept" authoritarianism. Although Wright acknowledges that this acceptance is perhaps most tenuous among migrant workers, I would counter that the lack of a well-articulated political opposition is not due to acceptance of the status quo but rather results from the continual threat of repression.

3. Field notes, October 2009.

4. The fact that Chen was willing to publicly admit that the enterprise-level chair had done nothing is noteworthy and unusual for Chinese union leaders.

5. "XXX guangzhou gongsi ni xiao yuangong liucheng gongzi; bu qian zi jiang bei chao" [Ascendant Guangzhou company plans to take away 60% of worker's salary; those who refuse to sign will be fired], *Xin kuai bao*, December 21, 2007.

6. "Shizong gonghui diaocha XXX 'hetongmen' weihu gongren quanyi" [GZFTU to investigate Ascendant's contract to protect the rights and interests of workers], *Guangzhou ribao*, December 22, 2007.

7. Interview with temporary worker at Ascendant Elevator, May 2009.

8. "Some union chairs are taking the wrong position," *Guangzhou ribao*, January 1, 2008.

9. Ibid.

10. Zhang 2008.

11. Interview with temp workers at Ascendant Elevator, May 2009.

12. The official name of this company is China Honda Auto Parts Manufacturing Co., Ltd. However, the plant has frequently been referred to as Nanhai Honda in the media, and so I will use this terminology.

13. "Dongfeng bentian: Wufa duoshan de hudie xiaoying" [Dongfeng Honda: No way to hide from the butterfly effect], *E'shang zazhi*, June 11, 2010.

14. "Honda Auto Parts Manufacturing Co., Ltd. Begins Operations in China," March 8, 2007, http://world.honda.com/news/2007/c070308AutoPartsManufacturing.

15. Ibid.

16. Field notes, December 2008.

17. This is a pseudonym. The same person also appeared as "Tan Zhiqing" in other reports.

18. David Barboza, "In China, Unlikely Labor Leader Just Wanted a Middle-Class Life," *New York Times*, June 13, 2010.

19. "Zhongguo bentian nanhai chang jin fugong, cong yuangong jiaodu kan laozi shi-jian" [China Honda Nanhai factory resumes production today, looking at labor conflicts from the perspective of employees], *Zhongguo Xinwen Zhoukan*, June 2, 2010.

20. Ibid.

21. Interview with Nanhai Honda worker, July, 2010.

22. "Bentian duzi lingbujian chang bagong zhi guangben tinggong" [Strike in Honda-owned factory results in stoppage for Guangzhou Honda], *Caixin*, May 27, 2010.

23. Interview with worker representative from Nanhai Honda union, July 18, 2010.

24. Interview with Nanhai Honda striker, July 2010.

25. "Zhongguo bentian nanhai chang jin fugong."

26. "Bentian jiaxin shi bagong chongji di chengben zhizaoye moshi" [Honda wage strikes are a shock to the low-cost manufacturing model], *Caixin*, May 31, 2010.

27. "Nanhai bentian tichu di-san ge tixin fang'an" [Nanhai Honda announces third proposal to raise wages], *Caixin*, May 30, 210.

28. Ibid.

29. Interview with Nanhai Honda strikers, July 2010.

30. In addition to interviews, much of the information from this section is derived from a detailed account written by a Honda worker that was posted online.

31. Interview with department foreman, Nanhai Honda, September 29, 2010.

32. "Open Letter from the Nanhai District Trade Union and Shishan Town General Trade Union to the Workers of Honda Motors Nanhai Component and Parts Factory," http://chinastudygroup.net/2010/6/translation-of-an-open-letter-from-the-nanhai-district-general-trade-union-and-shishan-town-general-trade-union-to-the-workers-of-honda-motors-nanhai-component-and-parts-factory.

33. Ibid.

34. Interview with Nanhai Honda striker, July 18, 2010.

35. The open letter from the worker representatives was posted online at http://zggr.cn/?action-viewnews-itemid-9411.

36. Ibid.

37. Thanks to Jonathan Hassid for advising on this; the leaked Department of Propaganda directive can be found at http://zhenlibu.wordpress.com/2010/05/29/%E4%B8%89%E4%B8%AA.

38. Chinese Worker, http://zggr.cn/?action-viewnews-itemid-9411.

39. It is important to note that in interviews with Nanhai strikers, there was hardly any evidence of anti-Japanese or overtly nationalist sentiment. And many strikers expressed great contempt for their Chinese managers.

40. "Riben dianzhuang zai hua qiye bufen fugong, laozi tanpan reng zai jinxing" [Japanese Denso company in China has partial resumption of work, negotiations continue], Reuters, June 24, 2010.

41. Ibid.

42. Ibid.

43. GZFTU, http://www.gzgh.org.cn/_layouts/ghpub09//Lists/Open.aspx?NavId=7&ID=2738.

44. Ibid.

45. "Dalian tinggong chao 7 wan ren canyu boji 73 jia qiye, yi gongzi zhang 34.5% gaozhong" [70k participate in Dalian strike wave affecting 73 enterprises, ends with 34.5% wage increases], Caixin, September 20, 2010.

46. "Yi lang gao guo yi lang, bentian zhi suo gongsi ye baofa bagong" [One wave is higher than the next, strike also erupts at Honda lock factory], Lianhe Zaobao, June 12, 2010.

47. "Shenzhen ji tiao zuidi gongzi zhi 1100 yuan" [Shenzhen makes emergency adjustment to minimum wage, now 1,100 yuan], Yikuo Meiri Caijing, June 10, 2010.

48. Ibid.

49. GZFTU, http://www.gzgh.org.cn/_layouts/ghpub09//Lists/Open.aspx?NavId=7&ID=2738.

50. "Guangzhou shizong: Gonghui yao zuowei gongren liyi daibiao canyu xietiao laodong guanxi" [GZFTU: The union should serve as workers' interest representative in participating in labor relations], October 12, 2010.

51. "Kekong de bagong shi hexie de yingyou zhi yi" [Controllable strikes are a right that should be enjoyed for harmony], Zhongguo Qiyejia, June 22, 2010.

52. Ibid.

53. "Guangdong sheng zong gonghui zhuxi: Qiye gonghui zhuxi duo bu shi minzhu xuanju" [GDFTU chair: Most enterprise union chairs are not democratically elected], Yangcheng Wanbao, July 3, 2010.

54. Xinmin Auto, http://auto.xinmin.cn/rollnews/2011/03/07/9639022.html.

55. Ibid., */9638257.html.*

56. "Bentian jiaxin shi bagong chongji di chengben zhizaoye moshi."

57. "Chen Weiguang Answers Questions from South China Normal University Student," http://www.gzgh.org.cn/_layouts/ghpub09//Lists/Open.aspx?NavId=7&ID=2738.

58. *Jiyu yu tiaozhan: Gonghui gongzuo 100 li* [Opportunity and challenge: 100 cases of union work] (Guangzhou: Guangzhou shi luogang qu zong gonghui, 2010), 91.

59. Interview with worker at Nanhai Honda, July 4, 2010.

60. Interview with Nanhai Honda workers, July 18, 2010.

61. "Nanhai bentian ni minxuan gonghui zhuxi" [Plans for Nanhai Honda to hold democratic elections for union chair], *Ta Kung Pao*, June 14, 2010.

62. Interview with Nanhai Honda worker, July 13, 2010.

63. Interview with Nanhai Honda worker, July 2010.

64. Interview with union representative from Nanhai Honda, September 29, 2010.

65. Interview with Nanhai Honda worker, July 18, 2010.

66. "Nanhai bentian tinggong shijian, rifang zuizhong jieshou zengjia gongzi fang'an [Nanhai Honda work stoppage, eventually the Japanese agree to a wage increase], *Nanfang Ribao*, March 3, 2011.

67. Ibid.

68. Without a doubt, the position of the provincial government vis-à-vis capital varies by industry. Even if the government became willing to sacrifice low-value-added industries, the threat of capital flight to both other countries and other regions of China remains a concern. But given the dense cluster of auto suppliers in Guangzhou and the relatively high costs of relocating production, the government likely felt greater confidence in dealing with foreign automakers.

69. Interview with Nanhai Honda striker, July 25, 2010.

70. Ibid.

CHAPTER 6

1. China of course experienced several decades of capitalist industrialization beginning in the late nineteenth century. However, this development was limited in geographic and social scope and was suspended once the Communists prevailed in the civil war.

2. These similarities should not be overstated and indeed are relatively superficial. But the comparison does reveal something about general tendencies in China's different regions and may help non-Chinese readers contextualize these developments.

3. I do not want to appear Pollyannaish about union democracy in the West or other developed countries during the period of industrialization. Although there was extensive corruption and "yellow" unionism in other countries, the point is that there are quite distinct *general* tendencies in China, which means that representation is a more acute problem at the class level.

4. There is some debate as to whether labor NGOs that have emerged in China since the mid-1990s count as worker organizations. Some view them more pessimistically as undemocratic and frequently controlled by external interests (Friedman 2009; Spires 2012; Lee and Shen 2011).

5. This number may seem high to those unfamiliar with the Taiwanese labor relations system. It includes occupational unions, which tend to be vehicles for buying insurance but do not engage in activities more typically associated with unions (e.g., collective bargaining, political mobilization).

6. I am sidestepping the debate of labor as an active subject (Negri 1984; Herod 2001) vs. passive object in the construction of capitalism. It is beyond the scope of this book to say definitively whether labor is following capital or the reverse in this instance.

7. See China Briefing, http://www.china-briefing.com/news/2012/01/27/chinas-provincial-gdp-figures-in-2011.html.

8. Like Arrighi and Silver (1999), I use the term "hegemony" in the specifically Gramscian sense—domination accomplished primarily by consent rather coercion. In the view of Arrighi and Silver, the period of American hegemony was notable for its brevity and quickly lapsed into coercion.

9. I have cited the original Italian version of the book where this passage appears. I drew this quote from an unofficial English translation of "The Strategy of Refusal," which can be found at http://operaismoinenglish.wordpress.com/2010/09/30/strategy-of-refusal. Since it was drawn from the Internet, there is no listed page number.

10. Working-class organizations have played an important role in democratization and redemocratization (Valenzuela 1989) in Europe (Rueschemeyer, Stephens, and Stephens 1992; Therborn 1977); Asia (Buchanan and Nicholls 2003); and Latin America (Collier and Mahoney 1997; Collier 1999), though it is worth noting this role has been inconsistent across cases (Bellin 2000).

11. As defined in the classic formulation by Skocpol (1979), a very different scenario than simple "democratization" as conceived of by Huntington (1991) and others.

12. This is true both because of so-called local protectionism and because officials' own career advancement can depend in large part on success with economic growth; see Li and Zhou 2005.

13. It is important to note that even if such a solution could address the immediate economic crisis, continual expansion of consumption in China poses an incredibly grave ecological threat (Hubacek et al. 2009; Peters et al. 2007).

14. I want to emphasize that I am *not* advocating a functionalist "social body" metaphor in the vein of Durkheim (1997) but simply want to indicate that previously (relatively) autarkic social units begin to be fused together, thereby increasing their strength.

15. See, for example, Seidman's (1994) account of the militancy of South African and Brazilian labor movements.

Bibliography

Abensour, Miguel. 2011. *Democracy against the State: Marx and the Machiavellian Moment.* Cambridge, UK: Polity.

Alden, Chris, and Daniel Large. 2011. "China's Exceptionalism and the Challenges of Delivering Difference in Africa." *Journal of Contemporary China* 20 (68): 21–38.

All China Federation of Trade Unions, ed. 1988. *Jianguo yilai zhonggong zhongyang guanyu gongren yundong wenjian xuanbian* [CCP Central Committee documents on the workers' movement since the establishment of the nation]. Beijing: Gongren chubanshe.

Arrighi, Giovanni. 2007a. *Adam Smith in Beijing: Lineages of the Twenty-First Century.* New York: Verso.

——. 2007b. "States, Markets, and Capitalism, East and West." *Positions: East Asia Cultures Critique* 15 (2): 251–84.

Arrighi, Giovanni, and Beverly J Silver. 1999. *Chaos and Governance in the Modern World System.* Minneapolis: University of Minnesota Press.

Asano, Hirokatsu, Takahiro Ito, and Daiji Kawaguchi. 2011. "Why Has the Fraction of Contingent Workers Increased? A Case Study of Japan." Hiroshima University, Graduate School for International Development and Cooperation (IDEC).

Averill, Stephen C. 1987. "Party, Society, and Local Elite in the Jiangxi Communist Movement." *Journal of Asian Studies* 46 (2): 279–303.

Bellin, Eva. 2000. "Contingent Democrats: Industrialists, Labor, and Democratization in Late-Developing Countries." *World Politics* 52 (2): 175–205.

Bianco, Lucien, and Muriel Bell. 1971. *Origins of the Chinese Revolution, 1915–1949.* Stanford: Stanford University Press.

Bickford, Thomas. 1994. "The Chinese Military and Its Business Operations: The PLA as Entrepreneur." *Asian Survey* 34 (5): 460–74.

Blanchard, Olivier, and Francesco Giavazzi. 2006. "Rebalancing Growth in China: A Three-Handed Approach." *China & World Economy* 14 (4): 1–20.

Blecher, Marc. 2002. "Hegemony and Workers' Politics in China." *China Quarterly* 170:283–303.

——. 2008. "When Wal-Mart Wimped Out: Globalization and Unionization in China." *Critical Asian Studies* 40 (2): 263–76.

Block, Fred. 2003. "Karl Polanyi and the Writing of *The Great Transformation.*" *Theory and Society* 32:275–306.

Bourdieu, Pierre. 1984. *Distinction: A Social Critique of the Judgment of Taste.* Cambridge, MA: Harvard University Press.

——. 1985. "The Social Space and the Genesis of Groups." *Theory and Society* 14 (6): 723–44.

Bramall, Chris. 1989. "The Wenzhou 'Miracle': An Assessment." In *Market Forces in China: Competition and Small Business—The Wenzhou Debate,* edited by Peter Nolan and Fureng Dong, 43–76. London: Zed Books.

Broadman, Harry G, and Xiaolun Sun. 1997. "The Distribution of Foreign Direct Investment in China." 339–61. World Bank report.

Brock, Andy. 2009. "Moving Mountains Stone by Stone: Reforming Rural Education in China." *International Journal of Educational Development* 29 (5): 454–62.

Brown, Philip, and Thomas Huff. 2011. "Willingess to Pay in China's New Cooperative Medical System." *Contemporary Economic Policy* 29 (1): 88–100.

Buchanan, Paul G, and Kate Nicholls. 2003. "Labour Politics and Democratic Transition in South Korea and Taiwan." *Government and Opposition* 38 (2): 203–37.

Burawoy, Michael. 1982. *Manufacturing Consent: Changes in Labor Process under Monopoly Capitalism.* Chicago: University of Chicago Press.

———. 1996. "The State and Economic Involution: Russia through a China Lens." *World Development* 24 (6): 1105–17.

———. 2003. "For a Sociological Marxism: The Complementary Convergence of Antonio Gramsci and Karl Polanyi." *Politics & Society* 31 (2): 193–261.

———. 2008. "What Is to Be Done? Theses on the Degradation of Social Existence in a Globalizing World." *Current Sociology* 56 (3): 351–59.

Burstein, Paul, and April Linton. 2002. "The Impact of Political Parties, Interest Groups, and Social Movement Organizations on Public Policy: Some Recent Evidence and Theoretical Concerns." *Social Forces* 81 (2): 380–408.

Cai, Yongshun. 2002. "The Resistance of Chinese Laid-Off Workers in the Reform Period." *China Quarterly* 170:327–44.

———. 2010. *Collective Resistance in China: Why Popular Protests Succeed or Fail.* Stanford: Stanford University Press.

Caraway, Teri. 2009. "Labor Rights in East Asia: Progress or Regress?" *Journal of East Asian Studies* 9 (2): 153–86.

Chan, Anita. 1993. "Revolution or Corporatism? Workers and Trade Unions in Post-Mao China." *Australian Journal of Chinese Affairs* 29:31–61.

———. 2001. *China's Workers under Assault: The Exploitation of Labor in a Globalizing Economy.* Armonk, NY: M.E. Sharpe.

———. 2007. "Organizing Wal-Mart in China: Two Steps Forward, One Step Back for China's Unions." *New Labor Forum* 16 (2): 87–96.

———. 2008. "Challenges and Possibilities for Democratic Grassroots Union Elections in China: A Case Study of Two Factory-Level Elections and Their Aftermath." *Labor Studies Journal* 34 (3): 293–317.

———. 2011a. "Strikes in China's Export Industries in Comparative Perspective." *China Journal* 65:27–51.

———. 2011b. "Unionizing Chinese Walmart Stores." In *Walmart in China,* edited by A. Chan, 199–216. Ithaca: Cornell University Press.

Chan, Anita, and Jonathan Unger. 2009. "A Chinese State Enterprise under the Reforms: What Model of Capitalism?" *China Journal* 62:1–26.

Chan, Chris King-Chi. 2010. *The Challenge of Labour in China: Strikes and the Changing Labour Regime in Global Factories.* London: Routledge.

Chan, Chris King-Chi, and Elaine Sio-leng Hui. 2012. "The Dynamics and Dilemma of Workplace Trade Union Reform in China: The Case of the Honda Workers' Strike." *Journal of Industrial Relations* 54 (5): 653–68.

Chan, Chris King-Chi, and Pun Ngai. 2009. "The Making of a New Working Class? A Study of Collective Action of Migrant Workers in South China." *China Quarterly* 198:287–303.

Chan, David, and Ka-Ho Mok. 2001. "Educational Reforms and Coping Strategies under the Tidal Wave of Marketisation: A Comparative Study of Hong Kong and the Mainland." *Comparative Education* 37 (1): 21–41.

Chan, Jenny Wai-ling. 2009. "Meaningful Progress or Illusory Reform? Analyzing China's Labor Contract Law." *New Labor Forum* 18 (2): 43–51.

Chan, Kam Wing. 2010. "The Global Financial Crisis and Migrant Workers in China: 'There is No Future as a Labourer; Returning to the Village Has No Meaning.'" *International Journal of Urban and Regional Research* 34 (3): 659–77.

Chan, Kam Wing, and Will Buckingham. 2008. "Is China Abolishing the Hukou System?" *China Quarterly* 195:582–606.

Chang, Chyi-herng, and Trevor Bain. 2006. "Employment Relations across the Taiwan Strait: Globalization and State Corporatism." *Journal of Industrial Relations* 48 (1): 99–115.

Chen, Calvin. 2008. *Some Assembly Required: Work, Community, and Politics in China's Rural Enterprises.* Cambridge, MA: Harvard University Press.

Chen, Chung, Lawrence Chang, and Yimin Zhang. 1995. "The Role of Foreign Direct Investment in China's Post-1978 Economic Development." *World Development* 23 (4): 691–703.

Chen Ding, and Huang Junyong. 2008. "Zhejiang wenlingshi tuixing hangye gongzi jiti xieshang zhidu de jingyan yu qishi" [The experience and inspiration of Wenling's implementation of a collective wage negotiation system]. *Tianjinshi gonghui guanli ganbu xueyuan xuebao* 16 (3): 30–32.

Chen, Feng. 2000. "Subsistence Crises, Managerial Corruption and Labour Protests in China." *China Journal* 44:41–63.

——. 2003. "Between the State and Labour: The Conflict of Chinese Trade Unions' Double Identity in Market Reform." *China Quarterly* 176:1006–1028.

——. 2004. "Legal Mobilization by Trade Unions: The Case of Shanghai." *China Journal* 52:27–45.

——. 2007. "Individual Rights and Collective Rights: Labor's Predicament in China." *Communist and Post-Communist Studies* 40:59–79.

——. 2009. "Union Power in China: Source, Operation, and Constraints." *Modern China* 35:662–89.

Chen, Feng, and Xin Xu. 2012. "'Active Judiciary': Judicial Dismantling of Workers' Collective Action in China." *China Journal* 67:87–108.

Chen, Shengjun. 2009. "Dui 'laodong hetong fa' shishi guocheng zhong ruogan wenti de sikao" [On some issues in the implementation of the Labor Contract Law]." *Hunan sheng gonghui ganbu xuexiao* 23 (3): 30–32.

Chen, Yiu Por, and Zai Liang. 2007. "Educational Attainment of Migrant Children: The Forgotten Story of China's Urbanization." In *Education and Reform in China,* edited by Emily Hannum and Albert Park, 117–32. New York: Routledge.

Cheng, Tun-jen. 1989. "Democratizing the Quasi-Leninist Regime in Taiwan." *World Politics* 41 (4): 471–99.

Chesneux, Jean. 1968. *The Chinese Labor Movement, 1919–1927.* Stanford: Stanford University Press.

Chibber, Vivek. 2003. *Locked in Place: State-Building and Late Industrialization in India.* Princeton: Princeton University Press.

——. 2012. *Postcolonial Theory and the Specter of Capital.* London: Verso.

Chin, Christine, and James Mittelman. 1997. "Conceptualising Resistance to Globalisation." *New Political Economy* 2 (1): 25–37.

Choi, Young-Jin. 2003. "Managerial Styles, Workforce Composition and Labor Unrest: East Asian-Invested Enterprises in China." *Comparative Sociology* 2 (2): 321–54.

Chu, Yin-wah. 1998. "Labor and Democratization in South Korea and Taiwan." *Journal of Contemporary Asia* 28 (2): 185–202.

Clarke, Simon. 2006. "The Changing Character of Strikes in Vietnam." *Post-Communist Economies* 18 (3): 345–61.

Clarke, Simon, Chang-Hee Lee, and Do Quynh Chi. 2007. "From Rights to Interests: The Challenge of Industrial Relations in Vietnam." *Journal of Industrial Relations* 49 (4): 545–69.

Clarke, Simon, Chang-Hee Lee, and Qi Li. 2004. "Collective Consultation and Industrial Relations in China." *British Journal of Industrial Relations* 42 (2): 235–254.

Clarke, Simon, and Tim Pringle. 2009. "Can Party-Led Trade Unions Represent Their Members?" *Post-Communist Economies* 21 (1): 85–101.

Cohen, Youssef. 1982. "'The Benevolent Leviathan': Political Consciousness among Urban Workers under State Corporatism." *American Political Science Review* 76 (1): 46–59.

Collier, Ruth. 1999. *Paths toward Democracy: The Working Class and Elites in Western Europe and South America.* New York: Cambridge University Press.

Collier, Ruth, and David Collier. 1991. *Shaping the Political Arena: Critical Junctures, the Labor Movement, and Regime Dynamics in Latin America.* Princeton: Princeton University Press.

Collier, Ruth, and James Mahoney. 1997. "Adding Collective Actors to Collective Outcomes: Labor and Recent Democratization in South America and Southern Europe." *Comparative Politics* 29 (3): 285–303.

Cooney, Sean. 2006. "Making Chinese Labor Law Work: The Prospects for Regulatory Innovation in the People's Republic of China." *Fordham International Law Journal* 30:1050–97.

Cooney, Sean. 2007. "China's Labour Law, Compliance and Flaws in Implementing Institutions." *Journal of Industrial Relations* 49 (5): 673–86.

Cooney, Sean, Sarah Biddulph, Kungang Li, and Ying Zhu. 2007. "China's New Labor Contract Law: Responding to the Growing Complexity of Labour Relations in the PRC." *University of New South Wales Law Journal* 30:786–801.

Cooney, Sean, Sarah Biddulph, and Ying Zhu. 2013. *Law and Fair Work in China.* New York: Routledge.

Crowley, Stephen. 2004. "Explaining Labor Weakness in Post-Communist Europe: Historical Legacies and Comparative Perspective." *East European Politics and Societies* 18 (3): 394–429.

Crowley, Stephen, and David Ost. 2001. *Workers after Workers' States: Labor and Politics in Postcommunist Eastern Europe.* Lanham, MD: Rowman & Littlefield.

Dale, G. 2012. "Double Movements and Pendular Forces: Polanyian Perspectives on the Neoliberal Age." *Current Sociology* 60 (1): 3–27.

David-Friedman, Ellen. 2009. "U.S. and Chinese Labor at a Changing Moment in the Global Neoliberal Economy." *Working USA* 12 (2): 219–234.

Deyo, Frederic C. 1987. "State and Labor: Modes of Political Exclusion in East Asian Development." In *The Political Economy of the New Asian Industrialism,* edited by Frederic C Deyo, 182–202. Ithaca: Cornell University Press.

———. 1989. *Beneath the Miracle: Labor Subordination in the New Asian Industrialism.* Berkeley: University of California Press.

Dong, Fureng. 1989. "The Wenzhou Model for Developing the Rural Commodity Economy." In *Market Forces in China: Competition and Small Business—The Wenzhou Debate,* edited by Fureng Dong and Peter Nolan, 77–96. London: Zed Books.

Duckett, Jane. 2001. "Bureaucrats in Business, Chinese-Style: The Lessons of Market Reform and State Entrepreneurialism in the People's Republic of China." *World Development* 29 (1): 23–37.

Durkheim, Emile. 1997. *The Division of Labor in Society*. New York: Free Press.

Eng, Irene. 1997. "The Rise of Manufacturing Towns: Externally Driven Industrialization and Urban Development in the Pearl River Delta of China." *International Journal of Urban and Regional Research* 21:554–68.

Esping-Andersen, Gosta. 1990. *The Three Worlds of Welfare Capitalism*. Princeton: Princeton University Press.

Evans, Peter. 1995. *Embedded Autonomy: States and Industrial Transformation*. Princeton: Princeton University Press.

——. 2000. "Fighting Marginalization with Transnational Networks: Counter-Hegemonic Globalization." *Contemporary Sociology* 29 (1): 230–41.

——. 2005. "Counter-Hegemonic Globalization: Transnational Social Movements in the Contemporary Global Political Economy." In *Handbook of Political Sociology*, edited by Thomas Janoski, Alexander M. Hicks, and Mildred Schwartz, 655–68. Cambridge: Cambridge University Press.

——. 2008. "Is an Alternative Globalization Possible?" *Politics & Society* 36:271–305.

——. 2010. "Is It Labor's Turn to Globalize? Twenty-First Century Opportunities and Strategic Responses." *Global Labour Journal* 1 (3): 352–79.

Fan, Cindy. 2006. "China's Eleventh Five-Year Plan (2006–2010): From 'Getting Rich First' to 'Common Prosperity.'" *Eurasian Geography and Economics* 47 (6): 708–23.

Fewsmith, Joseph. 2005. "Chambers of Commerce in Wenzhou Show Potential and Limits of 'Civil Society' in China." *China Leadership Monitor* 16:1–9.

Fine, Janice, and Jennifer Gordon. 2010. "Strengthening Labor Standards Enforcement through Partnerships with Workers' Organizations." *Politics & Society* 38 (4): 552–85.

Forster, Keith. 1990. "The Wenzhou Model for Economic Development: Impressions." *China Information* 5 (53): 53–64.

Forster, Keith, and Xianguo Yao. 1999. "A Comparative Analysis of Economic Reform and Development in Hangzhou and Wenzhou Cities." In *Cities in China: Recipes for Economic Development in the Reform Era*, edited by Jae Ho Chung, 51–102. New York: Routledge.

Frazier, Mark. 2010. *Socialist Insecurity: Pensions and the Politics of Uneven Development in China*. Ithaca: Cornell University Press.

Friedman, Eli. 2009. "External Pressure and Local Mobilization: Transnational Activism and the Emergence of the Chinese Labor Movement." *Mobilization: An International Journal* 14 (2): 199–218.

——. 2012. "Getting through the Hard Times Together? Chinese Workers and Unions Respond to the Economic Crisis." *Journal of Industrial Relations* 54 (4): 459–75.

——. 2013. "Insurgency and Institutionalization: The Polanyian Countermovement and Chinese Labor Politics." *Theory and Society* 42 (3): 295–327.

Friedman, Eli, and Ching Kwan Lee. 2010. "Remaking the World of Chinese Labour: A 30-Year Retrospective." *British Journal of Industrial Relations* 48 (3): 507–33.

Gallagher, Mary. 2002. "Reform and Openness: Why China's Economic Reforms Have Delayed Democracy." *World Politics* 54 (3): 338–72.

——. 2004. "Time Is Money, Efficiency Is Life: The Transformation of Labor Relations in China." *Studies in Comparative International Development* 39 (2): 11–44.

——. 2005. *Contagious Capitalism: Globalization and the Politics of Labor in China*. Princeton: Princeton University Press.

——. 2006. "Mobilizing the Law in China: 'Informed Disenchantment' and the Development of Legal Consciousness." *Law & Society Review* 40 (4): 783–816.

Ge, Wei. 1999. "Special Economic Zones and the Opening of the Chinese Economy: Some Lessons for Economic Liberalization." *World Development* 27 (7): 1267–85.

Gold, Thomas. 1990. "Tiananmen and Beyond, the Resurgence of Civil Society in China." *Journal of Democracy* 1:18–31.

Goldfield, Michael. 1989. "Worker Insurgency, Radical Organization, and New Deal Labor Legislation." *American Political Science Review* 83 (4): 1257–82.

Goldman, Rene. 1962. "The Rectification Campaign at Peking University: May–June 1957." *China Quarterly* 12:138–53.

Golley, Jane, and Xin Meng. 2011. "Has China Run Out of Surplus Labour?" *China Economic Review* 22 (4): 555–72.

Guha, Ranajit. 1983a. *Elementary Aspects of Peasant Insurgency in Colonial India.* Delhi: Oxford University Press.

———. 1983b. "The Prose of Counter-Insurgency." In *Subaltern Studies II: Writings on South Asian History and Society,* edited by Ranajit Guha, 1–43. Oxford: Oxford University Press.

Habermas, Jurgen. 1973. *Legitimation Crisis.* Boston: Beacon Press.

Hardt, Michael. 1995. "The Withering of Civil Society." *Social Text* 45 (45): 27.

Hardt, Michael, and Antonio Negri. 2004. *Multitude: War and Democracy in the Age of Empire.* New York: Penguin Press.

Harper, Paul. 1969. "The Party and Unions in Communist China." *China Quarterly* 37:84–119.

Harvey, David. 1982. *The Limits to Capital.* Chicago: University of Chicago Press.

Hassid, Jonathan. 2008. "Controlling the Media: An Uncertain Business." *Asian Survey* 48 (3): 414–30.

Hawkins, John N. 2000. "Centralization, Decentralization, Recentralization— Educational Reform in China." *Journal of Educational Administration* 38 (5): 442–55.

Herod, Andrew. 2001. *Labor Geographies: Workers and the Landscapes of Capitalism.* New York: Guilford Press.

Hinton, William. 1966. *Fanshen: A Documentary of Revolution in a Chinese Village.* New York: Monthly Review Press.

Hishida, Masaharu, Kazuko Kojima, Tomoaki Ishii, and Jian Qiao. 2010. *China's Trade Unions: How Autonomous Are They?* New York: Routledge.

Ho, Ming-sho. 2006. "Challenging State Corporatism: The Politics of Taiwan's Labor Federation Movement." *China Journal* 56:107–27.

———. 2010. "Manufacturing Loyalty: The Political Mobilization of Labor in Taiwan, 1950—1986." *Modern China* 36 (6): 559–88.

Howell, Jude. 2008. "All-China Federation of Trade Unions beyond Reform? The Slow March of Direct Elections." *China Quarterly* 196:845–63.

Hsing, You-tien. 2009. *The Great Urban Transformation: Politics of Land and Property in China.* Oxford: Oxford University Press.

———. 1998. *Making Capitalism in China? The Taiwan Connection.* New York: Oxford University Press.

Huang Anyu. 2010. *Taiwan jing ji zhuan xing zhong de lao gong wen ti yan jiu.* Beijing: Ren min chu ban she.

Huang, Yasheng, and Tarun Khanna. 2003. "Can India Overtake China?" *Foreign Policy* 137:74–81.

Hubacek, Klaus, Dabo Guan, John Barrett, and Thomas Wiedmann. 2009. "Environmental Implications of Urbanization and Lifestyle Change in China: Ecological and Water Footprints." *Journal of Cleaner Production* 17 (14): 1241–48.

Hung, Ho-fung. 2008. "Rise of China and the Global Overaccumulation Crisis." *Review of International Political Economy* 15 (2): 149–79.

——. 2009. *China and the Transformation of Global Capitalism.* Baltimore: Johns Hopkins University Press.

Huntington, Samuel P. 1991. "Democracy's Third Wave." *Journal of Democracy* 2 (2): 12–34.

Hurst, William. 2004. "Understanding Contentious Collective Action by Chinese Laid-Off Workers: The Importance of Regional Political Economy." *Studies in Comparative International Development* 39 (2): 94–120.

——. 2009. *The Chinese Worker after Socialism.* Cambridge: Cambridge University Press.

Jacobs, Paul. 1963. *The State of the Unions.* New York: Atheneum.

Katznelson, Ira. 1986. "Working-Class Formation: Constructing Cases and Comparisons." In *Working-Class Formation: Nineteenth-Century Patterns in Western Europe and the United States,* edited by Ira Katznelson and Aristide Zolberg, 1–41. Princeton: Princeton University Press.

Kay, Tamara. 2010. *NAFTA and the Politics of Labor Transnationalism.* Cambridge: Cambridge University Press.

Keck, Margaret, and Kathryn Sikkink. 1998. *Activists beyond Borders: Advocacy Networks in International Politics.*: Cornell University Press.

Keith, Ronald C. 1991. "Chinese Politics and the New Theory of 'Rule of Law.'" *China Quarterly* 125:109–18.

——. 1994. *China's Struggle for the Rule of Law.* New York: Macmillan.

Kong, Tat Yan. 2005. "Labour and Neo-Liberal Globalization in South Korea and Taiwan." *Modern Asian Studies* 39 (1): 155–88.

Koo, Hagen. 2001. *Korean Workers: The Culture and Politics of Class Formation.* Ithaca: Cornell University Press.

Kuruvilla, Sarosh, Subesh Das, Hyunji Kwon, and Soonwon Kwon. 2002. "Trade Union Growth and Decline in Asia." *British Journal of Industrial Relations* 40 (3): 431–61.

Kuruvilla, Sarosh, Ching Kwan Lee, and Mary Elizabeth Gallagher. 2011. *From Iron Rice Bowl to Informalization: Markets, Workers, and the State in a Changing China.* Ithaca: ILR Press.

Kwan, Daniel Y. K. 1997. *Marxist Intellectuals and the Chinese Labor Movement: A Study of Deng Zhongxia, 1894–1933.* Seattle: University of Washington Press.

Kwon, Seung-Ho, and Michael O'donnell. 1999. "Repression and Struggle: The State, the Chaebol, and Independent Trade Unions in South Korea." *Journal of Industrial Relations* 41 (2): 272–94.

Kwong, Julia. 2004. "Educating Migrant Children: Negotiations between the State and Civil Society." *China Quarterly* 19 (2): 1073–88.

Lardy, Nicholas R. 2007. "China: Rebalancing Economic Growth." Washington: Peterson Institute for International Economics and Center for Strategic International Studies.

Lau, Raymond W. K. 2001. "Socio-Political Control in Urban China: Changes and Crisis." *British Journal of Sociology* 52 (4): 605–20.

Lau, Raymond W. K. 2003. "The Habitus and 'Logic of Practice' of China's Trade Unionists." *Issues & Studies* 39 (3): 75–103.

Lee, Ching Kwan. 1995. "Engendering the Worlds of Labor: Women Workers, Labor Markets, and Production Politics in the South China Economic Miracle." *American Sociological Review* 60 (3): 378–97.

———. 1998. *Gender and the South China Miracle: Two Worlds of Factory Women*. Berkeley: University of California Press.

———. 2002. "From the Specter of Mao to the Spirit of the Law: Labor Insurgency in China." *Theory and Society* 31:189–228.

———. 2007. *Against the Law: Labor Protests in China's Rustbelt and Sunbelt*. Berkeley: University of California Press.

Lee, Ching Kwan, and Yuan Shen. 2011. "The Anti-Solidarity Machine? Labor Nongovernmental Organizations in China." In *From Iron Rice Bowl to Informalization: Markets, Workers, and the State in a Changing China*, edited by Sarosh Kuruvilla, Ching Kwan Lee, and Mary E. Gallagher, 173–87. Ithaca: Cornell University Press.

Lee, Lai To. 1984. *The Structure of the Trade Union System in China, 1949–1966*. Hong Kong: University of Hong Kong Press.

———. 1986. *Trade Unions in China: 1949 to the Present*. Singapore: Singapore University Press.

Lee, Yoonkyung. 2011. *Militants or Partisans: Labor Unions and Democratic Politics in Korea and Taiwan*. Stanford: Stanford University Press.

Leung, Pak Nang, and Pun Ngai. 2009. "The Radicalisation of the New Chinese Working Class: A Case Study of Collective Action in the Gemstone Industry." *Third World Quarterly* 30 (3): 551–65.

Li Faxian, and Wei Zhao. 2008. "Taiwan gonghui miandui minyinghua zhengce taidu bianhua yanjiu." *Taiwan yanjiu jikan* 101:24–30.

Li Guofang. 2001. "Tongyi zhanxian zhengce zai shenggang bagong zhong de zuoyong" [The function of the United Front policy during the Shenggang strike]. *Xingtai shifan gaozhuan xuebao* 16 (2): 38–45.

Li, Hongbin, and Li-An Zhou. 2005. "Political Turnover and Economic Performance: The Incentive Role of Personnel Control in China." *Journal of Public Economics* 89 (9–10): 1743–62.

Li Jianchang. 1991. "80 niandai de Taiwan laogong yundong: jiegou yu guocheng de fenxi." *Guoli Taiwan Daxue*. PhD diss.

Li, Minqi. 2005. "The Rise of China and the Demise of the Capitalist World-Economy: Exploring Historical Possibilities in the 21st century." *Science & Society* 69 (3): 420–48.

———. 2007. "Peak Oil, the Rise of China and India, and the Global Energy Crisis." *Journal of Contemporary Asia* 37 (4): 449–71.

———. 2009. *The Rise of China and the Demise of the Capitalist World Economy*. New York: Monthly Review Press.

Li Sishen, and Liu Zhikun. 2005. *Li Lisan zhi mi: Yi ge zhongcheng gemingzhe de quzhe rensheng* [The mystery of Li Lisan: The winding life of a loyal revolutionary]. Beijing: Renmin chubanshe.

Li Wei, ed. 2011. *Nongmingong shiminhua: Zhidu chuangxin yu dingceng zhengce sheji*. Beijing: Zhongguo fazhan chubanshe.

Li Zheng, and Chen Ji. 1988. *Quanmian shenhua gaige zhong de gonghui he gonghui de gaige* [The unions in deepening reforms and union reform]. Beijing: Gongren Chubanshe.

Liang, Guowei. 2012. "Nanhai Honda and the Institutional Fix." Unpublished manuscript.

Lin, Jing. 2007. "Emergence of Private Schools in China." In *Education and Reform in China*, edited by Emily Hannum and Albert Park, 44–63. New York: Routledge.

Lipset, Seymour Martin, Martin Trow, and James Coleman. 1956. *Union Democracy*. New York: Free Press.

Liu, Alan P. 1992. "The 'Wenzhou Model' of Development and China's Modernization." *Asian Survey* 32 (8): 696–711.

Liu, Hwa-Jen. 2011. "When Labor and Nature Strike Back: A Double Movement Saga in Taiwan." *Capitalism Nature Socialism* 22 (1): 22–39.

Liu, Mingwei. 2009. "Chinese Employment Relations and Trade Unions in Transition." PhD diss., Cornell University.

Liu, Yia-Ling. 1992. "Reform from Below: The Private Economy and Local Politics in the Rural Industrialization of Wenzhou." *China Quarterly* 130:293–316.

Liu, Yuanli. 2004. "Development of the Rural Health Insurance System in China." *Health Policy and Planning* 19 (3): 159–65.

Liu, Yuanli, William Hsiao, Qing Li, and Xingzhu Liu. 1995. "Transformation of China's Rural Health Care Financing." *Social Science & Medicine* 41 (8): 1085–93.

Locke, Richard M., Fei Qin, and Alberto Brause. 2007. "Does Monitoring Improve Labor Standards? Lessons from Nike." *Industrial and Labor Relations Review* 61 (1): 3–31.

Lubman, Stanley. 1999. *Bird in a Cage: Legal Reform in China after Mao.* Stanford: Stanford University Press.

Luce, Stephanie, and Edna Bonacich. 2009. "China and the U.S. Labor Movement." In *China and the Transformation of Global Capitalism,* edited by Ho-fung Hung, 153–72. Baltimore: Johns Hopkins University Press.

Ma, Zhining. 2011. *The ACFTU and Chinese Industrial Relations.* New York: Peter Lang.

MacFarquhar, Roderick. 1960. *The Hundred Flowers Campaign and the Chinese Intellectuals.* New York: Praeger.

Marx, Karl. 1978. "The Communist Manifesto." In *The Marx-Engels Reader,* edited by Robert C Tucker, 469–500. New York: Norton.

McAdam, Doug. 1982. *Political Process and the Development of Black Insurgency, 1930–1970.* Chicago: University of Chicago Press.

McAdam, Doug, Sidney Tarrow, and Charles Tilly. 2001. *Dynamics of Contention.* New York: Cambridge University Press.

Michels, Robert. 1962. *Political Parties: A Sociological Study of the Oligarchical Tendencies of Modern Democracy.* New York: Dover.

Milkman, Ruth. 2006. *L.A. Story: Immigrant Workers and the Future of the U.S. Labor Movement.* New York: Russell Sage Foundation.

Mok, Ka Ho. 2000. "Marketizing Higher Education in Post-Mao China." *International Journal of Educational Development* 20 (2): 109–126.

Mok, Ka Ho, Yu Cheung Wong, and Xiulan Zhang. 2009. "When Marketisation and Privatisation Clash with Socialist Ideals: Educational Inequality in Urban China." *International Journal of Educational Development* 29 (5): 505–12.

Munck, Ronaldo. 2004. "Globalization, Labor and the 'Polanyi Problem.'" *Labor History* 45 (3): 251–69.

Nee, Victor, and Sonja Opper. 2012. *Capitalism from Below: Markets and Institutional and Change in China.* Cambridge, MA: Harvard University Press.

Negri, Antonio. 1984. *Marx beyond Marx: Lessons on the Grundrisse.* Edited by Jim Fleming. South Hadley, MA: Bergin & Garvey.

No Chin-gwi. 2007. *8.15 Haebang ihu ui Han'guk nodong undong? Han'guk Noch'ong ch'ungmyon ui sironjok chaejomyong.* Seoul: Han'guk Nodong Chohap Ch'ongyonmaeng.

O'Brien, Kevin. 1996. "Rightful Resistance." *World Politics* 49 (1): 31–55.

O'Brien, Kevin, and Lianjiang Li. 1999. "Selective Policy Implementation in Rural China." *Comparative Politics* 31 (2): 167–86.

O'Brien, Kevin, and Lianjiang Li. 2006. *Rightful Resistance in Rural China.* Cambridge: Cambridge University Press.

Offe, Claus, and Helmut Wiesenthal. 1980. "Two Logics of Collective Action: Theoretical Notes on Social Class and Organizational Form." *Political Power and Social Theory* 1:67–115.

Ogle, George E. 1990. *South Korea: Dissent within the Economic Miracle.* London: Zed Books.

O'Rourke, Dara. 2003. "Outsourcing Regulation: Analyzing Nongovernmental Systems of Labor Standards and Monitoring." *Policy Studies Journal* 31 (2): 1–29.

Parris, Kristen. 1993. "Local Initiative and National Reforms: The Wenzhou Model of Development." *China Quarterly* 134:242–63.

Pearson, Margaret. 1994. "The Janus Face of Business Associations in China: Socialist Corporatism in Foreign Enterprises." *Australian Journal of Chinese Affairs* 31:25–46.

Pei, Minxin. 2006. *China's Trapped Transition: The Limits of Developmental Autocracy.* Cambridge, Mass.: Harvard University Press.

Perry, Elizabeth. 1993. *Shanghai on Strike: The Politics of Chinese Labor.* Stanford: Stanford University Press.

——. 1994. "Shanghai's Strike Wave of 1957." *China Quarterly* 137:1–27.

Perry, Elizabeth, and Xiaobo Lu. 1997. "Danwei: The Changing Chinese Workplace in Historical and Comparative Perspective."

Peters, Glen P., Christopher L. Weber, Dabo Guan, and Klaus Hubacek. 2007. "China's Growing CO_2 Emissions—A Race between Increasing Consumption and Efficiency Gains." *Environmental Science & Technology* 41 (17): 5939–44.

Polanyi, Karl. 1944. *The Great Transformation: The Political and Economic Origins of Our Time.* Boston: Beacon Press.

Pringle, Tim. 2011. *Trade Unions in China: The Challenge of Labour Unrest.* Abingdon, Oxon, UK: Routledge.

Pringle, Tim, and Simon Clarke. 2011. *The Challenge of Transition: Trade Unions in Russia, China and Vietnam.* New York: Palgrave Macmillan.

Przeworski, Adam. 1980. "Social Democracy as a Historical Phenomenon." *New Left Review* 122:28–58.

——. 1985. *Capitalism and Social Democracy.* Cambridge: Cambridge University Press.

Pun Ngai. 2005. *Made in China: Women Factory Workers in a Global Workplace.* Durham, NC: Duke University Press.

Pun Ngai, Chris King-Chi Chan, and Jenny Chan. 2009. "The Role of the State, Labour Policy and Migrant Workers' Struggles in Globalized China." *Global Labour Journal* 1 (1): 132–51.

Pun Ngai, and Huilin Lu. 2010. "A Culture of Violence: The Labor Subcontracting System and Collective Action by Construction Workers in Post-Socialist China." *China Journal* 64:143–58.

Qian, Xiaolei, and Russell Smyth. 2008. "Measuring Regional Inequality of Education in China: Widening Coast-Inland Gap or Widening Rural-Urban Gap?" *Journal of International Development* 20:132–44.

Reich, Michael, David M Gordon, and Richard C Edwards. 1973. "A Theory of Labor Market Segmentation." *American Economic Review* 63 (2): 359–65.

Rozman, Gilbert. 2012. "Invocations of Chinese Traditions in International Relations." *Journal of Chinese Political Science* 17 (2): 111–24.

Rueschemeyer, Dietrich, Evelyne Huber Stephens, and John D. Stephens. 1992. *Capitalist Development and Democracy.* Chicago: University of Chicago Press.

Sarti, Roland. 1971. *Fascism and the Industrial Leadership in Italy, 1919–1940.* Berkeley: University of California Press.

———. 1974. *The Ax Within: Italian Fascism in Action.* New York: New Viewpoints.

Schmitter, Philippe C. 1974. "Still the Century of Corporatism?" *Review of Politics* 36 (1): 85–131.

Seidman, Gay. 1994. *Manufacturing Militance: Workers' Movements in Brazil and South Africa, 1970–1985.* Berkeley: University of California Press.

Sheehan, Jackie. 1998. *Chinese Workers: A New History.* London: Routledge.

Shen, Ce, and John B. Williamson. 2010. "China's New Rural Pension Scheme: Can It Be Improved?" *International Journal of Sociology and Social Policy* 30 (5/6): 239–50.

Shenggang da bagong ziliao [Materials from the Guangdong-Hong Kong general strike].1980. Guangzhou: Guangdong Renmin Chubanshe.

Silver, Beverly J. 2003. *Forces of Labor: Workers' Movements and Globalization since 1870.* Cambridge: Cambridge University Press.

Silver, Beverly J., and Giovanni Arrighi. 2003. "Polanyi's 'Double Movement': The Belle Epoques of British and U.S. Hegemony Compared." *Politics & Society* 31 (2): 325–55.

Skocpol, Theda. 1979. *States and Social Revolution: A Comparative Analysis of France, Russia, and China.* Cambridge: Cambridge University Press.

Smith, S. A. 2000. *A Road Is Made: Communism in Shanghai, 1920–1927.* Honolulu: University of Hawai'i Press.

Smith, S. A. 2002. *Like Cattle and Horses: Nationalism and Labor in Shanghai, 1895–1927.* Durham, NC: Duke University Press.

Solinger, Dorothy J. 1995. "The Chinese Work Unit and Transient Labor in the Transition from Socialism." *Modern China* 21 (2): 155–83.

———. 1999. *Contesting Citizenship in Urban China: Peasant Migrants, the State, and the Logic of the Market.* Berkeley: University of California Press.

———. 2001. "Why We Cannot Count the 'Unemployed.'" *China Quarterly* 167: 671–88.

———. 2009. *States' Gains, Labor's Losses: China, France, and Mexico Choose Global Liaisons, 1980–2000.* Ithaca: Cornell University Press.

Spires, Anthony. 2012. "Lessons from Abroad: Foreign Influences on China's Emerging Civil Society." *China Journal* 68:125–46.

Stepan-Norris, Judith. 1997. "The Making of Union Democracy." *Social Forces* 76 (2): 475–510.

Stepan-Norris, Judith, and Maurice Zeitlin. 1991. "'Red' Unions and 'Bourgeois' Contracts?" *American Journal of Sociology* 96 (5): 1151–1200.

———. 1995. "Union Democracy, Radical Leadership, and the Hegemony of Capital." *American Sociological Review* 60 (6): 829–50.

———. 1996. "Insurgency, Radicalism, and Democracy in America's Industrial Unions." *Social Forces* 75 (1): 1–32.

———. 2002. *Left Out: Reds and America's Industrial Unions.* New York: Cambridge University Press.

Stranahan, Patricia. 1998. *Underground: The Shanghai Communist Party and the Politics of Survival, 1927–1937.* New York: Rowman & Littlefield.

Streeck, Wolfgang. 1991. "Interest Heterogeneity and Organising Capacity: Two Class Logics of Collective Action?" In *Political Choice: Institutions, Rules and the Limits of Rationality,* edited by Roland Czada and Adrienne Windhoff-Heritier, 161–98. Boulder, CO: Westview.

Tang Chunliang. 1989. *Li Lisan zhuan* [Biography of Li Lisan]. Ha'erbin: Heilongjiang Renmin Chubanshe.

Tarrow, Sidney. 1998. *Power in Movement: Social Movements and Contentious Politics.* Cambridge: Cambridge University Press.

Therborn, Goran. 1977. "The Rule of Capital and the Rise of Democracy." *New Left Review* 103:3–41.

Thireau, Isabelle, and Linshan Hua. 2003. "The Moral Universe of Aggrieved Chinese Workers: Workers' Appeals to Arbitration Committees and Letters and Visits Offices." *China Journal* 50:83–103.

Tilly, Charles. 2004. *Social Movements, 1768–2004.* Boulder, CO: Paradigm.

Tilly, Charles, and Sidney G. Tarrow. 2007. *Contentious Politics.* Boulder, CO: Paradigm.

Tran, Angie Ngoc. 2007a. "Alternatives to the 'Race to the Bottom' in Vietnam." *Labor Studies Journal* 32 (4): 430–51.

——. 2007b. "The Third Sleeve: Emerging Labor Newspapers and the Response of the Labor Unions and the State to Workers' Resistance in Vietnam." *Labor Studies Journal* 32:257–79.

Tran, Si Vy, and Brady Coleman. 2010. "Strikes and Resolutions to Strikes under Vietnamese Labor Law." *Currents: International Trade Law Journal* 18:49–61.

Traxler, Franz. 1993. "Business Associations and Labor Unions in Comparison: Theoretical Perspective and Empirical Findings on Social Class, Collective Action and Associational Organizability." *British Journal of Sociology* 44 (4): 673–91.

Tronti, Mario. 1971. *Operai e Capitale.* Turin: Einaudi.

Tsai, Kellee. 2002. *Back-Alley Banking.* Ithaca: Cornell University Press.

Tseng, Wanda, and Harm Zebregs. 2003. "Foreign Direct Investment in China: Some Lessons for Other Countries." In *China: Competing in the Global Economy,* edited by Wanda Tseng and Markus Rodlauer, 68–88. Washington, DC: International Monetary Fund.

Umney, Charles. 2011. "The International Labour Movement and China." *Industrial Relations Journal* 42 (4): 322–38.

Unger, Jonathan. 1996. "Bridges: Private Business, the Chinese Government and the Rise of New Associations." *China Quarterly* 147:795–819.

Unger, Jonathan, and Anita Chan. 1995. "China, Corporatism, and the East Asian Model." *Australian Journal of Chinese Affairs* 33:29–53.

Valenzuela, J. Samuel. 1989. "Labor Movements in Transitions to Democracy: A Framework for Analysis." *Comparative Politics* 21 (4): 445–72.

Voss, Kim, and Rachel Sherman. 2000. "Breaking the Iron Law of Oligarchy: Union Revitalization in the American Labor Movement." *American Journal of Sociology* 106:303–49.

Walder, Andrew G. 1983. "Organized Dependency and Cultures of Authority in Chinese Industry." *Journal of Asian Studies* 43 (1): 51–76.

Walder, Andrew G. 1984. *Communist Neo-Traditionalism: Work and Authority in Chinese Industry.* Berkeley: University of California Press.

Walder, Andrew G. 1991. "Workers, Managers and the State: The Reform Era and the Political Crisis of 1989." *China Quarterly* 127:467–92.

Walder, Andrew G., and Xiaoxia Gong. 1993. "Workers in the Tiananmen Protests: The Politics of the Beijing Workers' Autonomous Federation." *Australian Journal of Chinese Affairs* 29:1–29.

Wang, Fei-Ling. 2005. *Organizing through Division and Exclusion: China's Hukou System.* Stanford: Stanford University Press.

———. 2010. "Conflict, Resistance and the Transformation of the Hukou System." In *Chinese Society: Change, Conflict, and Resistance,* edited by Elizabeth J. Perry and Mark Selden, 80–100. New York: Routledge.

Wang, Haiyan, Richard P. Appelbaum, Francesca Degiuli, and Nelson Lichtenstein. 2009. "China's New Labour Contract Law: Is China Moving toward Increased Power for Workers?" *Third World Quarterly* 30 (3): 485–501.

Wang Hong. 1990. *Zhongguo gonghui zhongyao wenjian xuanbian* [selection of important Chinese union documents]. Beijing: Jixie Gongye Chubanshe.

Wang Jian. 2002. Gonghui gongzuo zhongyao wenjian xuanbian [Important trade union work document collection]. Beijing: Zhongguo Jinrong Chubanshe.

Wang Shaoguang. 2008. "The Great Transformation: The Double Movement in China." *Boundary 2,* 35 (2): 15–47.

Wang Shizong. 2004. "Hangye zuzhi de cunzai jichu he quanli laiyuan: Dui wenzhou shanghui de shehui hefaxing kaocha" [The origin of power and foundation of existence for industrial organizations: An investigation of the social legitimacy of Wenzhou employer associations]. *Zhonggong zhejiang sheng weidangxiao xuebao* 2:5–12.

Wang Yongxi, He Bufeng, and Cao Yanping. 2005. *Jianming zhongguo gonghui shi.* Beijing: Zhongguo gongren chubanshe.

Warner, Malcolm. 1995. *The Management of Human Resources in Chinese Industry.* Basingstoke, UK: Macmillan.

Weber, Max. 1946. "Bureaucracy." In *From Max Weber: Essays in Sociology,* edited by H. H. Gerth and C. Wright Mills. New York: Oxford University Press.

———. 1978. *Economy and Society.* Berkeley: University of California Press.

Wei, Yehua Dennis, Wangming Li, and Chunbin Wang. 2007. "Restructuring Industrial Districts, Scaling Up Regional Development: A Study of the Wenzhou Model, China." *Economic Geography* 83 (4): 421–44.

Wright, Erik Olin. 2000. "Working-Class Power, Capitalist-Class Interests, and Class Compromise." *American Journal of Sociology* 105 (4): 957–1002.

Wright, Teresa. 2010. *Accepting Authoritarianism: State-Society Relations in China's Reform Era.* Stanford: Stanford University Press.

Wu, David Yen-ho. 1991. "The Construction of Chinese and Non-Chinese Identities." *Daedalus* 120 (2): 159–79.

Wu Ganying. 2004. "Wenzhou shanghui zuoyong tuxiang: Qiangda minjian liliang zhutui jingji fazhan" [Promotion of the function of Wenzhou employer associations: Strong civil power promotes economic development]. *Qiye jingji* 11:152–53.

Wu, Tien-Wei. 1968. "Chiang Kai-shek's March Twentieth Coup d'Etat of 1926." *Journal of Asian Studies* 27 (3): 585–602.

Xiao Xinhuang. 1989. "Taiwan xin xing shehui yundong de pouxi." In *Longduan yu boxue: Weiquanzhuyi de zhengzhi jingji fenx.,* edited by Xiao Xinhuang and Wu Zhongji. Taipei: Taiwan yanjiu jijinhui.

Ye, Xinyue, and Yehua Dennis Wei. 2005. "Geospatial Analysis of Regional Development in China: The Case of Zhejiang Province and the Wenzhou Model." *Eurasian Geography and Economics* 46 (6): 445–64.

Yi Won-bo. 2005. *Han'guk nodong undongsa 100-yon ui kirok.* Seoul: Han'guk Nodong Sahoe Yon'guso.

Yu Jianxing, Xu Yueqian, and Jiang Hua. 2007. "Wenzhou shanghui de liwai yu bu liwai: Zhongguo gongmin shehui de fazhan yu tiaozhan" [The exceptionalness and unexceptionalness of Wenzhou employer associations: The development and challenges of civil society in China]. *Zhejiang daxue xuebao* 37 (6): 5–15.

Yu Jing. 2009. "Lun shixisheng laodong baozhang de zerenren ji xiangguan zeren" [On the obligations to labor and social security of intern]. *Zhongguo Laodong Guanxi Xueyuan Xuebao* 23:98–101.

Yu, Xiaomin. 2008. "Workplace Democracy in China's Foreign-Funded Enterprises: A Multilevel Case Study of Employee Representation." *Economic and Industrial Democracy* 29:274–300.

Zhan, Shaohua. 2011. "What Determines Migrant Workers' Life Chances in Contemporary China? Hukou, Social Exclusion, and the Market." *Modern China* 37 (3): 243–85.

Zhang, Lu. 2008. "Lean Production and Labor Controls in the Chinese Automobile Industry in an Age of Globalization." *International Labor and Working-Class History* 73 (1): 1–21.

Zhang, Yunqiu. 1997. "From State Corporatism to Social Representation." In *Civil Society in China,* edited by Timothy Brook and B. Michael Frolic, 124–48. Armonk, NY: M.E. Sharpe.

Zhao, Dingxin. 1998. "Ecologies of Social Movements: Student Mobilization during the 1989 Prodemocracy Movement in Beijing." *American Journal of Sociology* 103 (6): 1493–529.

——. 2001. *The Power of Tiananmen: State-Society Relations and the 1989 Beijing Student Movement.* Chicago: University of Chicago Press.

Zhao, Minghua, and Theo Nichols. 1996. "Management Control of Labour in State-Owned Enterprises: Cases from the Textile Industry." *China Journal* 36:1–21.

Zhongguo gonghui lishi wenxian [Historical documents of Chinese trade unions]. 1958. Beijing: Gongren Chubanshe.

Zhu Shengming. 2008. "Zhejiang wenling hangye gongzi jiti xieshang diaocha" [Investigation of Zhejiang's Wenling sectoral collective wage negotiation]." *Guangdong xingzheng xueyuan xuebao* 20 (6): 82–90.

Index

Page numbers followed by letters *f* and *t* refer to figures and tables, respectively.